# *The* Dodgers

## 60 YEARS IN LOS ANGELES

# The Dodgers

# 60 YEARS IN
# LOS ANGELES

## Michael Schiavone

SPORTS
PUBLISHING

Sports Publishing books may be purchased in bulk at special discounts for sales promotion, corporate gifts, fund-raising, or educational purposes. Special editions can also be created to specifications. For details, contact the Special Sales Department, Sports Publishing, 307 West 36th Street, 11th Floor, New York, NY 10018 or sportspubbooks@skyhorsepublishing.com.

Sports Publishing® is a registered trademark of Skyhorse Publishing, Inc.®, a Delaware corporation.

Visit our website at www.sportspubbooks.com.

10 9 8 7 6 5 4

Library of Congress Cataloging-in-Publication Data is available on file.

Cover design by Tom Lau
Cover photo credit: AP Images

Print ISBN: 978-1-68358-371-4
Ebook ISBN: 978-1-68358-194-9

Printed in the United States of America

For Su Lan and Valentina

# TABLE OF CONTENTS

# PREFACE

**IN 1988, I** was a fourteen year old living in Australia. As was the norm, on Sunday afternoons I would watch *Sports Sunday*. At the start of the program they promised extended highlights of Game One of the World Series between the Los Angeles Dodgers and the Oakland Athletics. While I am almost certain that I had once watched a baseball game, or at the very least viewed highlights of a game previously, almost thirty years later I cannot recall ever seeing one pitch prior to that day. I was a Los Angeles Lakers fan, so, naturally, I began supporting the Dodgers. As was the formula, *Sports Sunday* would show highlights of different sports throughout the show. One would see ten minutes of one sport before the show switched to another, and then another, before going back to the original sport. On this day I remember feeling impatient; I just wanted to watch highlights from the World Series. What is now folklore, in the bottom of the ninth trailing 4–3 facing the A's feared closer Dennis Eckersley, an injured Kirk Gibson blasted a two-run home run to win it for the Dodgers. People remember their first kiss, their wedding day, the day their children were born. I remember all of those and, if I close my eyes, can still see the home run and Gibson pumping his arm while circling the bases. I also can hear Vin Scully's call of the home run: "High fly ball into right field, she is gone! In a year that has been so improbable, the impossible has happened."

The emotion, the drama, and Scully's call made me a baseball fan—it made me a Dodgers' fan. Another television network showed the rest of the series on delay. I begged my dad to record the games. After school I would rush home and watch the World Series. Following the Dodgers' World Series–clinching victory in Game Five, I jumped up and down with excitement. The Los Angeles Dodgers became, and still are, my favorite sporting team. I am privileged and thankful that almost 30 years later I am able to write the history of the Los Angeles Dodgers to mark the 60th year since the team relocated from Brooklyn.

# 1

# THE BROOKLYN DODGERS

THE HISTORY OF the Dodgers can be traced back to the formation of the Brooklyn Grays in 1883. The team originally played in the Inter-State Association of Professional Baseball Clubs before joining the American Association the following year.[1] The team (now known as the Bridegrooms) won the American Association championship in 1889 before losing to the New York Giants in an early version of the World Series. The World Series that we know today, a match-up between the National League and American League champions, did not begin until 1903. In 1890, the team left the American Association and joined the National League. Even though they had the less-than-flattering nickname of Bridegrooms, they managed to win the National League pennant, compiling a 86–43 record—well ahead of the Chicago Colts (6½ games) and the Philadelphia Phillies (9 games). Legend has it the team

---

[1] Upon joining the AA, they would go by the Brooklyn Atlantics but went back to the Grays the following season.

chose the Bridegrooms moniker because seven members of the team got married in 1888. The Bridegrooms went on to tie with the American Association champion Louisville Colonels in the World Series. Both teams won three games, and there was one tie. The weather continually worsened during the Series, which led to the managers deciding that Game Seven would be the last game, which Louisville won to tie the Series. While a deciding game was meant to be played the following year, it never occurred due to the respective leagues being at loggerheads due to the formation of the Players League.

During the 1890s and into the new century, the Brooklyn squad also had other informal monikers such as Ward's Wonders (based on John Montgomery Ward, who was the skipper from 1891 to 1892), Foutz's Fillies (based on Dave Foutz, who was the skipper from 1893 to 1896), and Hanlon's Superbas (based on Ned Hanlon, who was the skipper from 1899 to 1905). Another moniker was attached to the Brooklyn side in the 1890s: the Trolley Dodgers.

The term "Trolley Dodgers" first appeared in print in May 1895 and was picked up by other publications throughout the season. In the 1800s, when the city had a number of trolleys, they were initially pulled by horses. Brooklyn residents did not bother to look when they crossed the street because they "knew" that horses would not run them over. However, when horse trolleys were replaced by electric ones, many Brooklyn residents still did not bother to look when they crossed the street. As a result, they often had to jump out of the way to prevent being hit. Of course, not all Brooklyn residents were lucky; eight people were killed in 1892, fifty-one in 1893, and in thirty-four in 1894. In a wonderful article, "The Crim Reality of the 'Trolley Dodgers,'" Peter Jensen Brown elaborates:

The name 'trolley dodgers' would not and could not have been used to describe the baseball team or anyone else from Brooklyn until 1892. The frequent appearance of the verb 'to dodge,' in association with trolleys in Brooklyn between 1892 and 1894, and the lack of evidence of 'trolley dodger' during the same period, suggests that the phrase had not achieved a significant level of use, if any, before 1895. The description of 'trolley dodger' as the 'new' name of the Brooklyn team shortly after opening day in 1895, and the repeated reporting of the name as 'new' throughout 1895 and into 1896, suggests that the name was likely first applied to the team in 1895. The name seems to have been extended to people from Brooklyn only later, and then not in a pejorative sense.

The moniker was frequently used by a wide variety of newspapers in 1896. Eventually, "Trolley" was dropped from the name, and the local baseball team simply was known as the Brooklyn Dodgers. However, it was still an informal nickname. From 1899 to 1910, the team was more formally known as the Brooklyn Superbas. In 1911 and 1912, the team was known as the Brooklyn Dodgers, but the following year it was once again known as the Superbas. From 1914 until 1931 it went by the Brooklyn Robins. In 1932, the team was formally known once again as the Brooklyn Dodgers. And it was not until 1933 it the nickname became permanent, with the Dodgers name being put on the team's jerseys.

There was another informal nickname bestowed upon the Dodgers in the mid-1930s. The Dodgers of this era were more known for their less-than-stellar approach to the game. It would be wrong to claim that the players did not care, but they were seemingly lacking in the basic fundamentals of the game. The

Dodgers continually committed basic errors, and defeat was more common than victory.[2] Legend has it that sports cartoonist Willard Mullin heard a cab driver ask, "So how did those bums do today?" and drew a cartoon based on circus clown Emmett Kelly with the heading "Dem Bums." Rather than take offense at the carton, Brooklyn fans loved it, and the Dodgers were dubbed "Dem Bums" by the Brooklyn faithful. No one berated and abused the Dodgers more than the Brooklyn faithful, but at the same time no one loved their baseball team more than they did. The Dodgers were a part of Brooklyn, and the city was a part of them.

While the "Dem Bums" nickname was somewhat fitting, the team did have some successful seasons. Indeed, the team won the National League pennant in 1890, 1899, 1900, 1916, 1920, 1941, 1947, 1949, 1952, 1953, 1955, and 1956. However, apart from 1955, the Dodgers always came up short in the World Series. In 1916, they lost four games to one to the Boston Red Sox. In 1920, they lost five games to two to the Cleveland Indians. In 1941, they lost four games to one to the New York Yankees. In 1947, they lost four games to three—again to the Yankees. In 1949, it was four games to one in a loss to the Yankees.

In fact, the Yankees beat them *again* in the 1952, 1953, and 1956 World Series (four games to three, four games to two, and four games to three, respectively). The 1955 season, however, was a different story.

With the World Series tied at three heading into the seventh and deciding game, most people expected the Yankees to once

---

2  From 1933 to 1938, the Dodgers went 404–510–12 (.436 winning percentage) and averaged 85 losses a season.

again triumph—especially as the game was being held at Yankee Stadium. If history does indeed repeat itself, with the first time being a tragedy and the second time a farce, the Dodgers were always destined to not be good enough. However, this year the Dodgers were not to be denied. With Gil Hodges driving in two runs and eventual World Series MVP Johnny Podres throwing a complete-game shutout, the Dodgers finally defeated the Yankees to claim their first World Series crown. There was pandemonium on the Brooklyn streets as long-suffering Dodger fans could finally celebrate a World Series triumph. What the fans did not realize at the time is that this would be the last Brooklyn Dodger World Series victory.

## WALTER O'MALLEY AND THE DODGERS MOVE TO LA

Walter Francis O'Malley was a New Yorker to his core. He was born in the Bronx on October 9, 1903, and grew up in Queens. After obtaining a Bachelor of Arts degree with a focus on engineering from the University of Pennsylvania, O'Malley attended Columbia Law School. However, following his father losing his job, O'Malley worked during the day (as an engineer, surveyor, as well as business owner) and attended Fordham University at night. After graduating, O'Malley moved away from engineering and concentrated on practicing law. In addition to law, he also became a part-owner of J. O. Duffy Building Materials. In an event that would change Brooklyn and Los Angeles baseball history, Brooklyn Trust Company President George V. McLaughlin asked O'Malley to monitor the Dodgers' legal and business affairs, as the team was behind in its payments to Brooklyn Trust.

In 1943, O'Malley went to work for the Dodgers full-time as their vice president and general counsel. In 1944, O'Malley, along with Branch Rickey and Andrew Schmitz, purchased 25 percent of the Dodgers. The following year, O'Malley, Rickey, and John L. Smith bought another 50 percent of the Dodgers. In October 1950, Rickey purchased an additional stake in the team. This meant that O'Malley was now the president and majority owner of the Dodgers. One of his stated goals, along with finally brining a World Series triumph to Brooklyn, was building a new stadium.

The Dodgers played their home games at Ebbets Field. It is fair to say that, by the 1950s, the conditions at the stadium were not the best. As Michael D'Antonio outlines in *Forever Blue*,

> Periodically, visits by various city inspectors had required the team to make emergency fixes to avoid losing the occupancy permit for the stadium. The electrical system, taxed by the addition of lights for night games, was especially troublesome. Years later [Dodgers GM] Buzzie Bavasi would admit that he used his influence with a distant relative—his sister's father-in-law, who ranked high in the fire department—to avoid citations and shutdowns.

Other stadiums around the country also had to deal with similar issues that could potentially be overcome. What could not be overcome for O'Malley was that Ebbets Field could only hold 32,000 spectators, and there was no room to expand. The 1955 world champion Brooklyn Dodgers attracted 1,033,589 fans to their home games, second best in the NL, but O'Malley had grander visions. Even if it was possible to expand the capacity of the stadium there were only, at most, 700 parking spaces close to the stadium. As a result, in 1946, O'Malley raised the possibility of the Dodgers potentially moving to a new stadium and, by 1953, began formally negotiating with the city. Unlike modern owners, O'Malley was not looking for the city to finance or even partly finance the stadium. In a letter to the vice chairman of the Triborough Bridge and Tunnel Authority, O'Malley wrote,

> It is my belief that a new ball park should be built, financed and owned by the ball club. It should occupy land on the tax roll. The only assistance I am looking for is in the assembling of a suitable plot and I hope that the mechanics of Title I (of the Housing Act of 1949) could be used if the ball park were also to be used as a parking garage.

Yet even though O'Malley was willing to have the Dodgers finance the stadium themselves, New York City officials were seemingly not interested in accommodating the team. While the New York media vilified O'Malley for moving the Dodgers to Los Angeles, New York City officials had a large role in forcing the owner's hand.

After negotiations were seemingly going nowhere, O'Malley stated in August 1955 that the Dodgers would not play at Ebbets Field after the 1957 season. They would either play in a new stadium in New York or would not be playing in New York. Despite numerous meetings, pronouncements, and the like, O'Malley and New York City officials could not come to any agreement. Both New York Mayor Robert Wagner and the planning chief Robert Moses were seemingly indifferent to the Dodgers staying in Brooklyn. Writing in the *New York Times* in 2015, a mere 58 years after the Dodgers left Brooklyn, Michael Beschloss noted that

O'Malley wanted the city to help him clear suitable land for a privately funded new stadium in the borough. When O'Malley focused on one particular site, he found that Moses was already working with the real estate mogul Fred Trump (father of the current US president). During their cat-and-mouse game, which lasted for years, Moses suggested that the Dodgers build a ballpark in Flushing Meadows, Queens (near where Citi Field now stands). At one point, Moses angered O'Malley by counseling him to simply fix up Ebbets Field.

Likewise, when directly asked about the possibility of the Dodgers leaving Brooklyn, Wagner replied, "I don't get emotional about it."

Thus, by the start of Spring Training in 1957, it was becoming all the more likely that the Dodgers would be moving to Los Angeles. Indeed, as Jim Gordon, writing for the *Society for American Baseball Research,* noted,

On February 21, 1957, the Los Angeles baseball world exploded when the Brooklyn Dodgers announced that they had bought Wrigley Field [not the famed Chicago stadium, but one with the same name that was situated in Los Angeles], the Los Angeles Angels, their territorial rights and Pacific Coast League franchise for $3,000,000, and the Fort Worth franchise of the Texas League. "It is my considered opinion that Los Angeles will have major league baseball by 1960," said Brooklyn president Walter O'Malley. Only ten days earlier, O'Malley had given New York officials six months to do something on an acceptable new stadium for the Dodgers. The next day, the Dodgers announced that they would schedule some spring training games at Wrigley in 1958. O'Malley had inspected Wrigley Field and other Los Angeles baseball sites in January.

The Dodgers were already halfway to California.

In May of '58, the National League owners gave formal approval for the Dodgers to move to Los Angeles if O'Malley so desired. The last home game in Brooklyn was scheduled for September 24, 1957. The Dodgers beat the Pittsburgh Pirates, 2–0, on the back of a complete-game shutout by Danny McDevitt. The Dodger faithful were already resigned to the team leaving Brooklyn, as there were only 6,702 fans in attendance. And on September 29, the Philadelphia Phillies beat the Dodgers at home, 2–1. This was the last Brooklyn Dodger game. In a precursor of what was to come, Sandy Koufax pitched a scoreless final inning for the Dodgers. On October 8 at 4 p.m., the Dodgers officially announced that they were moving to Los Angeles. However, it was not O'Malley who alerted the media or even attended the announcement. It was Arthur Patterson, whom the *New York Daily News* called a "third-string club official," that read a one-sentence statement:

> In view of the action of the Los Angeles City Council yesterday, and in accordance with the resolution of the National League made October 1, the stockholders and directors of the Brooklyn Baseball Club have today met and unanimously agreed that the necessary steps be taken to draft the Los Angeles territory.

The New York media never forgave O'Malley for his perceived treachery. Writing in the *Daily News*, Dick Young opened his article on the team leaving for Los Angeles by stating that

"Walter O'Malley, the most momentous manipulator baseball has ever known, yesterday officially moved the Brooklyn Dodger franchise to Los Angeles." Despite the hatred and vitriol, the reality was that the Brooklyn Dodgers were no more; indeed, as of 2020, there has not been another Major League Baseball team to call Brooklyn home, and there is exceedingly unlikely to be one in the foreseeable future. In contrast to the hostility of the New York press, the Los Angeles media coverage was one of jubilation. As the *Los Angeles Times* roared, "At long last, we've got the Dodgers!"

# 2

# 1950S: A NEW BEGINNING AND WORLD SERIES TRIUMPH

**A**MONG THE JUBILATION and despair of the Dodgers moving west, the reality was that the team did not have a home stadium. Before building a new stadium, the team needed a temporary home. The stadiums under consideration were the Rose Bowl, Wrigley Field (the minor-league stadium located in Los Angeles that the Dodgers purchased), and the Los Angeles Coliseum. The Rose Bowl was one of the preferred options due to the stadium seating capacity being more than 100,000. Following a visit to the stadium in late 1957, O'Malley stated that "The people of Pasadena were kind enough to invite us . . . and I feel very sure we can arrive at an intelligent basis for an agreement to play in the Rose Bowl." However, that idea soon went nowhere as it was claimed that for-profit groups were forbidden to use the stadium, and the more likely deal breaker was that it was estimated to cost upwards of three-quarters of a million dollars to renovate the stadium to meet Major League requirements. O'Malley certainly wanted the Dodgers to play to as many people as possible, but spending a sizable amount to upgrade the stadium for what was always going to be a temporary home was not in the cards.

Another option for the Dodgers was the then minor-league stadium Wrigley Field, which the team bought in 1957 and moved their offices to. The name came from Chicago Cubs owner William Wrigley Jr., who paid over $1.1 million for the stadium to be built. However, even as a temporary solution, the option was not that palatable. Wrigley Field's capacity was only 20,500 (with Ebbets's being 31,902). Moreover, as Brian M. Endsley wrote in *Bums No More*,

> At first glance, the park appeared normal: 340 feet down the foul lines and 412 feet to dead center field. But these measurements were misleading due to the park's strange angles. The distances from home plate usually increase rapidly idly from the foul lines toward center, thus forming natural "power alleys." In Wrigley Field, the outfield fences were angled slightly toward the infield instead of away from it. As a result, the power alleys were a cozy 345 feet from home plate, only five feet deeper than down the foul lines, clearly inadequate when compared to the 15 other major league parks.

The power alleys were certainly conducive to home runs. In 1961, the Los Angeles Angels played their home games at Wrigley Field during their inaugural season. There were 248 home runs at Wrigley that year—a major-league record that would last until 1996. The ease in which to hit home runs at Wrigley Field is clear, as the record was only broken by Coors Field in Denver (which is situated 5,200 feet above sea level).

Nevertheless, despite its obvious drawbacks, as Gordon claimed, an option being considered was to play

> weekend and holiday games in the [Los Angeles] Coliseum and weekday night games at Wrigley Field. Enlarging Wrigley to [a capacity of] 26,000 to 27,000 was being considered, but only if it cost less than $250,000. In early November [1957], the Coliseum Commission told the Dodgers that they would not modify the stadium for baseball unless the team played at least 35 games there. After a crowd of 102,368 attended the Rams-49ers game on November 10 [1957], and because of the large early ticket requests, the Dodgers next said that their preference was to play all their games in the Coliseum and drop Wrigley Field.

However, to add only an extra 2,500 seats and to make stadium improvements would cost at least $250,000. Due to the limited seating, Wrigley Field was only ever going to be seriously considered if there was no other viable option. Quite simply, O'Malley did not move to Los Angeles to play in a stadium that held less than 30,000 fans. He did not move the team to Los Angeles out of the kindness in his heart; he wanted to make as much money as possible. The stadium that could hold the most fans and was willing to accommodate the Dodgers was the Los Angeles Coliseum.

Construction of the Coliseum cost $900,000, and it opened in 1923. It was modified in 1932 to add more seating and for improvements for the upcoming Olympics. Even though the Coliseum was willing to accommodate the Dodgers, this did not mean they would accept any offer from O'Malley. After several proposals were rejected and it was looking like the Dodgers may indeed have to play games at Wrigley Field, O'Malley offered to rent the Coliseum for two years at a cost of $600,000, but home plate had to be situated at the "west end of the stadium" so outfielders would not be looking into the sun. The situating of home plate bothered the football teams who used the Coliseum, as they believed it "would cause most damage to their field." Nonetheless, in this case money talked, and the commission did not want to have to deal with the fallout if they rejected the Dodgers. Following the agreement being reached, O'Malley stated, "This ended my longest losing streak." The Dodgers had found a temporary home, but the commission did ban beer sales at Dodger home games, which, arguably, cost O'Malley a small fortune.

The Coliseum may have been good stadium for football and other athletics, but it left a lot to be desired as a baseball stadium. As Endsley noted, "Essentially a football field gerry-rigged with chain-link fences into a baseball park, it was 301 feet down the right-field line, a fantastic 440 feet to right-center, 425 feet to dead center, but only 250 foot down the left-field line, and 320 feet to left-center." Considering the incredibly short dimensions in left field, a

> 42-foot-high screen was attached to the left-field foul pole at the 250-foot sign, and stretched 140 feet across to a support tower in left-center to neutralize the 320-foot "power alley." Then, for 30 more feet, it was reduced in four "steps" to eight feet. In dead center field, it joined a six-foot chain-link fence that extended across the field to the right-field foul pole.

However, even with the barrier, routine fly outs in every other major-league stadium were home runs at the Coliseum. In contrast, due to a fence at right field being angled toward the vast confines of right-center, it made it incredibly difficult to hit home runs to right. Indeed, only nine home runs were hit to right in 1958 during 77 games at the Coliseum. The dimensions of the Coliseum hurt Dodger great and Hall of Famer Duke Snider. Snider hit forty or more home runs in each of his previous five seasons. However, in 1958, Snider only hit 15 home runs. While a knee injury certainly played a part, Snider was never the same power threat as he was in Ebbets Field. The most home runs he hit as a Los Angeles Dodger was only 23 in 1959. As the legendary Willie Mays said to Snider when they saw each for the first game at the Coliseum, "Duke, they killed you. Man they took the bat right out of your hands."

Of course it was not just left-handed hitters complaining about the Coliseum. Before the start of the season, opposing pitchers were already upset about the ease in which batters could hit home runs to left. Giants pitcher Johnny Antonelli vented that "It's the biggest farce I've ever heard of." It was not just opposing pitchers complaining about playing at the Coliseum. Dodgers ace Don Drysdale stated that "It's nothing but a sideshow. Who feels like playing baseball in this place?" while infielder Randy Jackson years later commented that "It was weird, weird, weird playing in the Coliseum."

Unfortunately, one Dodger star would never play in the Coliseum or indeed play another baseball game again. On January 28, 1958, eight-time All-Star, three-time National League MVP, future member of the Hall of Fame, and the Dodgers' starting catcher Roy Campanella closed his liquor store in Harlem for the night. (It would be many more years and industrial disputes before players did not need to work another job(s) to survive.) While driving home, Campanella's car hit a patch of ice, overturned, and crashed into a telephone pole, breaking his neck and leaving him paralyzed. There was hope Campanella could eventually walk again. However, despite the best efforts of everyone involved, Campanella never regained the use of his legs; he was dependent on a wheelchair for the rest of his life. It was a very sad start to the year for the Dodgers.

The team honored Campanella on May 7, 1959. Roy Campanella Night saw a record crowd of 93,103 fans in attendance to see an exhibition game between the Dodgers and the New York Yankees. As Houston Mitchell recounted in *If These Walls Could Talk*, former Dodgers' shortstop and the heart and soul of the ball club Pee Wee Reese wheeled Campanella to home plate. Campanella then spoke to the crowd:

> I thank each and every one of you from the bottom of my heart. This is something I'll never forget as long as I live. I want to thank the Yankees for playing this game, and my old Dodgers team too. It's a wonderful tribute. I thank God I'm able to be here and see it.

The crowd gave Campanella a standing ovation, and, while it would be wrong to claim that there was not a dry eye in the house, more than a few tears were shed. Rather than forget about the plight of Campanella, O'Malley made sure the former Dodger was taken care of and employed him for a number of years. Speaking to the *Los Angeles Times* in August 1979 following O'Malley's death, Campanella stated,

> A lot of people didn't know the man for what he was. He stood by me every minute after my accident, helping me to see my way through. No one knows that after that wonderful night he had for me in the Coliseum when 93,000 showed up, he gave me a check for $50,000. And

he continued my salary, which was more than $50,000 a year, for years after that. He was a great pioneer in integrating baseball. He was the attorney and part owner of the Brooklyn Dodgers when Jackie Robinson, Dan Bankhead, Don Newcombe and Roy Campanella were signed. If we had more people like Walter O'Malley, this world would be a much better place.

While never playing a game in Los Angeles, players like Roy Campanella were what the Dodgers were built upon. In his autobiography, Campanella wrote that Brooklyn was "where I wanted to finish my playing career. I got my wish all right, but in a much different way." Campanella died on June 26, 1993. He was seventy-two years old.

## 1958: THE FIRST SEASON IN LA

After all the turmoil and upheaval of leaving Brooklyn, the headache of trying to find a stadium to play in, as well as dealing with the aftermath of Campanella's paralysis, the team was thankful for the 1958 season to finally begin. After compiling a 15–16 record during Spring Training, expectations were muted about how the Dodgers' season would unfold.

The team began on the road with a visit to the San Francisco Giants, who also moved from New York in the offseason. Unlike the vitriol thrown at O'Malley for moving the Dodgers to California, the Giants only received a fraction of the hatred from the New York media.

On April 15, 1958, the Dodgers faced the Giants in the first major-league game ever played in California—indeed, the first game ever on the West Coast. A crowd of 23,448 packed into Seals Stadium to witness history being made. Don Drysdale was the opening day starter for the Dodgers, while Ruben Gomez took the mound for the Giants. It was a great day for the Giants and a bad beginning for the Dodgers.

Drysdale could not make it out of the fourth, giving up six runs on five hits. In contrast, Gomez threw a complete-game shutout, as the Giants won, 8–0. The Dodgers, however, did not have to wait long for their first win, as they defeated the Giants the following day, 13–1, with Duke Snider hitting two home runs. The Giants came back and defeated the Dodgers 7–4, taking the opening series, with Dodgers pitching great Don Newcombe suffering the loss and hurting his shoulder in the process.

The Dodgers were now ready for their home opener on April 18. Once again, they would be facing the Giants. A major-league-record crowd of 78,672 witnessed the first Dodger home game and the first major-league game at the Los Angeles Coliseum. Before they could take the field, or even get to the stadium, Dodger players and management had to attend a welcoming parade at City Hall. As Endsley eloquently wrote, "With what must have been a dagger to the hearts of Brooklyn Dodger fans, Walter O'Malley presented Los Angeles Mayor Norris Poulson with the actual home plate ripped from Ebbets Field." While one would assume that the players could then get ready to play the actual ballgame, they were then driven in a motorcade to the Coliseum in convertibles. The route was packed almost the entire way, not with the usual Los Angeles gridlock, but with people wanting to catch a sight of their hometown team. The players finally arrived at the stadium after 11:30 a.m.; the Dodgers were finally home—well, their home for the next few years.

Even before the game began, eight people were forced to seek medical attention because they "collapsed from excitement."

Of course, "collapsed from excitement" could also be a euphemism for having too much to drink. A highlight, if you can call it that, was when Mayor Poulson pitched to San Francisco Mayor George Christopher. Christopher could not get a hit from the "hard"-throwing Poulson. The true highlight of the pregame ceremony was when the players from the Dodgers and Giants were introduced to the crowd, with a massive cheer when Campanella's name was called.

After all the hoopla, at long last there was finally a major-league game in Los Angeles. Dodger veteran Carl Erksine took the mound and threw the first pitch at the Coliseum. The first home run at the Coliseum belonged to Giant veteran Hank Sauer, who hit a "mammoth" 275-foot homer in the fourth. What would have been an easy fly out in all other stadiums easily cleared the fence at the Coliseum. The first Dodger home run at the Coliseum belonged to Dick Gray, this being a more legitimate home run, measured at 350 feet. After all was said and done, the Dodgers defeated the Giants, 6–5. The victory was in a large part thanks to Giants rookie third baseman Jim Davenport. Trailing 6–4 in the ninth, Davenport failed to touch third base in the ninth before coming home. He was called out, and even though the great Willie Mays singled home a run later in the inning, Dodger pitcher Clem Labine retired the final two Giants to record the first Dodger victory in Los Angeles. Yet even with the victory and record attendance, Erksine thought the crowd was subdued. D'Antonio noted that Erksine had recalled that the crowd "didn't make half as much noise as thirty thousand in Ebbets Field."

Two great personal milestones occurred on April 23. Dodgers great Gil Hodges hit his 300th home run, while on the same day the legendary Pee Wee Reese, who played his first game for the Dodgers back in 1940, played in his 2,000th game. However, the Dodgers lost to the Chicago Cubs, 7–6.

While fans could not get enough of Dodger baseball, as 1,845,556 attended home games (a Dodger record), the team was not that good. The Dodgers finished the 1958 season with a losing record of 71–83, a mere 21 games behind the Milwaukee Braves. The pitching staff that led the league in ERA the previous year was now last. Playing home games in the Coliseum and the cheap home runs it allowed certainly contributed to the pitchers' less-than-stellar season. While baseball in Los Angeles was a success, it was one of disappointment on the field. More-over, in addition to the tragic accident of Campanella, another all-time Dodger great was not long for LA.

Don Newcombe pitched for the Brooklyn Dodgers from 1949 until 1951. After two years of military service, he rejoined the Dodgers in 1954. He was a four-time All-Star, Rookie of the Year, and the National League Cy Young winner in 1956, as well as an MVP. With the Dodgers decline in 1957, he was not as formidable as he once was but was still a fearsome pitcher. While finishing the season with a 11–12 record, he threw four complete-game shutouts (one less than 1956), and his ERA was 3.49 (only 0.43 higher than the previous season). Though struggling a bit on the field, he found Los Angeles to his liking. He dated numerous celebrities and was a fixture at the best nightclubs in town. However, what may have been "good" for his personal life was not as good for his baseball career. In 11 games with the Los Angeles Dodgers in '58, he compiled a 0–6 record and a whopping 7.86 ERA. Nevertheless, considering his previous success, one would have assumed that the team would not cut ties with "Newk," as he was known. However, baseball is a business above all else, and winning is paramount. While players are expected to be loyal to their team, teams are rarely loyal to their players. Just before the trade deadline of June 15, the Dodgers traded Newcombe, who had no advance notice of his impending trade, to the Cincinnati Reds. Newcombe eventually admitted he was an alcoholic by 1958 and had started drinking heavily due to not only the stress of playing baseball but also having to deal with the pure hatred of many Americans because he was black. By 1961, Newcombe was out of the majors, and even though he was the first former major leaguer to play in the Japanese League in 1962, he only lasted a single season. He felt if it was not for his drinking he could have played for another five years. Newcombe managed to turn his life around and, in 1970, rejoined the Dodgers and helped set up and run their Community Relations department, the first in Major League Baseball. Beginning in 2009, Newcombe was employed by the Dodgers as a special adviser to the chairman. Newcombe passed away on February 19 2019. It was a sad day for the Dodgers.

## 1959: WORLD SERIES CHAMPIONS

Following the disappointing 1957 and 1958 seasons, expectations were not high going into the '59 season. Indeed, the overwhelming majority of the media thought the team would finish near the middle of the pack again, if not even lower. Before the start of the season, O'Malley wanted to fire Dodgers' manager Walter Alston. Only the intervention of Dodger great and now coach Pee Wee Reese and Dodgers general manager Emil Joseph

"Buzzie" Bavasi, who both threatened to quit if Alston was fired, saved Alston's job.[3] However, following a promising Spring Training, there was optimism in the Dodgers' camp. Moreover, after a season playing in the Coliseum, Dodger pitchers were more comfortable playing there. In addition, outfielder Wally Moon, who was acquired in the offseason from the St. Louis Cardinals, mastered the art of hitting home runs to left field using a flick-of-the-wrist technique he learned from Cardinal great Stan Musial.

The Dodgers started off well in April, compiling an 11–6 record. They won or split every series and were tied with Milwaukee for the NL lead. In a highlight for the month, Don Demeter hit three home runs (including an inside-the-park home run) on April 21, driving in six runs—with his third home run coming in the bottom of the 11th to help the Dodgers beat the Giants, 9–7, at the Coliseum. However, all the promise in April dissipated in May with a 14–17 record as the team had slipped to fourth place. However, it was still relatively early in the season, and they were only five games behind Milwaukee in the standings. Indeed, May was the only month the Dodgers had a losing record. And heading into August, they were 13 games above .500 and in second place in the standings, tied with Milwaukee, only half a game behind the Giants. Coming into the last day of August, the Dodgers were trailing the Giants by two games—who they were scheduled to play at the Coliseum. Taking the mound for the Dodgers was twenty-three-year-old Sanford Braun Koufax, more commonly known as Sandy

---

3  Alston would go on to coach the Dodgers until 1976, a total of 23 years as the team's skipper. He would finish was a 2,040–1,613 record (.523) to go along with seven NL pennants and four World Series championships.

Koufax. At this stage of his career, the young pitcher lacked control and still needed time to develop. However, on this day he put it all together. In a precursor for what was to come in the 1960s, before a crowd of 82,794, Koufax struck out 18 Giants (tying the major-league record) as the Dodgers won 5–2, with Moon hitting a three-run home run in the bottom of the ninth, which cut the Giants lead in the standings to a single game.

The Dodgers led the division going into the final week of the season, but Milwaukee was only half a game behind, and the Giants one behind. The final week was not kind to the Giants, who ended the season in third place after losing seven of their last eight games. However, both the Dodgers and Braves had reason to rejoice as they ended the season with similar 86–68 records. Thus, the National League pennant would be decided by a three-game playoff.

On September 28, in the first game of the playoff in Milwaukee, the Dodgers started with Danny McDevitt, who had gone 10–8 on the season. Dodgers manager Walter Alston could have started Koufax, but he did not have faith in the left-hander. Game One was played to a half-empty stadium; Milwaukee fans evidently assumed the Braves would triumph and head to the World Series. It looked promising early on, as McDevitt only lasted 1⅓ innings before the Dodgers brought in rookie Larry Sherry with the score tied 1–1. Following an error and a groundout, the Braves took a 2–1 lead. However, Sherry pitched a great 7⅔ innings, only allowing four hits, and the offense did enough, as the Dodgers triumphed 3–2. Don Drysdale, who had a record of 17–13, started for the Dodgers in Game Two in Los Angeles. Drysdale only fared a little better than McDevitt, giving up four runs (three earned) in

4⅓ innings. Heading into the bottom of the ninth, the Dodgers were trailing 5–2. However, with almost everyone expecting Milwaukee to even the series, the Dodgers scored three runs to send the game into extra innings. And in the bottom of the 12th, the Dodgers started a two-out rally. With men on first and second, Carl Furillo hit the ball to Milwaukee shortstop Felix Mantila, who made a throwing error that allowed the winning run to score, sending the Dodgers to the World Series. It was one of the greatest comebacks in postseason history.

With the Braves out of the way, the Dodgers were set to face the Chicago White Sox, who had won their first American League pennant since the infamous 1919 "Black Sox" team. As Vin Scully proclaimed on the Dodgers' radio broadcast, "We go to Chicago!"

One Dodger was "disappointed" there would be no third game—namely, starting pitcher Roger Craig. Craig was scheduled to start the decider, and, as there was no game, it may well have prevented him from securing the National League ERA title. In *Bums No More*, Endsley recounted Craig stating,

> I had pitched 152⅓ innings and, back then, you had to pitch 154 to qualify for the ERA championship. My ERA was 2.06 and Sam Jones was at 2.89. In 1959, the playoff counted in the regular season statistics. I probably could have given up 13 earned runs and still won the ERA title. But I'd rather win the National League pennant, anyway.

Though disappointed, Craig could take solace in the fact that he was the starting pitcher for Game One of the 1959 World Series.

Game One, however, did not go well for Craig and the Dodgers. Craig gave up five runs in just 2⅓ innings. He was relieved by Chuck Churn, who in turn proceeded to give up six runs in ⅔ of an inning (though only two of those runs were earned). In contrast, American League Cy Young winner Early Wynn did not give up a run over seven innings. The Dodgers ended up losing Game One, 11–0. Craig noted to Endsley that "I was completely out of sync that day. I left too many balls in the middle of the plate. I was a low-ball pitcher, and [Ted] Kluszewski [who drove in five runs] was a good low fastball hitter—not a good matchup from my point of view."

Game Two, however, would go much better for the Dodgers. Trailing 2–1 after six, the Dodgers scored three runs in the top of the seventh with pinch-hitter Chuck Essegian hitting a solo shot to tie the game and Chuck Neal hitting a two-run shot (after a Gilliam walk) to give the Dodgers a 4–2 lead. Essegian would later claim that was the best ball he had ever hit. The Dodgers would end up winning the game, 4–3, with starter Johnny Podres pitching six strong innings and Sherry getting the save with three innings of one-run ball.[4]

The teams then headed to Los Angeles for Game Three. A crowd of 92,394 saw a scoreless game through six innings. Once again it was a pinch-hitter who had the biggest impact in the game. After two walks and the bases loaded, the Sox brought in pitcher Gerry Staley to face Dodger veteran Carl Furillo, who hit a two-run single to give the Dodgers a 2–0 lead—one they would hold on to for the victory. For the Dodgers, Don Drysdale only gave up a run in seven innings and, once again, Sherry got the save by only giving up one hit in two innings.

Game Four saw 92,650 pack the Coliseum. The Dodgers blew the game open in the bottom of the third by recording five

---

4  Saves were not officially recognized until 1969. However, the indispensable Baseball-reference lists saves prior to that date.

straight hits, scoring four runs. Craig, hoping to redeem himself from his Game One outing, pitched six scoreless innings. Unfortunately, he pitched seven innings. Craig gave up four runs in the seventh, including a three-run shot to White Sox catcher Sherm Lollar, as Chicago tied the game. Gil Hodges, however, settled the outcome in the bottom of the eighth with a home run leading off the inning. Sherry got the win for the Dodgers by pitching two innings of scoreless ball while only giving up one walk.

Hoping to see the Dodgers capture the World Series, 92,706 fans were in attendance for Game Five. In a great pitching duel, Koufax only gave up only one run over seven innings while striking out six, and Stan Williams did not give up a run in two innings of relief. Unfortunately for the home side, White Sox pitcher Bob Shaw did not give up a run over seven, and neither did the White Sox bullpen, as Chicago won, 1–0.

With the series at 3–2, the teams headed back to Chicago. In Game Six, held on October 8, 1959, the Los Angeles Dodgers captured their first World Series crown. The Dodgers broke the game open by with a two-run home run from Duke Snider in the third, and the team scored an additional six runs in the fourth. After Podres gave up three runs in 3⅓ innings, Sherry pitched 5⅔ innings while only giving up four hits and no runs, as the Los Angeles Dodgers defeated the Chicago White Sox, 9–3, to win the World Series four games to two. Not surprisingly, Sherry was named World Series MVP.

The Dodgers were now world champions. And for the players, who almost all had jobs in the offseason to make ends meet, being World Series champions meant more money. Years later, shortstop Maury Wills, as retold by Steve Delsohn in *True Blue*, proclaimed, "That was my rookie year after eight and half years in the minors. And the winner's share was $11,000 [actually, a record $11,231]! That was more than twice what I was making. Man, I was going to retire, get that place in the country I always wanted. Wow, an $11,000 check!" Winning, of course, is fundamental, but so is being able to support oneself and family. The extra income was welcomed by all Dodgers.

The '59 Dodgers were not an all-time great team. Indeed, in 1997 Bill James wrote that the 1959 Dodgers "were, in my opinion, the weakest World Championship team of all time." Such a sentiment was shared by Dodgers general manager Bavasi. In *True Blue*, Bavasi claimed that the 1959 Dodgers "was the worst club ever to win a World Series. But it's also my favorite club. Those kids won on sheer courage and fortitude. That's really all it was." Alston proclaimed after the game, "This is the greatest team I ever was connected with, or any manager was ever connected with. This team never quit. It came from behind all the way. It won against big odds."

Indeed, with the pressure on, the batters delivered. Over the six games the Dodgers scored 21 runs, 19 of them coming with two outs. They came through in the clutch. The 1959 Dodgers may or may not be the worst World Series champion of all time, and, I would argue that there were a number of worse World Series champions. But, in the end, all that matters is the 1959 Los Angeles Dodgers, unlike the White Sox, Giants, Yankees, or the twelve other Major League teams, *were* World Series champions.

## THE FIGHT FOR CHAVEZ RAVINE

In addition to the battle on the baseball field, the Dodgers were facing a battle off it—namely, to build a stadium at Chavez

Ravine. In October 1957, the Los Angeles City Council, besotted with the idea of the Dodgers playing in the city, agreed to give O'Malley and the team a 315-acre site to build their ballpark. In addition to giving the Dodgers Chavez Ravine, the city council also offered a $4.7 million package to improve access routes and the like around the area. All the city council wanted in return was Wrigley Field. Even though O'Malley would be using his own funds to build the actual stadium, the city council's offer was too good to refuse. There was only one problem for the Dodgers: the offer did not sit too well with a large segment of the city's population. This eventually led to a referendum, known as Proposition B, to determine whether the land-swap deal would go ahead. Before the referendum, the Dodgers bought television time and hosted an almost five-hour "Dodgerthon" that included appearances from players, as well as a number of celebrities. In the end, the Los Angeles voters approved the land-swap deal. As described by D'Antonio, "The voting pattern, which showed that many districts voted against the position held by their city council representatives, suggested a very independent electorate. Most surprising was the huge yes vote in the very district where the ravine was located. Represented by an opponent of the land swap, Edward Roybal, the area was home to a relatively poor and mostly black and Hispanic population. Given the demographics, one might expect them to resent the notion of families being displaced. However, the people of the district knew the ravine and its history better than others, and apparently preferred to have baseball there. The main opposition came from the mainly middle-class and white districts of the San Fernando Valley, but it was not strong enough to overcome overwhelming approval for the proposition in places like

South Central and Downtown." Of course, the Dodgers' propaganda efforts through the Dodgerthon, and the united support from the media for baseball at Chavez Ravine, undoubtedly had a major effect in swaying voter opinion.

O'Malley's excitement that the proposition passed did not last long, as a California court ruled that the city council "exceeded its authority and violated rules requiring that development of Chavez property serve a public purpose." The issue would be decided in the California Supreme Court. The court ruled in favor of the Dodgers, but those opposed to the Chavez Ravine deal appealed the decision. While defeating the White Sox in the 1959 World Series may have been the highlight of the Dodgers year, O'Malley would have been equally pleased on October 18, as the United States Supreme Court threw out all the challenges to the land-swap deal. The Dodgers were at long last able to build a stadium at Chavez Ravine.

In a decade that saw them win the first, and only, World Series in Brooklyn, the upheaval of moving to LA, and the paralysis of Roy Campanella, the 1950s ended on a very positive note. The Dodgers were world champions after only their second season in Los Angeles and were victorious in the courts—finally cleared to build their own stadium. For O'Malley and the Dodgers, they were eagerly awaiting the new decade and hoping and expecting continued success both on and off the field.

# 3

## 1960S: THE GOLDEN AGE OF LA DODGER BASEBALL AND ITS DECLINE

**T**HE 1960S STARTED with great promise for the Dodgers; they were World Series champions, they were finally able to start construction on their new stadium, and, while they may not have had a star-studded roster, they had high hopes for the upcoming season. Indeed, by mid-April the Dodgers were tied for first in the National League. However, April 21 was the last day the Dodgers would lead the league all season. They posted a lackluster 8–7 record in April, followed by two losing months in May (12–14) and June (13–14). Things picked up again in July, as the Dodgers had a 19–7 record. Once again, optimism filled the hearts of Dodger fans. But for the remainder of the season, they played .500 ball, with a 15–15 record in August, 14–14 in September, and 1–1 in October.

On a positive note, the Dodgers had a winning record for the year, going 82–72. But they finished in fourth, 13 games behind the Pittsburgh Pirates. Individually, first baseman Norm Larker posted a .323 batting average and made the All-Star team. Maury Wills had a breakthrough season, batting .295 while having 50 stolen bases, which led the NL. Another positive was right fielder Frank Howard hitting 23 home runs and winning the NL Rookie of the Year Award.

On the pitching side, Drysdale led the team with 15 wins and an ERA of 2.84, while striking out 246 to lead the league. Nevertheless, the season was one of disappointment for the Dodgers, especially Sandy Koufax.

The 1960 season was Koufax's sixth season pitching for the Dodgers. However, as in all the other years, he was frustrated. It is fair to say that Koufax should have learned his trade in the minors. However, because he was a "bonus baby" and was required to spend at least two seasons with the major league team, Koufax never pitched in the minors. Thus, for all his promise, Koufax was a wild left-hander and, by the end of the 1960 season, had a record of 36–40, with an ERA of 4.10. For Koufax, he believed Alston was not giving him a fair chance to be the pitcher he could be. In contrast, people close to Alston claim that very few managers would have had the patience for Koufax to put it all together. In an infamous exchange at the Coliseum during the 1960 season, Koufax got into an argument with Bavasi. Delsohn recounted the exchange:

"I want to pitch," Koufax screamed at Bavasi, "and you guys aren't giving me a chance!"

"How can you pitch," Bavasi answered, "when you can't get the side out?"

"How can I get anyone out sitting in the dugout?" Sandy snapped.

Koufax was so frustrated during the season that he began giving serious consideration to quitting baseball altogether. Bavasi stated that "Koufax came to me during the '60 season. He said, 'Alston's not pitching me. I'm going home.' I said, 'When do you want to go?' Koufax said, 'Tomorrow.' I said, 'Fine, I'll get you a ticket.'"

While Koufax did not take Bavasi up on his offer, at the end of the season Koufax threw his glove, among other things, in the bin and left the clubhouse. It was a good thing for the Dodgers and for Koufax himself that he stayed with the team, as in the 1961 season he was about to become the pitcher he was destined to be.

\* \* \*

The 1961 season was one of promise for the Dodgers. After having winning months in April, May, June, and July, there was hope that the team might possibly return to the World Series. They battled the Cincinnati Reds for the league lead from late May onward. However, the Dodgers suffered a lackluster August (11–15) and, while they had a winning September, ended up finishing at 89–65, four games behind the first-place Reds. Wally Moon led the team with a .328 batting average, and Wills stole 35 bases, while catcher John Roseboro hit 18 home runs. For the pitching staff, Podres went 18–5 with an ERA of 3.74, Drysdale went 13–10 with an ERA of 3.69, and Koufax went 18–13 with a team-leading ERA of 3.52 and made his first All-Star team.

What led to Koufax starting to put it all together? Apart from Koufax figuring things out, most of the credit has to go to his roommate and back-up Dodger catcher Norm Sherry. During a flight to a Spring Training game, Koufax told Sherry that he wanted to work on his change-up and curve ball. Koufax was meant to only pitch five innings, but as another pitcher missed the flight to the game Koufax would likely have to go about seven. After a less-than-promising start and unable to throw strikes, Koufax walked the bases loaded. Sherry then visited the mound. He told Delsohn about his conversation with Koufax: "Sandy, we only got one other pitcher here. And at this rate, you're gonna be out here all day. Why don't you take something off the ball? Don't even try and strike these next guys out. Just throw it over the plate and let them hit it."

Koufax then proceeded to strike out the side and throw a no-hitter for seven innings. The proverbial lightbulb went off in Koufax's head. He started to master his command, and, while 1961 was a good season (he still walked 96 batters in 255 2/3 innings, but this was a marked improvement from the previous season where he walked 100 in 175 innings), he truly came into his own as one of the best pitchers ever the following season.

## 1962: INTEGRATION, A NEW STADIUM, AND A COLLAPSE

Despite Jackie Robinson breaking the color barrier in baseball and paving the way for players like Newcombe and Wills, the reality was that American society was still a long way from being integrated. The black Dodger players knew that many people would cheer them at games but would be mortified if they moved next door or even into the same neighborhood. There were many Los Angeles neighborhoods that black Dodger players understood they should not live in if they wanted a quiet, peaceful life. Moreover, it was every aspect of society that was still unofficially segregated. As Michael Leahy wrote in *The Last Innocents* about Wills,

> Being the honored guest at a country club's banquet, where he usually would be the only black invitee, remained as awkward for him as ever. Never would he feel quite as small at such events as when hugely successful white people sang his praises as an outstanding ballplayer, an excellent role model, and a credit to everyone who knew him. Something faintly patronizing about it left him wanting to be gone.

At least, at the Coliseum or at Dodger Stadium, people could sit wherever they wanted, and, heaven forbid, blacks and whites could even sit next to each other.

The same was not true at Holman Stadium, the Dodgers' Spring Training venue. Black fans were only allowed to sit in the right-field corner and next to the left foul pole. Moreover, there were segregated bathrooms, entrances, and water fountains. In 1962, the black Dodger players had enough of this disgraceful situation. As Tommy Davis recounts in *The Last Innocents*, "We just thought, No more . . . . We were the Dodgers. We were the team that had broken barriers. We weren't going to put up with this stuff Vero Beach was doing with our ballpark. We were going to have to get him to do something about it." "Him" was Walter O'Malley's son, Peter. Part of Peter O'Malley's responsibilities was managing Holman Stadium. Davis notes that "we told him, 'This was the place where Jackie came to play for our team—this is where Jackie stood . . . We are the Dodgers. We don't do this. We don't stand for this. Vero Beach can do what it wants, but this is Dodgertown—we don't do things like that here.' We kept talking, and Peter listened very respectfully." To Peter O'Malley's credit, within two days the bathrooms were integrated and the word *colored* was painted over throughout the stadium. Vero Beach officials could have forced the Dodgers to revert back to segregation due to a racist ordinance that separated blacks and whites. However, in this case money was more important than racism, and Vero Beach officials allowed the desegregation with nary a word.

There were also changes with the Dodgers' home stadium in 1962—namely, the opening of the stadium in Chavez Ravine or, as it was known later, Dodger Stadium. On April 10, the Dodgers played their first game at their new stadium against the Cincinnati Reds. The players were happy to be finally having home games at a real baseball stadium, with the dimensions being 400 feet to center, 370 feet to the power alleys, and 330 feet to both the left and right foul poles. The pitchers were particularly happy, as there was no longer any prospect of cheap home runs—especially as the cool night air made it even more difficult for batters to hit the ball out. While the players were happy to be in a true ballpark, the home opener did not go according to the plan, as the Reds beat the Dodgers, 6–3. Los Angeles would have to wait until the following day for their first victory at Chavez Ravine. On the back of a complete game from Koufax, the Dodgers beat the Reds 6–2.

As for the rest of the season, the Dodgers finished the schedule with a 101–61, record, tied with the Giants. The Dodgers then proceeded to lose a three-game playoff against San Francisco, two games to one. Individually, Tommy Davis had a great year, leading the league in batting average (.346), hits (230), and RBIs (153). Frank Howard smashed 31 home runs while driving in

119. And in the best performance for the Dodgers, Wills hit .299, lead the league in triples (10), and incredibly stole 104 bases while only being caught 13 times. Wills broke Ty Cobb's stolen-base record of 96. Set in 1915, the record was thought by many to be unbeatable.

It was a breathtaking year for Wills. Every time he got on base, Dodger—and sometimes even opposing—fans would yell, "Go, go, go!" Wills payed a high price, with his legs and feet being a constant shade of purple due to the pounding they took every time he stole a base, yet, in a testament to his fortitude and resilience, he kept running. Wills was named the National League MVP.

On the pitching side, Drysdale had a magnificent year, going 25–9 (leading the league in wins) with an ERA of 2.83 while striking out a league-leading 232. He was a very worthy recipient of the Cy Young Award. Koufax went 14–7 with an ERA of 2.54—which led the league—while striking out 216.

The 1962 season was shaping up to be a monumental one for Koufax. On April 24 versus the Cubs, Koufax pitched a complete game, only giving up six hits and two runs while striking out 18. On June 30 at Dodger Stadium, in front of a crowd of 29,797, he struck out 13 Mets while giving up five walks on his way to his first no-hitter. It was a thing of beauty.

Unfortunately, tragedy was about to strike. Early in the 1961 season, Koufax decided to bat left-handed (he usually batted right-handed), and during an at-bat his hands got jammed. Come 1962, Koufax started feeling something was wrong by May, while in June his hand started to go numb. In a 1963 *Sports Illustrated* article by Robert Creamer, Koufax noted that "The trouble was down here in the palm, here where the fleshy part of the thumb joins the palm. There was a blood clot right there, and that cut off the circulation to the index finger and partly to the next finger and thumb." In early July, Koufax pulled himself out of a game after seven innings because of the issue. On July 17, he had to leave after the first. Koufax recalled that "The doctors told me later that at the time they weren't worried so much about when I was going to pitch again as they were that they might have to amputate the finger." While Koufax returned in late September, the finger still bothered him, and he was largely ineffective, giving up ten earned runs in only 8⅔ innings spread across four games. That Koufax was basically unable to pitch from July onward arguably led to the Dodgers failing to win the pennant and the infamous collapse at the end of the season.

With seven games remaining, the Dodgers lead the Giants by four full games. Most observers were already salivating at the prospect of a Dodger-Yankee World Series.[5] However, the Dodgers could only record one solitary win in their last seven games, while the Giants went 5–2. A three-game playoff would decide who would be facing the Yankees. In Game One, Koufax started for the Dodgers, but as previously noted he was not the same pitcher as before the finger injury. He only lasted an inning, giving up three runs on two homers. The Giants ended up trouncing the Dodgers, 8–0.

As Houston Mitchell recounted in *If These Walls Could Talk*, after the game Koufax claimed that "I had an idea what I wanted to do out there, but I couldn't seem to do it. . . . I try to throw hard, but the ball doesn't come out hard and my control was way off."

---

5  The teams had already met in seven World Series match-ups, with the Yankees winning all but one (1955).

In the second game, Cy Young winner Drysdale started for LA; he only lasted 5⅓ innings while giving up five runs. After the Giants scored four runs in the top of the sixth, the Dodgers were trailing 5–0. However, the Dodgers had a seven-run reply to give them a 7–5 lead. The Giants, not to be denied, scored two more in the top of the eighth to tie the score.

In the bottom of the ninth, the Dodgers loaded the bases with only one out and Wills at third. To the plate stepped first baseman Ron Fairly. Giants' pitcher Mike McCormick quickly got ahead in the count, 0-2. On the third pitch, Fairly hit a fly ball to center field that was easily caught by Willie Mays. Wills just beat the throw from Mays to home and the Dodgers walked off with an 8–7 victory. Mitchell wrote that Fairly joked that "If I had been on third base instead of Wills, we'd still be playing." LA would not be so fortunate in the deciding game at Dodger stadium.

The Dodgers were leading the Giants 4–2 following eight innings. Alston sent out reliever Ed Roebuck, who had pitched the previous three innings without giving up a run despite relieving Podres in the sixth with the bases loaded and none out. At the urging of Snider, Drysdale went to Alston and told him he wanted to pitch the ninth. Alston replied that he would be starting the next day in Game One of the World Series. Following a single and a failed double-play ball, Roebuck then proceeded to walk Willie McCovey and Felipe Alou to load the bases. With Willie Mays up, he gave up a single to score a run, and the lead was down to one. Once again instead of going to Drysdale, Alston turned to Stan Williams. The Giants tied the game with a sacrifice fly by Orlando Cepeda, and, following a wild pitch, Williams intentionally walked Ed Bailey to again load the bases. Williams then walked in Jim Davenport, the go-ahead run. He was mercifully replaced by Ron Perranoski.

The proverbial wheels had truly fallen off for the Dodgers by this stage, as another run scored through an error to give the Giants a 6–4 lead. They would make short work of LA in the bottom of the ninth. Thus, not only did the Dodgers collapse during the regular season, they collapsed in the ninth inning of the deciding playoff game, which handed the Giants a World Series appearance.

Understandably, several LA players blamed the loss on Alston. Another person blaming Alston was the third-base coach and former Brooklyn Dodger manager, Leo Durocher. Durocher was hired by O'Malley in November 1960 and never got along with Alston. It turned into outright conflict in 1962, especially when the Dodgers began to struggle down the stretch. Wills argued that the reason why Alston never allowed Drysdale to pitch in the ninth was because Durocher was vocally advocating it in the dugout. Rather than keep the conflict internal, Durocher allegedly told the media that the Dodgers would have won the pennant if he was their manager. As soon as he was told of Durocher's comments, Bavasi fired him. However, Alston would not allow it. The most likely explanation is that he probably knew O'Malley would likely stop Bavasi from firing Durocher. Indeed, O'Malley wanted to fire Alston. However, once again Bavasi told O'Malley that he would resign if he fired Alston. Thus, neither Alston nor Durocher were fired, and the conflict was set to continue for the 1963 season.

## 1963: WORLD SERIES TRIUMPH

Before the season got underway, the conflict between Alston and Durocher roared back to life due to the media and Drysdale. The magazine *Sport* had an article "Will Dissension Destroy the

Dodgers?" focusing on the managerial conflict. Adding fuel to the fire was Drysdale, who was quoted as saying in regard to the disastrous top of the ninth in the third playoff game, "You're damn right I would have liked to pitch. Only they [meaning Alston] didn't ask me."

If LA had a good start to the season, the conflict would have gone away. After all, a winning team is a happy team. Unfortunately for Alston, the Dodgers only went 10–11 in April and, by May 3, were in sixth place in the standings. The next day they proceeded to lose again to Pittsburgh, only winning one game in the four-game series. As one could imagine, there was dissension in the clubhouse, and the media was continually calling for O'Malley to fire Alston. However, the series loss turned the season around. Following the games, the team took an old bus without air-conditioning from the stadium to the airport. Several players were unhappy with this situation and let the traveling secretary know about it. As fate would have it, the Dodger bus passed the Pirates new air-conditioned bus. This further upset the players. Finally, Alston had enough and told the driver to pull the bus over. As Fairly recounted in *True Blue*, Alston said, "Anybody who doesn't like this bus? Get off it and come outside. We'll settle it right there." Alston then proceeded to get off the bus and walked back and forth looking at the players through the windows. Nobody got off. He eventually got back on the bus, looked directly at the biggest Dodgers in size, including Frank Howard, and said, "Anybody got anything to say?" Not one player said at word. Coincidence or not, LA then proceeded to go on a 13–2 run.

However, even with the great run in May, the Dodgers lost their last two games for the month and the first three in June.

As a result, once again the press began calling for Alston's head. Indeed, before a game with Chicago in early June, the Cubs head coach predicted if the Dodgers lose that day's game that Durocher would take over. LA swept the series in Chicago but were inconsistent in June, going 16–12. The pressure on Alston was still firmly in place. The team responded by going 21–10 in July, and while they had an up-and-down August they were still six games up heading into September. After a bad start to the month, their lead was cut to a single game on September 15, and, once again, there was fear of a collapse to rival the previous seasons. This would not happen in 1963, however, as the Dodgers then won nine of their next ten games and clinched the National League pennant. The World Series that many had hoped for the previous year would now be happening: the Los Angeles Dodgers vs. the New York Yankees.

Individually, Davis had another great year to lead the NL in batting with a .326 average. Wills hit .302 while stealing 40 bases (quite simply, his body was not in condition to try to steal as many bases after last year's record-breaking season), and Howard lead the team with 28 home runs while batting .273.

On the pitching side, Drysdale had an average year in regard to wins and losses, going 19–17, but his ERA was 2.83 (his lowest since 1957), and he threw 17 complete games (only two less than in 1962). Veteran Johnny Podres went 14–12 with an ERA of 3.54 (his best since 1960), while closer Ron Perranoski saved 21 games and went 16–3 with an ERA of 1.67. And then there was Koufax.

If the 1961 and 1962 seasons showed a glimpse of what he was capable of, 1963 was the start of arguably the greatest four-year run a pitcher has ever had. In 1963, Koufax went 25–5 with an ERA of 1.88, while striking out 306 with 11 shutouts. Koufax did not just lead the NL in these categories, but all of baseball. It was truly an extraordinary season. Moreover, on May 11 versus the Giants in front of a crowd of 49,807 at Dodger Stadium, Koufax was at his best. After eight innings of giving up only a walk, Koufax returned to the mound seeking his second no-hitter. After making short work of Joey Amalfitano and Jose Pagan, Koufax walked Willie McCovey. However, Koufax was not to be denied this day. On an 0-1 count, he got Harvey Kuenn to ground out. Koufax had thrown his second no-hitter as LA beat their hated rivals, 8–0. It was an odd outing for Koufax in the sense that he only struck out four Giants, but it was another masterful performance. Koufax was fast becoming a must-see attraction. At the end of the season, Koufax was duly rewarded as the Cy Young Award winner and NL MVP. In addition, the fans recognized his greatness. Every time Koufax pitched, it meant an extra five to ten thousand fans would attend Dodger Stadium. The extra fans meant approximately $1.05 million in revenue for O'Malley. In return, O'Malley "rewarded" Koufax by paying him a measly $35,000 to pitch for the Dodgers for the 1963 season, with no guarantee he would ever receive another contract. By way of comparison, Wally Moon's salary was $36,000, Wills $45,000, and Drysdale's $46,000. Giants legend Willie Mays was the highest paid player in the game, receiving $105,000. Quite simply, before the Major League Players' Association (MLBPA) came under the leadership of Marvin Miller, the players were not adequately rewarded for their labor. That was, however, in the future. For now, Koufax would have to "accept" being under-paid (but as we shall see, he did not meekly accept the situation). And also, there was still a World Series to win.

In the lead-up to Game One of the World Series, LA was the underdog—even with Koufax scheduled to pitch. Pitching for the Yankees was the veteran and legendary player Whitey Ford. That the Dodgers were the underdogs amused their players—especially Wills, who expected his team to not only win but dominate the Yankees. In Game One at Yankee Stadium, Wills, despite his confidence, was nervous before the game. To calm his nerves, he drank some brandy that Roseboro brought. While Roseboro was taking a couple of sips of his own, he saw Alston staring at him, smiling.

As for the game itself, LA got to Ford early, scoring four runs in the second and another in the third. And giving Koufax a five-run lead meant the game was as good as over. Koufax did not have a bad game; he gave up two runs on six hits while striking out 15 (a World Series record) as the Dodgers won, 5–2. While Koufax was already a hero in Los Angeles, his performance in Game One made him a national star. The Yankees were mesmerized. As Leahy recounted, Yankee starter Jim Bouton remembered,

> It wasn't just the speed of Koufax's pitches but the smoothness of his motion . . . It was easy for him—it was like playing catch. He didn't seem to be throwing hard. The ball just seemed to explode at the last second. It seemed so big coming out of his hand, like it's floating. Then it just explodes—it's like an optical illusion. Wham, it's past you and on the ground.

Yet Koufax told the media following the game, "I felt a little weak. . . . I just felt a little tired in general early in the game. Then I felt a little weak in the middle of the game. Then I got some of my strength back, but I was a little weak again at the end."

Despite their setback, the Yankees were confident going in Game Two. This confidence was misplaced, however. Once again, LA scored early, with Davis driving in two in the first. That would be more than enough, as Podres pitched a gem, going 8 ⅓ innings while giving up only a single run on six hits, as the Dodgers won, 4–1. The Dodgers had come into Yankee Stadium and dominated the home team.

The Series now headed to Los Angeles, and, despite this, the Yankees were still seemingly confident—at least publicly—on winning. Ford claimed that his team would be leaving LA with the series tied at two. On the day of his start in Game Three, Bouton and backup infielder Phil Linz printed a fake newspaper with the headline "Bouton Shuts Out the Dodgers, Linz Wins Game with Homer." On the way to Dodger Stadium, Bouton showed the rest of the Yankees, which led to great mirth. The Yankees were very confident that they would have no trouble getting hits off Game Three starter Don Drysdale. Once again, the Dodgers jumped out to an early lead, with Davis driving in third baseman Jim Gilliam with a single in the first. Following the first, Bouton settled down and pitched a superb seven innings while only giving up that solidarity run. Hal Reniff pitched a scoreless eighth for the Yankees. Unfortunately for the Yankees, they did not get to Drysdale. "Big D" pitched magnificently, throwing a complete-game shutout while only allowing three hits and one walk to nine strikeouts. Mitchell noted that Drysdale claimed, "I don't know if this was the best I've ever pitched, but I had real good stuff and I was able to put almost every pitch right where I wanted it to go." The Dodgers won the game, 1–0, and took a 3–0 Series lead with Koufax scheduled to pitch in Game Four the following day. Yet the Yankees—well, at least Bouton—were still confident that they were going to come back. Bouton later told Leahy that "The history of our team said we came back all the time. Even after losing the third game, we thought we could still win the Series, that we were going to score whatever runs were needed and win. The dynasty would continue: that was our attitude."

Once again, Koufax would be facing Ford. This time LA did not get to Ford early. Indeed, scores were tied at zero following the top of the fifth. But in the bottom of the inning, Frank Howard hit a towering home run to deep left field to give the Dodgers a 1–0 lead. This was the first time a ball had reached the second deck since the stadium had opened. Many in the crowd expected that was all the Dodgers needed; after all, Koufax was on the mound. However, in the top of the seventh, a hobbled Mickey Mantle hit a tracer-bullet home run to left-center to tie the game. The tie would not last long, however. In the bottom of the seventh, Jim Gilliam hit a ball to third, but while the throw was accurate to Yankee first baseman Joe Pepitone, he lost sight of the ball, and it bounced off his arm, allowing Gilliam to reach third. Up to the plate came center fielder Willie Davis, who promptly hit a fly ball to deep center, allowing Gilliam to score easily. That was all Koufax needed; he only allowed two more hits (a single in the eighth and the ninth) for the rest of the game. In another outstanding display of pitching, Koufax only gave up one run on six hits and no walks, while striking out eight.

The Dodgers had swept the Yankees on the back of sublime pitching from Podres, Drysdale, and Koufax. Not surprisingly, Koufax was named World Series MVP. While the Dodger players were justifiably overjoyed, they only held subdued celebrations. Wills later told Leahy, "We were just happy . . . really happy and glad it was over. You were always glad when it was over." As was Alston. After ending the previous year with a large segment of the team, Durocher, and the media calling for his head, Alston was vindicated. The Los Angeles Dodgers were once again World Series champions.

# 1964: BASEBALL IS NOT EVERYTHING

The 1964 season is not a year fondly remembered. After their dominance over the Yankees in the World Series, many people began thinking about a dynasty. However, the Dodgers played inconsistent ball all year, and the only time they were in first place was after a 4–0 victory over the St. Louis Cardinals on Opening Day, with Koufax pitching a complete game shutout. They fell to fourth in the standings the next day following a loss. Amazingly, for the rest of the season they got no higher than fifth and ended up in sixth place, 13 games behind the Cardinals. Injuries to Roseboro, Podres, and Davis hammered the Dodgers' chances, not to mention Koufax injuring his elbow on August 8 (to be noted). What happened off the field had a great bearing on the Dodgers season and subsequent seasons. While baseball may seem like life-and-death to the fans, the reality is that the players are human. They have the same failings that we all do.

Frank Howard was a man-mountain. At his peak, he was 6-foot-8 and weighed 275 pounds, yet he was wary of others. In a 1964 profile in *Sports Illustrated*, he noted, "Five years ago I couldn't sit down and talk to anyone I didn't know well. I would run and hide to avoid publicity. I still don't get on easily with people that I don't know. I'm a moody guy, and I've done some stupid things."

Even though he and LA were playing well at the end of the 1963 season, Howard wanted to quit baseball. While he was talked out of it, he wanted out once again before the start of the 1964 season. He noted,

> A combination of things hit me all at once. I had some personal problems which had to be ironed out. The way I felt, mentally and physically, it would have been an injustice to the club and to myself to try and play baseball. Some people began writing things off the top of their heads about a matter which they knew nothing about. My wife became the brunt of unfair criticism, but she hadn't done anything. It was my fault, and I was confused. I went to several priests to see what I should do. Finally George Mackin, a vice president of the Green Bay Packaging Company where I work as a sales trainee, gave me some good advice. He said, "Frank, a man should do what his abilities show he should do. Right now you don't know much about the box business, but you know baseball, and deep down you love it. If I were you, Frank, I would go back." So I did.

While ill-informed fans and the media would label Howard as soft, among other less-flattering terms (after all, who would not want to play professional baseball?), players are not machines. They are human beings who share the strengths and weaknesses we all have.

As for his season, Howard had averaged .282 and 24 home runs over his previous four seasons. He still hit 24 home runs in 1964, but his batting average dropped to .226. Howard was unhappy that he was being platooned, and Alston and Bavasi thought that power hitters were pointless at Dodger Stadium. Thus, when Howard asked to be traded following the season, LA management duly obliged. Howard was traded to the

Washington Senators for Claude Osteen, John Kennedy, and cash considerations. Howard ended up playing until the end of the 1973 season, was a four-time All-Star, and had a great career. He eventually became a major-league manager. Frank Howard was a great Dodger and, more importantly, was able to overcome the problems that plagued him in 1963 and 1964.

\* \* \*

Respect is essential; we all want to be respected. One Dodger who did not believe the organization respected him was Sandy Koufax. Prior to the start of the 1964 season, Koufax wanted a substantial raise on his relatively meager income. After all, if he was worth at least $1 million to the Dodgers, it was only fair that he receive a fair proportion of that. Koufax was the reigning Cy Young winner, NL MVP, and World Series MVP. It could be argued that there was no better baseball player on the planet. Koufax was not asking for the world, but rather seeking $85,000. As it currently stood, Drysdale and Wills were the highest paid Dodgers, each earning less than $50,000. Bavasi was telling the media that the Dodgers would have trouble paying Koufax even $50,000 and implied that the lefty was seeking $100,000. Once negotiations began, Bavasi offered Koufax $65,000. After arguing for over 2½ hours, Koufax signed for $70,000. The reality was before the advent of free agency the teams truly owned the players. If Koufax wanted to keep playing baseball, he had to do it with the Dodgers. In contrast to the heated negotiations with Koufax, LA management gave Drysdale a similar salary without any anguish. While Koufax was not happy with the outcome, he was willing to put the acrimonious negotiations behind him. However, the next day the *Los Angeles Herald-Examiner* claimed that Koufax had demanded $90,000 or he would quit baseball. Koufax was convinced that Bavasi or someone with Dodger management had fed the story to the Dodger beat writer at the *Examiner*, Bob Hunter.

Quite simply, Koufax felt disrespected. As Koufax's roommate and teammate Dick Tracewski told Leahy,

> He wanted to be respected for what he did, and part of that respect meant a fair salary and being treated fairly. I liked Buzzie [Bavasi]. But I'm not sure Sandy holds the same opinion. It always seemed Buzzie and the Dodgers had some reporters writing what they wanted to be written. Bob Hunter was in bed with the Dodgers, we always thought. It bothered Sandy when he read things in the paper that he knew were just wrong and that had to be coming from the Dodgers. It showed no respect, he thought. The respect to him was bigger than the money.

Koufax was still fuming on the opening day of Spring Training. He talked to several reporters about the anger and disrespect he felt. This led O'Malley to try to defuse the situation. It is fair to say that he was unsuccessful. While O'Malley claimed LA management did not plant the story, he basically insulted Koufax by claiming that the lefty's father would understand the reality of bargaining better and Koufax was young and, by implication, naive. Eventually, Koufax and Bavasi had a meeting, and while nothing was resolved they claimed that everything was settled. It was not as the following season would demonstrate.

As for Koufax's 1964 season, he went 19–5 with a league-leading ERA of 1.74 to go along with seven shutouts, also best in the NL. However, Koufax had injured his elbow in the first inning of a game on April 22, which caused him to miss two scheduled starts. He returned to action after twelve days. Incredibly, Alston did not protect Koufax in the slightest, as he ended up pitching ten innings as the Dodgers beat the Cubs, 2–1. Moreover, on May 24, after pitching another complete game three days earlier, Koufax came in on relief and pitched three innings as LA shut out the Phillies, 3–0, with Koufax earning the save. Considering that Koufax was still recovering from injury and the Dodgers were 6½ games out of first place, the treatment of Koufax was reprehensible. He was the Dodger's ace and should have been protected. Nevertheless, Koufax was still at the height of his powers. On June 4 against the Phillies, in front of 29,709 fans at Connie Mack Stadium, Koufax only gave up one walk while striking out 12 as he recorded his third career no-hitter.

Unfortunately for baseball fans across the country and for Koufax himself, he would suffer a more serious injury later in the season. On August 8, Koufax hurt his elbow sliding into second base. Koufax claimed that it hurt as expected, but it had all but dissipated when he went back out to pitch. The following morning Koufax had a lump on his elbow and could not even brush his teeth without pain. However, even though the team knew the pain Koufax was in, nothing was done to try to remedy the situation. One would assume that the Dodgers would try to protect the best pitcher in the majors; they did not. Indeed, on August 12, Koufax pitched a complete game, as the Dodgers beat Cincinnati, 4–1, and on August 16 he pitched a complete-game shutout, striking out 13 (tied his season high) as the Dodgers won, 3–0.

On August 17, Koufax awakened to swelling not just in his elbow but also in his entire arm. It was so bad that he could not bend or straighten his arm. This time, even though Koufax still wanted to pitch, the font office acted. An X-ray revealed Koufax had traumatic arthritis. The ailment was almost certainly due to pitching. There was no cure, and the arthritis would only get worse. Koufax was prescribed phenylbutazone, which would eventually be banned for use by humans by the Food and Drug Administration because of very serious side effects. A couple weeks later, Koufax tried throwing the ball to Dodgers coach Joe Becker. The elbow swelled up almost immediately. Koufax did not pitch again for the rest of the season. It was the "perfect" end to a horrible season, both on and off the field.

There was, however, one positive for Dodger players. The 1964 season was the last time that Durocher would coach the team. During the season, players were becoming increasingly annoyed that Durocher openly advocated fining them for their mistakes, continually attempted to undermine Alston, and remained a loud, abrasive bully. Two incidents sealed his fate. During the middle of the season, Durocher, while talking to the media, started hitting the shins of Howard with a bat. Even though Howard told him to stop in no uncertain terms, Durocher, acting like a bully, did not. Howard finally had enough, lifted Durocher up, and threw him backward. While Durocher got the message on that day, he still was the clubhouse bully. Later that year, he challenged Dodger backup catcher Jeff Torborg, saying that he could knock the ball from Torborg's glove while the catcher was blocking home plate. Dodger coach Pete Reiser threw the ball to Torborg, who blocked home plate, and running in came Durocher, who was knocked out cold in the collision. He was lying on the ground with one of his legs quivering.

The players did not respect Durocher. At the end of the year, he was let go by the Dodgers, with neither Bavasi nor Alston saying a word to prevent his firing. The Dodger players, and indeed players across baseball, were becoming sick of the way they were treated. The players were meant to be professional, but *all* players were underpaid; the majority had to work in the offseason to survive and had to deal with coaches and management who thought they were better than them. Change would eventually come, starting in the 1966 season, but before then the 1965 season would be remembered as one for the ages.

## 1965: A BRAWL AND WORLD SERIES CHAMPIONS ONCE AGAIN

The 1965 Dodgers finished the season with a 97–65 record. For much of the season they were in first place, but a bad run in September saw them drop to 4½ games back, with the Giants going on their own 14–0 run in the month. However, a 13–0 run in late September saw them once again take the NL lead. Then on October 2, in front of 41,574 fans at Dodger Stadium, Koufax pitched a complete game, giving up four hits and a walk while striking out 13 as the Dodgers defeated the Milwaukee Braves, 3–1, to clinch the National League pennant. The Dodgers were headed to the World Series once again.

Individually, Wills had another outstanding year, hitting .286 while leading the NL in stolen bases once again, this time with 94. Jim Lefebvre hit .250 with 12 home runs while winning the NL Rookie of the Year Award. Drysdale had also another stellar season on the mound, going 23–12 with an ERA of 2.77.

Condemning the Giants to second place must have been particularly sweet for the players because, in addition to the natural rivalry, they were still fuming after a horrendous brawl involving the teams on August 22.

Trouble had been brewing since August 19. Wills had deliberately hit Giants catcher Tom Haller in the mask with his bat on a bunt to try to get the umpire to call catcher's interference. The plan worked, as Wills was awarded first base. This, understandably, infuriated the Giants. Later in the game, Giant Felipe Alou tried the same thing. This greatly annoyed Dodger catcher Roseboro, who told Alou in no uncertain terms never to do that again. This led to Giants' pitcher Juan Marichal yelling at Roseboro from the dugout. While there were no further incidents in that game, the stage was set for bloodshed.

On August 22 in the second inning, Marichal threw two pitches high and tight on Wills, though he would end up lining out to end the inning. In the third inning, with two outs, Marichal threw very close pitches—now to Fairly (who would ground out). The Dodgers were irate at this point, but, and as fortune would have it, Marichal was due to lead off in the bottom of the third. Koufax was on the mound for the Dodgers. However, it was very rare for him to deliberately hit a batter. While Drysdale hit 154 batters in his career, Koufax only ever hit 18. His teammates claim that Koufax was afraid that he could seriously injure or even kill an opposing batter if he set out to hit him. Roseboro claimed that if Drysdale was pitching, the brawl would never have happened because Drysdale would have retaliated by knocking Giants' batters off their feet. Because Koufax was on the mound and did not want to hit Marichal, the Dodgers went to Plan B. Koufax threw high and inside to Marichal. Then, when returning the ball to Koufax, Roseboro threw a bullet back very close to Marichal's ear; Marichal would later claim that the ball hit him. Marichal then said a few choice words to Roseboro, who took a step toward the Giant. Marichal did not respond in kind. In fact, Marichal did not even throw a punch at Roseboro. Instead, in a heinous display, he hit Roseboro as hard as he could with his bat. Not surprisingly, the Dodger players were beyond incensed, as blood was pouring from Roseboro's eyes. Willie Mays tried to calm the situation by holding on to Roseboro; Mays, as did several other players, believed that Roseboro's eye was knocked out of his head. Marichal had, in fact, missed Roseboro's eye by a matter of inches. The blood, through a two-inch cut in Roseboro's forehead, was what was running into his eye. Roseboro would require fourteen stitches to close the cut. San Francisco police were forced to intervene and stop the brawl, as Marichal went toward the mound—with bat still in hand—looking for more Dodgers to attack.

Shockingly, Marichal was only suspended for eight game days and was fined the maximum allowable amount of $1,750. If the same thing happened today, Marichal would be facing a lengthy suspension. The Dodgers were disgusted that Marichal got off so easily; quite simply, he should have faced criminal proceedings for his actions. Roseboro launched a civil suit again Marichal seeking $110,000 in damages; the case was settled with Roseboro receiving $7,500. Eventually, and somewhat shockingly, Roseboro and Marichal reconciled and were on friendly terms for the rest of their lives.

It is fair to say that Roseboro and Marichal, despite the brawl, respected each other. It was through mutual respect that they could overcome their animosity and become friends.

\* \* \*

For whatever reason, despite his greatness, the Dodger front office and sections of the media did not truly respect Sandy Koufax. A 1965 *Time* magazine article had this to say about Koufax: "Just because a man does his job better than anybody else doesn't mean that he has to take it seriously—or even like it." It goes on to claim that "Alone among ballplayers, Koufax is an anti-athlete."

To claim that Koufax did not like baseball or even take the game seriously is laughable. Somewhat shockingly, such an opinion was shared by at least some in the Dodger organization. In the article, Dodger executive Fresco Thompson had the audacity to state that Koufax did not even like baseball: "What kind of a line is he drawing anyway—between himself and the world, between himself and the team?" Dodger management and O'Malley responded to the article—and especially Thompson's comments—by doing nothing. That a Dodger executive could so disparage such a great player is telling what management thought of Koufax the person. Koufax was a Dodger if he continued to play well, but to management he was never one of "them."

It is difficult to escape the notion that the reason why Koufax was painted as different by the media and even Dodger management was because he is Jewish. One just has to look at how Koufax was viewed as money-hungry prior to the start of the 1964 season. The front office had to be dragged kicking and screaming to give Koufax a substantial rise, while Drysdale got almost as much money without any animosity or planted stories about him quitting the game if he was not paid. As Leahy correctly claimed, there were several "anti-Semitic stereotypes and prejudices occasionally evident in newspaper references to Koufax's supposed business shrewdness and inferences that Koufax might be less committed to the Dodgers than to getting more money, in and out of the sport. (No other player in the game suffered through such veiled and repugnant speculation about his motives—there can be no reasonable doubt about its cause and effect.)" Koufax was singled out, and the only thing different about him, apart from being the best player on the planet, was that he is Jewish.

On the field, Koufax had another stellar season. He went 26–8 with an ERA of 2.04, tallying up a stunning 382 strikeouts.[6] He led the NL in wins, win-loss record, ERA, complete games, innings pitched, and strikeouts. It was an amazing season for Koufax who, with all the accolades, pitched what is still considered *the* perfect game. On September 9, in front of only 29,139 fans at Dodger Stadium, Koufax went head-to-head with Cubs' pitcher Bob Hendley. In a game that only lasted one hour and forty-three minutes, Hendley only gave up one hit and one walk while giving up a single run in a great pitching performance. Unfortunately for Hendley and the Cubs, Koufax was simply perfect. One out away from a perfect game, Koufax faced Harvey Kuenn who was pitch-hitting for Hendley. Following a 2-2 count, Koufax struck out Kuenn—his 14th on the day—on the way to a perfect game. Legendary broadcaster Vin Scully had the pleasure of calling the game. Following the final out and after thirty-eight seconds of wild applause from the crowd, Scully spoke:

---

6  This was the highest amount in the twentieth century, breaking Rube Waddell's 1904 record of 349.

> On the scoreboard in right field it is 9:46 p.m. in the City of the Angels, Los Angeles, California. And a crowd of 29,139 just sitting in to see the only pitcher in baseball history to hurl four no-hit, no-run games. He has done it four straight years, and now he caps it—on his fourth no-hitter he made it a perfect game. And Sandy Koufax, whose name will always remind you of strikeouts, did it with a flurry. He struck out the last six consecutive batters. So when he wrote his name in capital letters in the record books, that k stands out even more than the o-u-f-a-x.

It was the perfect call to what the Society of American Baseball Research, and many including this author, considers *the* perfect game.

Now all the Dodgers had to do to cap off a memorable year was win the World Series. Facing the Dodgers were the Minnesota Twins, who had an even better year than the Dodgers, going 102–60 to win the American League pennant by seven games over the White Sox. Taking the mound for the Twins in Game One would be Mudcat Grant, with Drysdale pitching for the Dodgers.

While one would have expected Koufax to start Game One, it was scheduled for October 6, which happened to fall on the Jewish holiday of Yom Kippur. While Koufax claimed he had not pitched on Yom Kippur in the previous ten seasons, that was not technically correct. As a 2015 *Sports Illustrated* article by John Rosengren notes:

> In 1960, Koufax pitched two innings of scoreless relief on Oct. 1, the day of Yom Kippur, not long after the holiday ended at sundown, in an otherwise forgettable loss to the Cubs on the next-to-last day of the

season with the Dodgers 13 games out of first place. The following year, Koufax started for Los Angeles on Sept. 20, with the first pitch coming mere minutes after sundown ended on Yom Kippur. He threw 205 pitches that night and went all 13 innings to beat the Cubs, even though the Dodgers were again out of contention for the pennant. For both games he showed up at work before the holiday—and its restrictions—ended.

The difference is that in 1960 and 1961, Koufax was not yet Koufax; he was a good pitcher struggling to find his way. If Koufax had pitched in the World Series on Yom Kippur, this would have hurt Jewish people. The best take of the situation belongs to Sarah Wexler, a writer at *Dodgers Digest*. She argues: "Though it was not his intention to do so, Koufax revealed something about what it meant to be ethnically and culturally (as opposed to just religiously) Jewish in America. In effect, he demonstrated that cultural Jewishness was just as legitimate a part of Jewish identity as religiosity was." Considering his stature on the team and that Drysdale was a great pitcher in his own right, Koufax's teammates accepted his decision.

LA took an early lead in Game One, with Fairly hitting a solo home run to give the team the lead in the top of the second. However, the Twins tied it up in the bottom of the inning when Don Mincher countered with a solo home run of his own. The proverbial wheels fell apart for Drysdale and the Dodgers in the bottom of the third, and the Twins piled on six runs to blow the game wide open. The Dodgers never recovered and ended up losing, 8–2. Despite the loss, the Dodger players were not perturbed; after all, Koufax would be starting Game Two.

## THE DODGERS

Unfortunately for LA, things did not go as planned. After five scoreless innings, the Twins scored two runs (one earned) in the bottom of the sixth. The Dodgers were able to get one back in the top of the seventh. However, somewhat inexplicably, Alston got Drysdale to pinch-hit for Koufax in the inning, and he proceeded to strike out. Ron Perranoski replaced Koufax on the mound and gave up one run in the seventh and two runs in the eighth. The Twins beat the Dodgers, 5–1, to take a two-games-to-none lead. The series then traveled to Los Angeles. Taking the mound for the Dodgers in Game Three was Claude Osteen, who was acquired in the trade that sent Frank Howard to the Senators. Osteen had a good year for LA. While his record was 15–15, his ERA was only 2.79— he suffered due to a lack of run support. In front of 55,934 rabid fans at Dodger Stadium, Osteen pitched arguably the game of his life as he threw a complete-game shutout as the Dodgers beat the Twins, 4–0. With Drysdale scheduled to start Game Four and Koufax Game Five, and with both games at home, the Dodger players were confident of taking a 3–2 lead before heading back to Minnesota. The players were right to be confident.

In Game Four, LA jumped out to an early lead by scoring a run in the first and the second, and Drysdale returned to form. He pitched a complete game, striking out 11 while only giving up two runs, as the Dodgers beat the Twins, 7–2, to level the World Series at two games apiece.

If Drysdale pitched brilliantly in Game Four, Koufax pitched even better in Game Five. Once again the Dodgers scored early; this time with two runs in the bottom of the first. That was all the support Koufax needed. He threw a complete-game shutout while only giving up four hits and a walk to go along with 10 strikeouts. The Dodgers defeated the Twins, 7–0.

Games Six and Seven (if required) were due to be played at Metropolitan Stadium in Minnesota. In Game Six, Osteen took the mound for LA but could not recapture his Game Three form. While he only gave up two runs (one earned in five innings of work), the Twins took to reliever Howie Reed, scoring three runs off him in two innings. The Dodgers were never in the contest, as the Twins won handily, 5–1. The stage was set for the deciding Game Seven.

The main issue for the Dodgers heading into Game Seven was who would take the mound: Drysdale, who would be pitching on three-days' rest, or Koufax, who would be pitching on only two-days' rest. Even though it was Drysdale's turn to pitch and he was fresher, the players—and, in an unselfish act, even Drysdale—wanted Koufax to start. Drysdale said he would pitch out of the bullpen if needed. Koufax duly responded to the challenge.

The Dodgers scored two runs in the top of the fourth, thanks to a solo home run by left fielder Lou Johnson, followed by a double by Fairly, who was promptly cashed in by first baseman Wes Parker. Once again, two runs were all that Koufax needed. He threw another complete-game shutout, giving up three hits and three walks while striking out 10 as the Dodgers won, 2–0, and captured the World Series. What made the performance more remarkable is that Koufax could not locate his curveball. After the game he said, "When I threw it I couldn't get it over. And those first few innings I really didn't know how long I was going to last."

Koufax admitted there were other occasions when he could not locate his curveball, but never in a high-stakes situation. Koufax won the game for LA even though he almost exclusively threw fastballs.

However, not everything was perfect for Koufax on that day. When announcing who would be pitching later that day, Alston told the players that they would be starting the left-hander. Alston did not even bother to say his name. Koufax viewed it as another reminder that he would never have a good relationship with the manager. O'Malley's interview with Scully following the game provided another reminder to the players about how management viewed them. As recapped by Leahy, O'Malley told Scully,

> You never know what's gonna happen with these boys. I wish it could've been finished in Los Angeles so all our wonderful fans out there could've been in on the end of it. But they got the picture. It was a great Series. We're very proud of our manager, our team, and Buzzie. And you, Vinny. And Jerry [Doggett; play-by play announcer, along with Scully for the Dodgers] too.

O'Malley never bothered to thank the players, instead claiming they were unpredictable. It would be impossible for any player not to view the interview as a slight. The players are the heart-and-soul of the game, and O'Malley not publicly thanking the players following their World Series victory was incredibly disrespectful. The stage was set for the following season, when baseball players had enough of being treated as second-class citizens and, in a simple vote, paved the way for future generations to be fairly rewarded. And for Dodger management, they had to deal with their two star pitchers deciding to be united in seeking a better contract, as well as their star shortstop deciding enough was enough. The 1965 season should have been the start of a dynasty. Instead, it was a peak that would take well over a decade for them to reach again.

## 1966: A SIGN OF REVOLT AND THE UNRAVELING OF A CHAMPIONSHIP TEAM

It is fair to say that, for a long time, baseball players were exploited, not earning anywhere close to a fair wage. In addition, owners have been crying poverty ever since the advent of professional baseball. In 1881, Chicago White Stockings owner Albert Spalding derided the amount players were earning: "Salaries must come down or bankruptcy stares every team in the face." At the time, the owners and the various leagues had the overwhelming power. The first players' association in baseball—and indeed the first in professional sports—formed in 1885. It did not last, nor did all player associations before the formation of the Major League Baseball Players Association (MLBPA) in 1954. However, while securing some gains for the players, the MLBPA was largely ineffectual. Former player Steve Boros noted that, despite the MLBPA, "players had no leverage . . . They were taken advantage of, but nothing to do. There were lots of horror stories, distrust, and anger, but we had no weapons." This was the situation players faced before Marvin Miller became head of the MLBPA. Miller, who previously was an official for the United Steelworkers, believed that owners would never willingly give their employees decent wages and working conditions. Employees had to fight to secure gains.

Prior to Spring Training in 1966, Miller was asked to become the executive director of the MLBPA. Despite some initial hesitation, Miller agreed to run. Campaigning for the directorship, Miller decided to meet with as many players as he could during Spring Training. In a resounding endorsement of his candidacy, the players voted 489–136 to elect Miller as the head of the MLBPA. The "no" votes came overwhelmingly from a few teams, such as the San Francisco Giants, whose players voted 27–0 against. Considering that he was a longtime Dodger fan, Miller was greatly amused that the Giants players initially responded very negatively toward him.

When meeting with the Dodger players during Spring Training, Miller specifically brought up how the card manufacturer Topps was taking advantage of the players. For years, Topps had signed contracts with individual players; in return for a small fee, the company could sell a card bearing the likeness of the player. In some choice words, he questioned the players' intelligence in agreeing to such a deal. He pointed out that only through solidarity and militancy could the players achieve gains. As Dodger outfielder Al Ferrara told Leahy about his first impressions of Miller,

> I liked him—I liked his competitive fire. He grew on people. We needed Marvin. A lot of us were dumb fucking guys when it came to all that stuff. We weren't businessmen. I was an uneducated guy. We were getting screwed by all kinds of people, starting with baseball owners and all the way down to Topps. We were looking for someone smart and tough to lead us out of the woods, because we didn't even know where the woods were.

Also helping Miller was that Bavasi talked to the players the day before they met Miller and implored them not to elect him. Ferrara claimed, "We all knew Buzzie was a mouthpiece for O'Malley and that Buzzie was there to make money for O'Malley . . . You could tell Buzzie and O'Malley wanted no part of Miller educating us. Buzzie's attitude was: 'Who is this guy?' Well, that did it. Now we're really interested in what this guy has to say."

One of the first things in Miller's sights once he was elected was attempting to get a better deal for the players from Topps. After some heated negotiations with the MLBPA, the company agreed to a new deal whereby players received royalties on the cards sold. As Miller wrote in his autobiography, "Topps agreed to double the payment from $125 to $250 per member and, more importantly, pay 8 percent on sales up to $4 million a year and 10 percent on sales above that figure." Miller's long-term goal was the elimination of the reserve clause, which tied a player to a team so long as he played professional baseball. Also, there were no multiyear contracts; players had to negotiate a new contract every single year. Miller and the MLBPA set about making major positive change for *all* Major League players.

O'Malley and Dodgers management were arguably fearful of what a union would mean for the players and the team's profits due to the actions of Drysdale and Koufax prior to the start of Spring Training. Bavasi told the players that the playing budget for 1966 would increase by $100,000 and that the money would have to cover an increase in salary for *all* twenty-three players. Thus, if someone like Koufax received a large salary bump, which he certainly deserved, it would mean the remaining players would only receive a modest increase. While O'Malley and Bavasi may have assumed that the players would begrudge Koufax, Drysdale, or whoever received a large increase in salary, the players were outraged that management thought they would accept such obvious divide-and-conquer tactics. The Dodgers were the defending World Series champions, and this is how they were being treated? Indeed, such a tactic arguably made the players more prounion and Koufax and Drysdale more likely to engage in collective action.

After fruitless negotiations with Bavasi individually over a new contract, Drysdale and Koufax decided to be united in seeking a better deal for both. They each sought a three-year deal worth $500,000 over the length of the contract. Considering the previous year Koufax earned $85,000 and Drysdale $80,000, they wanted substantial raises as well as security—which a three-year contract would provide. When management did not come close to matching what the players wanted, Drysdale and Koufax did not show up for the start of Spring Training.

Another Dodger was also holding out for a better deal. Despite being a lynchpin of the team for many years, Maury Wills rightfully believed he was being underpaid with a salary of only $60,000. For the 1966 season, he wanted his income to increase to $100,000. However, while Koufax and Drysdale were united, Wills was acting without any support. Thus, he was susceptible to a fear campaign organized by Bavasi, who told Wills that O'Malley knew that he was acting in cahoots with Koufax and Drysdale and, as such, the owner was mad and implied that his actions would have serious consequences. This unnerved Wills, who flew to Vero Beach the following day, paying for the flight himself, then signed for somewhere between $75,000 and $85,000. Without anyone supporting Wills and no strong union to protect him, Wills had to accept what was offered if he wanted to continue his career. As Wills told Leahy,

It was the same old thing . . . Buzzie used scare tactics on me. He tried to do that with everyone. But Sandy didn't back down. He had leverage to do that. The scare tactics worked on me. After I signed, I told reporters I was ready to win another pennant and play hard, and all that was true—I always played hard. But the whole thing hurt. The way they could scare you like that: it hurt your pride as a man. That was the worst thing: what it took out of you.

Koufax understood if he held out by himself he would likely lose the battle. But by being united with Drysdale they had a much better chance to achieve their demands. While the team could have potentially traded one player or refuse to bargain, it was highly unlikely they would do such a thing to their top two pitchers. To help their negotiating position, Koufax and Drysdale signed a deal with Paramount Pictures to appear in films and television shows. Moreover, unbeknownst to anyone, Koufax knew that 1966 would be his final season. He was in incredible pain, and the drugs he had to take just to pitch were jeopardizing his health. Koufax was willing to walk away from the game he loved if he did not receive a substantial raise. While he did not expect to receive a multiyear offer—especially as O'Malley had never offered one or even paid a player $100,000 or more—Koufax wanted a significant raise in his final year as a Dodger. As Spring Training was nearing an end, Drysdale and Koufax had yet to sign new contracts and were rehearsing for their parts in a film. In this high-stakes game it was the front office who blinked first. O'Malley made a final offer to the players: $125,000 for Koufax and $110,000 for Drysdale. The players duly accepted; their collective actions had yielded substantial, and well-deserved, raises. Now that the off-field matters were settled, the players sought to once again be crowned World Series champions.

* * *

Just like in 1964, once again following a World Series victory, the Dodgers were inconsistent for most the 1966 season. Unlike in 1964, though, they were never that far off the league lead. The furthest back they were was seven games on May 13. But two weeks later, on May 28, they were only 1½ games from the lead. Yet they tumbled and, by July 1, were 6½ games back. LA then proceeded to go 18–10 in July to be tied for the NL lead by the end of the month. Come September, the Dodgers battled with the Giants and the Pittsburgh Pirates for the pennant. In their final three games, the Dodgers only had to win one against the Phillies in Philadelphia to secure the NL pennant. After dropping the first game of the series, the teams were unable to play the following day due to rain. Thus, on the final day of the season, the Dodgers were scheduled to play a doubleheader on October 2. They only had to win one, and the pennant was theirs. Drysdale was scheduled to pitch the opening game. However, he only lasted two innings and failed to get an out in the third. Nevertheless, the Dodgers were still ahead, leading 3–2 after seven innings. They then proceeded to blow the game by committing two errors in the bottom of the eighth, as the Phillies scored twice to take the lead; they would hold on and win the game, 4–3. Thus, the Dodgers had to win the final game of the season to clinch the NL pennant.

Instead of starting Game One of the World Series, Koufax had to pitch in the final regular season game on only two days' rest. If the Giants lost their final game in Pittsburgh, this would have meant the Dodgers would have won the pennant irrespective of their result. However, the Giants tied their game in the top of the ninth and eventually won in eleven innings.

In another gem of a performance, Koufax entered the ninth looking at another complete-game shutout, as LA was ahead, 6–0. Considering that the Dodgers were all but headed to the World Series, one would have expected Alston to turn to a reliever to finish the game. This was especially true, as the Phillies scored three runs off Koufax with nobody out in the ninth. However, Koufax stayed in and eventually wrapped up the game with the Dodgers winning, 6–3, securing another trip to the World Series. The question asked after the game: Should Alston have pulled Koufax? Quite simply, that was never a possibility; Alston seemingly always allowed his star players to pitch complete games. Moreover, the players wanted Koufax in the ninth. As left fielder Lou Johnson told Leahy,

> Sandy never came out of a big game in the ninth . . . never. Don't care how tired somebody thought he looked. We'd be worried to have anybody else out there. It was more than just Sandy being the best pitcher. He was Sandy. He never let you down. So what if he gives up a couple runs. We go down fightin' with him if we go down. And we weren't goin' down. This was Sandy pitching. Come on now.

And with that, the Dodgers were set to face the Baltimore Orioles in the World Series. Unlike LA, who had to fight to win the NL pennant, the Orioles won the AL over the Twins by a nine-game margin. In contrast to 1963 and 1965, when the players were confident going into the World Series, the 1966 season was anything but—they were tired. The pennant race had totally exhausted the players, both mentally and physically. Indeed, following the NL clinching victory in Philadelphia, there was no big celebration in the dressing room; the players were obviously happy they won the NL but were happier the regular season was over.

In Game One of the World Series at Dodger Stadium, Dave McNally took the mound for the Orioles. He only lasted 2⅔ innings, giving up two runs. Unfortunately, Drysdale had an even worse day, giving up four runs in just two innings of work. The Dodgers ended up losing the game, 5–2. Though down 1–0, Koufax was scheduled to start Game Two.

Koufax did not pitch badly, but it was clear he did not have his best stuff. The Orioles scored four runs off him (one earned) in six innings. Koufax was undone in the fifth by center fielder Willie Davis, as Davis committed an astonishing three errors in the inning and the Orioles scored three runs. For the Orioles, twenty-year-old Jim Palmer was outstanding, pitching a complete-game shutout while only giving up four hits and three walks, as the Orioles were again triumphant, 6–0.

The Series then headed to Baltimore. In Game Three, Osteen pitched a great game; in seven innings of work, the Orioles only scored one run. However, Wally Bunker was even better, pitching a complete-game shutout as the Orioles won, 1–0. Thus, heading into Game Four, the Dodgers were shut out twice and had failed to score since the third inning of Game One. Nobody expected the Dodgers to be swept, but swept they were, as the Orioles beat the Dodgers the following night, 1–0. Drysdale was heroic, going eight innings, but the offense was nonexistent. The Orioles were World Series champions for the first time in franchise history. That the Dodgers were swept was obviously disappointing, but the biggest disappointment of the season was yet to come.

Confirming his thoughts, 1966 was indeed Koufax's last season. It was, without a doubt, the greatest final season of a pitcher ever. Koufax finished the season with a 27–9 record and a miniscule ERA of 1.73 (the lowest of his career). He pitched 323 innings, started 41 games, had 27 complete games—with five complete-game shutouts—and struck out 317. He led the NL in these categories.

Koufax was once again rewarded with the Cy Young Award and finished second in MVP voting behind the legendary Pirate Roberto Clemente. What makes Koufax's season even more remarkable is that he was in constant pain the entire time and knew 1966 would be his finale. The first anyone in the organization knew about Koufax retiring was on the plane ride home after the World Series. Koufax was talking to Ferrara when mentioned he would be retiring. Ferrara told Leahy, "He wasn't confiding in me. . . . I think I was just there and he said it. It just came out. There weren't any throwaway lines from him. He kept it simple. Knowing him, the decision wasn't spur of the moment. He didn't do anything spur of the moment. But he just said it to me and that was pretty much it." Ferrara did not mention to anyone else what he knew.

On November 18, Koufax officially announced his retirement while most the Dodger players were on a goodwill tour of Japan following the World Series. While O'Malley was with the players on the goodwill tour, neither Bavasi (who was upset Koufax would not delay his announcement until O'Malley was back from Japan) nor anyone from Dodger management attended Koufax's press conference when he made his announcement. Koufax stated that he the main reason was his fear of jeopardizing his long-term health. Koufax stated that "I don't know if cortisone is good for you or not. But to take a shot every other ballgame is more than I wanted to do, and to walk around with a constant upset stomach because of the pills and to be high half the time during a ballgame because you're taking painkillers, I don't want to have to do that." Koufax admitted that "I feel I am doing the right thing, and I don't regret one minute of the past 12 years. The only regret is leaving baseball." Koufax was thirty years old at the time of his announcement. If he played today, it is highly likely that Koufax's arm could have been healed through surgery. However, at the time, Koufax had the choice of playing on while being in considerable pain and taking a bevy of prescription medication or retiring.

Losing Koufax was a huge blow to the team; they would also soon lose Maury Wills. Wills did not have the best season in '66. His batting average dropped to .273 (his lowest since his rookie year), and while he stole 38 bases, that was a dramatic decline from the 94 he swiped the previous season. Moreover, he was caught 24 times. Wills was hurting after a long season, yet he, unlike Koufax and Drysdale, was forced to embark on the good-will tour of Japan. Unlike goodwill tours today, where the players may play three or so games, the Dodgers were scheduled to play 18 exhibition games. Quite simply, almost all the players did not want to go to Japan. They were incredibly tired, and the last thing they wanted after such a long season was to travel overseas, play more games, and be away from their families. Throughout the season, Wills continually told management that his trouble-some right knee could not handle any more games, especially at the end of an arduous season. However, O'Malley and Bavasi told Wills that he *had* to go to Japan. In a compromise, Bavasi and Wills came to an agreement: Wills would only play in one to two innings in a select number of games. For the rest of the tour, all he had to do was smile in photos and be at the games.

Prior to the first game, Wills was told he would be the starting shortstop; he would be playing most innings in almost all the games. Dodger management had lied to him. Wills played but was in great pain, and, in a game in the Japanese city of Sapporo, he injured his knee even worse. Nevertheless, he was expected to play in the remaining games. Wills had finally had enough; for almost his entire career he felt disrespected by the Dodgers and did not want to jeopardize his career by playing from an injury in meaningless games. He went to call Alston and tell him that he was leaving the tour. However, the hotel operator connected Wills with O'Malley. Unperturbed, Wills told O'Malley that his knee was in very bad shape and he needed to go back to the United States to seek medical attention. Rather than support Wills, O'Malley told him that he had to stay on the tour. O'Malley viewed the publicity the team was getting in Japan as more important than the health of their starting short-stop. Indeed, during the tour he basically told Alston that the games were not mere exhibitions—the Dodgers *had* to perform well. For the players, they did not care in the slightest whether they won or lost. This time Wills did not back down and he left Japan, stopping in Hawaii for a few days before going back to Los Angeles. Now, while Wills probably should not have spent time in Hawaii, the reality was the Japan tour was meaningless and the Dodgers were jeopardizing his health and had lied to him about how much he was expected to play. O'Malley was furious at Wills' insubordination and told the *Los Angeles Times* that the shortstop had breached his contract.

Wills was not the only player who had promises broken during the Japanese tour. Osteen's wife was due to give birth during the tour. Osteen, understandably, wanted to stay home with his family. However, O'Malley told him that he only had to play in the opening game, as it would be televised by the ABC network. However, the game was not televised. And with Wills leaving Japan and the Dodgers not performing well, O'Malley ordered Osteen to remain in Japan and play. Osteen was not happy but believed there was nothing he could do. Once again, O'Malley put his own interests above what was best for the players. Osteen's wife gave birth while Osteen was in Japan.

As for Wills, while the team was still in Japan, O'Malley called Bavasi in America and told him, "It looks to me as though the boy's asking for it, and I think we'll have to give it to him." On December 1, the Dodgers traded their captain and starting shortstop to Pittsburgh. The players were incredibly scornful of the decision to trade Wills; Ferrara told Leahy,

> Let's face it: players' rights weren't at all respected then. .
> . . Maury had every right to do what he did in Japan and
> get the hell out of there. He was hurting. But the atti-
> tude of everybody in management was, "How dare you?"
> You didn't do something like that then. People didn't
> have the balls. But Maury had the balls. That trade was
> made to show everybody on the Dodgers who was boss.
> It was vengeance. Everybody in the organization knew it.
> Getting rid of Maury destroyed us the next season.

What should have been a dynasty or, at the very least, a contending side for years to come came to a crashing halt. Koufax was gone, Wills was gone, and Tommy Davis, who after injury derailed his year in 1965 had a good 1966 in limited opportunities, was traded to the New York Mets. Overall, 1966 was not a good year for the Los Angeles Dodgers.

# 1967–69: JUST DOING TIME

If the end of the 1966 season was bad for the Dodgers, 1967 was a lot worse on the field of play. Dodgers management never expected the team to contend. In April 1967, Bavasi told the *Cincinnati Enquirer* that "We always want to win the pennant and we always expect to, but we don't think the public expects us to win this year." He went on to claim, "So we think we're free to experiment, to play with a young team." Under such illogic, it was the Los Angeles public that was at fault that the team was not contenders, not O'Malley and Bavasi for dismantling a pennant-contending team.

The season started with the team losing their first four games, and it was all downhill from there, not being in contention at any point during the season. The Dodgers finished the season with a record of 73–89, their worst since moving to Los Angeles and came in eighth in the National League; only the Houston Astros and Mets had a worse season. LA finished an astonishing 28½ games behind the St. Louis Cardinals.[7]

No player had a particularly great year, although Roseboro hit .272 and was decent behind the plate (and was promptly traded to the Twins in a five-man deal), and Ferrara led the team with a miserly 16 home runs while batting .277. As for the pitching staff, Bill Singer had an ERA of 2.64 while going 12–8, Osteen went 17–17 with an ERA of 3.22, and Drysdale, after a down 1966, bounced back with an ERA of 2.74 even though he had a 13–16 record. Even without Koufax, the pitching staff was still capable of a pennant chase. However, the pitchers were badly let

---

7  The Cardinals then went on to defeat the Boston Red in seven games to win the World Series.

down by the lack of offense—as they were in the 1966 World Series. In the 16 games Drysdale lost, the offense combined for a grand total of 15 runs. Indeed, in 1966 the Dodgers scored 606 runs; in 1967 they only scored 519 runs.[8]

As for the Dodgers who were traded away, Wills only stole 29 bases for Pittsburgh but hit .302 (tied for a career high), while Tommy Davis also hit .302 with 16 home runs and 32 doubles. In contrast, Gene Michael, the Dodgers' current shortstop, only hit .202 with four extra-base hits.

The Dodgers also suffered off the field, as the team's lack of success resulted in attendance dropping 952,667 from the previous year, though they were only behind the Cardinals in total attendance.[9] In a lowlight for the season, on September 28, only 9,253 fans bore witness to the Dodgers beating the Mets, 3–0, with Osteen pitching a complete-game shutout. The fans in Los Angeles were used to seeing World Series champions or, at the very least, competitive teams. The 1967 Dodgers, however, were a long way from being championship-caliber or even competitive. It was not their fault the 1967 side were also-rans and unlikely to contend for several years; the Dodgers were also-rans because of O'Malley and Bavasi.

* * *

With the MLBPA negotiating the first Basic Agreement with Major League Baseball, everyone knew that 1968 was going to be an important year. While only achieving moderate gains, it

---

8  In 1966, the Dodgers averaged 3.74 runs per game, as opposed to 67 when they averaged 3.20. That's a half run less each game.
9  It was the first time the Dodgers did not finish first in total attendance since 1958, which was their first year in Los Angeles.

was a precursor for the coming years. Some key terms agreed upon were the minimum salary increased by $3,000 to $10,000, the spring-training per diem increased to $40 per day, daily meal money for the season increased from $12 to $15, and players now flew first-class.

As for the Dodgers, 1968 did not start on the best note. On April 4, tragedy struck as Dr. Martin Luther King Jr. was murdered. While other teams canceled their scheduled games, the Dodgers did not. Instead, they played a meaningless exhibition game against Cleveland. Moreover, Dr. King's funeral was scheduled for April 9; the same day as Opening Day. The Dodgers did not plan to cancel the game even though their opponents, the Phillies, wanted the game to be postponed. All other home teams across baseball made it clear they were going to reschedule. Bavasi claimed he discussed the issue with the team's black players and coaches. He told the players that if they did not want to play, they did not have to. As Glenn Stout notes in *The Dodgers*, Bavasi argued that the Dodgers should play because it would "give people some sort of amusement when they need it most. It may help keep people off the streets and to forget their anger," and the funeral was scheduled for the morning while the home opener was to be a night game. Eventually, after outrage across the community, the Dodgers agreed to postpone their home opener, but it was more a public-relations move than anything else.

There was further upheaval off the field the following month. After almost eighteen years, Bavasi announced that he would be leaving the team in June to join the expansion San Diego Padres, who were scheduled to join the NL in 1969. Bavasi was at the helm for the triumphant years but also oversaw LA's disastrous decline following the 1966 season, and the team's farm system was average at best. Bavasi likely jumped before he was pushed out, as it was clear that O'Malley was grooming his son Peter to run the team. And by joining the Padres, Bavasi received a 30 percent ownership stake. Despite his years of service with the Dodgers and hinting about it on more than once occasion, O'Malley never gave Bavasi a piece of the Dodgers. As Bavasi told Delsohn, "Arnholt Smith, the owner in San Diego, gave me 30 percent of the ballclub. Well, I never got a piece of the club with the Dodgers. Nobody got a piece but Walter O'Malley." The likelihood that Bavasi knew he was to be replaced is seen in the number of mean-spirited comments he made about O'Malley's frugalness once leaving the Dodgers. Bavasi stayed with the Padres until the end of the 1977 season, then joined the California Angels as executive vice president and GM. He retired following the 1984 season.

Regarding the farm system, it was rejuvenated due to the 1968 draft, which was held a few weeks after Fresco Thompson took over from Bavasi and became GM. In the draft, the Dodgers selected, among others, Bobby Valentine, Steve Garvey, Bill Buckner, and Ron Cey. It was a great draft for the Dodgers and served them well for several years. Dodger draft pick and future major leaguer Tom Paciorek even went as far as to claim, "That might have been the best draft in the history of baseball, because everyone [who made an MLB team] played a long time in the big leagues." The Dodgers made 101 selections in the draft. Out of those 101, 14 made the major leagues—ten position players and four pitchers. Unfortunately, Thompson never saw the players develop into major leaguers. He was diagnosed with cancer shortly after becoming GM and passed away in November of that year. He was sixty-six. Thompson was then replaced as GM by Al Campanis.

On the field, 1968 was a "better" year for the team after the disastrous 1967; they won three more games than then previous year and went 76–86, 21 games behind the Cardinals. While there was only a very minor improvement in the win column, the offense receded. While the team only scored 519 runs in 1967, the 1968 offense could only muster 470 runs, which was dead last in the NL. Newly acquired catcher Tom Haller hit .285 with 27 doubles, and Len Gabrielson led the team in home runs, hitting 10. The Dodgers were ranked tenth in home runs (67), batting average (.230), and hits (1,234).

The 1968 season was not the finest offensive performance in the Dodgers' illustrious history. In contrast, the pitching staff once again had a fine year, albeit not in wins due to the horrible offense. Don Sutton had a record of 11–15 with an ERA of 2.60, and Bill Singer went 13–17 with an ERA of 2.88, while closer Jim Brewer saved 15 games with an ERA 2.49. Indeed, the Dodgers' ERA was a combined 2.69, second best in the NL. Once again, with better offense LA could have been contenders. Overall, 1968 was one of resigned disappointment. This was reflected in the turnstiles, as attendance declined by more than 83,000. The Dodgers slipped to third in total NL attendance, this despite Drysdale's record-breaking streak.

On May 14, Drysdale pitched a complete-game shutout while only giving up two hits and three walks, as the Dodgers beat the Cubs, 1–0. While it was another great performance from the future Hall of Famer, it was just the beginning of something special. In his next start on May 18, he threw another complete-game shutout, as the Dodgers beat the Astros, 1–0. He was just getting started. On May 22, in St. Louis, Drysdale pitched another gem, only giving up five hits while striking out eight as he shut out the Cardinals, 2–0. In Houston on May 26, he pitched another complete-game shutout as the Dodgers won, 5–0. Drysdale had now pitched four complete-game shutouts in a row.

Facing Drysdale in his next start would be the Giants, who would have loved nothing more than to stop his scoreless-inning and complete-game-shutout streak. Unfortunately for them, they were having little to no effect, as Drysdale was cruising through eight innings of shutout ball. However, he ran into trouble in the ninth by giving up two walks and a single to load the bases with nobody out. The likelihood that Drysdale's streak would be over was incredibly high. Into the batter's box stepped Giants catcher Dick Dietz. On a 2-2 count, Drysdale hit Dietz in the elbow. It should have forced in a run and ended the streak. However, in an extremely controversial call, umpire Harry Wendelstedt ruled that Dietz made no attempt to get out of the way of the pitch and instead ruled it a ball. The Giants were furious, and Giants manager Herman Franks was tossed from the game for arguing. Did Wendelstedt make the correct decision? Technically yes, but if Drysdale did not have his streak going it is unlikely Wendelstedt would have made that ruling. Nevertheless, the Giants still had ample opportunity to score. However, it was not to be. On a 3-2 pitch Dietz hit a shallow fly to the outfield—not deep enough to score the runner from third. The next batter was Ty Cline, who hit a grounder to first and Wes Parker got the force out at home. Finally, Jack Hiatt popped the ball up in the infield for the third and final out. Drysdale got out of a bases-loaded jam in the ninth and completed another complete-game shutout, his fifth in a row, as the Dodgers won, 3–0. The Giants were still furious after the game. One unnamed Giant said, "Somewhere in that routine he gets it—the Vaseline or whatever it is he puts on the ball to make it jump around." While Dietz claimed, "Wendelstedt said I stuck my arm out on purpose. . . . What am I? Crazy? I'm not going to let him hit me—not Drysdale. He'll cut you in two out there. I just couldn't move." Even the Dodger players were bemused by the ruling.

At Dodger Stadium on June 4, Drysdale was attempting to break the record for the most number of complete-game shutouts in a row—and he did not disappoint. Drysdale was simply magnificent. In front of a disappointing crowd of 30,422, Drysdale allowed three hits while striking out eight as he pitched his sixth complete-game shutout in a row, leading the Dodgers to a 5–0 victory. History was made, and Drysdale was also close to claiming the scoreless-inning streak record held by Walter Johnson since 1933 at 55⅔ innings. Unfortunately, history was also made in a tragic way later that night. June 4 was also primary night in California, in which Robert F. Kennedy was victorious. A few days earlier Kennedy had a conversation with Drysdale, one that Drysdale cherished. Kennedy began his victory speech with "I first want to express my high regard for Don Drysdale, who pitched his sixth straight shutout tonight, and I hope that we have as good fortune in our campaign." He did not. Just after midnight, Kennedy was shot and killed. The Dodger players, and the rest of the county, were in shock.

As fate would have it, Drysdale was set to go for the scoreless-inning-streak record on the same day as Kennedy's funeral, June 8. Kennedy's funeral was scheduled for the day, while the Dodgers were due to play at night against the Phillies. In the first inning, Drysdale was clearly nervous but managed to escape unscathed despite issuing a walk. The second inning was largely stress-free, although a Philly missed a home run by inches as it went foul. Upon completing the inning, Drysdale had tied the fifty-five-year scoreless-innings record. In the top of the third, Drysdale pitched to Phillies shortstop Roberto Pena, quickly getting ahead 0–2. He then got Pena to hit a routine grounder to third. Dodger third baseman Ken Boyer threw to first baseman Wes Parker to record the easy out. Don Drysdale was now in the record books with the scoreless-innings record and also got through the third inning unscathed.

There was, however, additional controversy. Following the third inning, Phillies manager Gene Mauch had a talk with home-plate umpire Augie Donatelli. Mauch claimed that Drysdale was using Vaseline. Donatelli told *Sports Illustrated* in June 1968,

> Mauch started to complain and said, "He's putting grease on the ball." I asked him where he was getting it from and Mauch said, "The back of his head." I went to Drysdale and said, "Don, do you have Vaseline on the back of your head?" He said, "What do you mean?" I said, "You know the rule, and if you touch the back of your head again I'm going to have to fine you." Don said, "Augie, I'm sweating like hell out here. That isn't Vaseline; that's sweat. Just tell me what the hell I can't do." When Drysdale first came up to the majors he was no bargain, but he changed and we umpires appreciate that. He could have punched me in the mouth when I started to inspect him.

In the top of the fourth, Donatelli reminded Drysdale not to touch the back of his head. Drysdale did not and retired the side in order. However, another shutout was not on the cards. In the top of the fifth, Drysdale gave up two singles to the first two batters he faced. While he managed to strike out the next batter, a sacrifice fly to pinch-hitter Howie Bedell drove in a run.[10] Drysdale's scoreless inning streak ended at 58⅔ innings. The Baseball Writers Association of America would later rule that "in terms of a scoreless or hitless streak a starting pitcher should not be credited with a partial inning if the opposition scores in that inning." As such, the record was officially credited at 58 innings. The Dodgers wound up winning the game, 5–3. Following the victory, Drysdale told the *Los Angeles Times,* "I wanted the record so bad. . . . But I'm relieved that it's over. I could feel myself go 'blah' when the run scored. I just let down completely. I'm sure it was the mental strain." It was a remarkable stretch of pitching from one of the all-time greats. While 1968 was not good for the team, it will always be fondly remembered by baseball fans due to Drysdale's record-breaking run.

\* \* \*

There were some major changes to baseball before the start of the 1969 season. The NL added two expansion teams: the Montreal Expos and the San Diego Padres. Likewise, the AL added the Kanas City Royals and the Seattle Pilots.[11] The NL, as did the AL, split into two divisions: East and West. The Dodgers were put in the West Division with the Padres, Giants, Reds, and Astros. Moreover, the winner of the West and East divisions would have a best-of-five playoff series at the end of the season, with the winner going on to the World Series. Splitting the NL in two increased the chances that the Dodgers would make the postseason.

---

10  Interestingly enough, Bedell never drove in another run in the majors.
11  The Pilots relocated to Milwaukee in 1970 and became the Brewers.

## THE DODGERS

If you just look at the standings, the team had another disappointing year. They finished in fourth place, eight games behind the Atlanta Braves. However, they vastly improved with a 85–77 record. Indeed, they were still very much in contention by mid-September. They then proceeded to lose 11 out of 13 games and tumble down the standings. Nevertheless, there were still several positives of note. Rookie Ted Sizemore hit .271 with good defense (at second, not so much at shortstop) on the way to winning Rookie of the Year honors, and Willie Davis had a career resurgence, hitting .311 (compared to .250 the previous year). Moreover, under the reign of Campanis, the Dodgers made several significant midseason trades. The team picked up Manny Mota from Montreal, who proceeded to hit .323, and in a hell-freezing-over moment, O'Malley agreed to Campanis's continued requests to bring back Maury Wills. Wills was languishing in Montreal, only hitting .222, and said he was going to retire as a tactic in an attempt to be traded. He only returned to the Expos when he was alerted that if he did indeed retire he could not be traded to another team. Wills was ecstatic to return to the Dodgers—he never wanted to leave in the first place. Wills went on to hit .297, stealing 25 bases in 104 games and once again electrifying the Dodgers.

The pitching staff had, as was the norm, another good season with the third-best ERA in the NL. Osteen went 20–15 with an ERA of 2.66 (the best of his career up to that point), Bill Singer had a record of 20–12 with a career-best 2.34 ERA, while closer Jim Brewer saved 20 games with an ERA of 2.55. Overall, the pitching staff had another fine year. There was, however, one disappointment: Dodgers ace Don Drysdale was forced to retire.

A shoulder injury following his great scoreless-inning streak of 1968 forced Drysdale to miss the last six weeks of the season. In May of 1969, Drysdale hurt his shoulder again. As he told *Sports Illustrated* at the time, "I just won't go out and embarrass myself or the ball club when I'm not 100 percent. It is now between my arm and medical science. If I could come back and help this team win, I would rate it as one of the finest things that ever happened to me." Drysdale did come back in mid-June, but he was not the same. There was one final hurrah, as he pitched a complete-game shutout against the Padres in San Diego on June 28. However, he was forced to go back on the disabled list in July. Drysdale came back later that month, but he knew he was done. On August 1, he only lasted two innings while giving up five runs. On August 5, Drysdale pitched against the Pirates. In six innings of work he gave up three runs (two earned) on eight hits and a walk. While technically a quality start (three earned runs or less in at least six innings), Drysdale knew his body could not handle the strain anymore. *Los Angeles Times* journalist Dan Berger went up to Drysdale after the game and asked him how he was doing. "'Awful,' he said. 'This is it.' It? I asked. 'I can't take any more medication for the arm. It's not responding. I believe I should be taken off the active list to make room for a pitcher who can help the club.' I asked if he was retiring. He shook his head yes. 'I've spoken with Ginger [his wife] and Mr. O'Malley about this.'" In addition to the medication not helping his shoulder, he felt he "was becoming dopey" and was worried that the police would believe he was on illegal drugs and arrest him. While the players may not have been taking steroids and the like back in the 1960s, doctors were pumping players full of every other drug imaginable so they could get out on the field and perform. Drysdale, like Koufax before him, had enough of the pain, *as well* as the medication he was forced to take to try to play. Later that month, Drysdale officially announced his retirement.

Following his retirement, Drysdale stayed in baseball as a broadcaster, beginning in 1970—first with the Expos and eventually with the Dodgers starting in 1988. On July 3, 1993, Drysdale was in Montreal, as he was due to call the Dodger-Expo game later that day. However, he did not show up for the bus to take him to the stadium. Drysdale was later found in his hotel room. He had suffered a heart attack and passed away in his sleep at the age of fifty-six. Among his possessions was a recording of Robert F. Kennedy's speech, where he congratulated Drysdale on the complete-game-shutout record. Drysdale's broadcast partner, Vin Scully, broke the news of Drysdale's death to the listening audience: "Never have I been asked to make an announcement that hurts me as much as this one. And I say it to you as best I can with a broken heart."

The 1960s ended up having some very big highs for the Dodgers, including World Series triumphs and the total dominance of Koufax, but also some very big lows, such as the 1967–68 seasons, the trade of Wills, and the forced retirements of Koufax and Drysdale. With the more than respectable showing in the 1969 season, the 1960s ended on a positive note for the Dodgers. The team was hoping for continued momentum in the 1970s. As we shall see, despite some very good seasons and individual performances, they could not quite reach the mountaintop.

# 4

# 1970S: LABOR TURMOIL AND WORLD SERIES HEARTACHE

**O**N THE SURFACE, the 1970s were a successful time for the Dodgers. As the Dodgers themselves note, "The Los Angeles Dodgers of the 1970s were a team of winners. Three National League pennants and three appearances in the World Series (1974, 1977, and 1978), along with 910 victories (second-best decade in Dodger history), are certainly enough credentials for a successful decade." During the decade, they also never finished lower than third in the NL West. However, the 1970s was a decade of disappointment for the team—a sense, like the 1960s, of what could have been. Off the field, the 1970s was marked with the inevitable conflict between players and owners that had been brewing for decades.

## 1970–71: NL WEST BRIDESMAIDS

The 1970 season was a good one for almost all baseball players, as the MLBPA signed a second Basic Agreement with MLB.

The minimum salary increased to $12,000 with a further increase of $3,000 scheduled for 1972. In addition, the players achieved the right for grievance procedures (arbitration) not controlled by the commissioner. While players were still subjected to the reserve clause, there was now a major challenge to it. St. Louis Cardinal star player Curt Flood was informed by the team in late 1969 that he was traded to the Philadelphia Phillies. Flood was not happy and, after discussing the issue with Miller and the MLBPA, wrote to Baseball Commissioner Bowie Kuhn expressing his desire for free agency and declaring he was not property to be owned.

Kuhn responded to Flood's letter by writing one of his own: "I certainly agree with you that you, as a human being, are not a piece of property to be bought and sold. . . . [However,] I cannot see its applicability to the situation at hand." This led the MLBPA to challenge baseball's antitrust exemption and as such the reserve clause, in court. In an interview, Flood categorized himself as a "well-paid slave."

Flood lost the initial court case, but baseball's lawyers inadvertently led to the elimination of the reserve clause, as they claimed that the issue between Flood and MLB was "only a labor dispute over a mandatory collective bargaining issue." In other words, the union would be able to challenge the reserve clause in negotiations with MLB. Flood and the MLBPA initially decided to appeal the decision.

On June 18, 1972, the Supreme Court ruled against Flood by a 5-to-3 margin. The Court claimed that the 1922 decision that baseball was not subject to the Sherman Act was wrongly decided, but that they would not overturn it, as their ruling was based on adherence to principle. It was up to Congress, not the courts, to overturn baseball's antitrust exemption. Flood paid a steep price of standing up to injustice, not playing in the 1970 season and only lasting a few weeks with the Washington Senators in 1971 (as the long layoff hampered his ability to perform up to his previous high standards). The reserve clause in its current form was still intact. However, major changes were coming.

* * *

There was a major change at the top of the Dodgers organization, as Walter O'Malley decided to promote his son Peter to team president. Peter O'Malley was now responsible for the day-to-day operation of the team, while the elder O'Malley stayed on as chairman. There was optimism at the start of the 1970 season due to the team's improvement the previous year. They would open the season at home against the Cincinnati Reds. Unfortunately for the Dodgers, the Reds defeated them 4–0 in the first game, 5–2 in the second, and 3–0 in the third to complete the series sweep—certainly not the best start to the year.

However, the less-than-stellar San Diego Padres were next on the schedule, so the Dodgers were feeling confident. As with the first series, it was not to be—in game one of a three-game series, the Padres defeated the Dodgers 7–2 and then followed it up the next day, winning 4–0. A five-game losing streak was not the way the Dodgers expected to start off their season. They finally broke through for their maiden win in 1970 by defeating the Padres, 6–0, with Bill Singer pitching a complete-game shutout. The Dodgers then went on a mini-tear, winning two in a row in Houston against the Astros. Alas, they then lost both games of a two-game series against the Reds in Cincinnati to fall to a record of 3–7. While the team recovered to post a winning season

(87–74) and finish second in the NL West, they were never in contention, finishing 14½ games back of the first-place Reds.

Individually, Wes Parker had another fine season along the way to winning his fourth Gold Glove. He hit .319 and led the NL with 47 doubles and 111 RBIs. Thirty-seven-year-old Maury Wills hit .270 while stealing 28 bases (although he was caught 13 times). Second-year player Billy Grabarkewitz made the All-Star team while leading the Dodgers with 17 home runs.

Overall, it was a much better offensive output compared to the previous years, as the team was ranked second in hits in the NL, fourth in runs, first in batting average, but dead last in home runs. The pitching staff had another solid year, if slightly down from previous seasons; the team ERA was 3.82 in 1970 (fifth in the NL), compared to 3.08 in 1969 (third in the NL) and 2.69 in 1968 (second in the NL). Osteen had a record of 16–14 with an ERA of 3.83, and Sutton had a record of 15–13 with an ERA of 4.08. In both cases, Osteen and Sutton's ERA were substantially higher than in 1969.

There was a major pitching individual highlight for the season, as Bill Singer pitched a no-hitter. Since being brought up full-time in 1967 as a twenty-three year old, Singer was developing into a dependable frontline pitcher. In 1969, he made the All-Star team and had a 20-win season with an ERA of 2.34. While he suffered a loss in his first game of the year on April 8, he bounced back by throwing a complete-game shutout against the Padres on April 12. However, in his next start he lasted only four innings and was badly fatigued. It was determined that he was suffering from hepatitis. He did not pitch again for the team until June 14, when he gave up four runs in only two innings of work. However, come July he was seemingly back to full health.

On July 5, he pitched a complete-game shutout against the Giants. On July 10, he pitched 8⅔ innings and picked up the win. In his next start, on July 16, Singer pitched a complete game and only gave up a single run.

Singer was on a roll, and it would continue through July 20 against the Astros at Dodger Stadium. The crowd of only 12,454 on a Monday afternoon saw history being made. Singer struck out 10 and walked none on the way to a no-hitter. Singer hit an Astro in the first and committed errors in the first (pickoff attempt) and in the seventh (throw to first base). The no-hitter was the highlight of Singer's Dodgers career. Following mediocre 1971 and 1972 seasons, Singer was part of a megatrade to the California Angeles in November 1972 (see below).

Overall, while the 1970 season was not bad, it was not that good either. While the offense improved, the pitching regressed. Though finishing second in the NL West was an improvement, they were seemingly a long way from challenging their traditional rival Giants and the emerging powerhouse that was the Cincinnati Reds.

The number one priority for the Dodgers in the offseason was to acquire a bonafide slugger. To improve their power hitting, the Dodgers acquired third baseman Dick Allen. Allen was indeed a great power hitter. Since joining the majors he had never hit less than 20 home runs in a full season. In the previous three seasons he hit 33, 32, and 34 home runs. Allen was a star player and a great pickup.

There was just one issue: Allen marched to his own beat. It is fair to say that he enjoyed drinking and only participated in batting practice if he felt like doing so. He once fought a teammate and was late to a game because he was at a racetrack.

Nevertheless, he performed when it mattered and was ecstatic to be a Dodger. He told the *Oakland Tribune*, "Putting on a Dodger uniform is something special for me. My family, we used to go to Forbes Field in Pittsburgh every time the Dodgers would come there. And we lived 30 miles away."

In 1971 for the Dodgers, he led the team with 23 home runs, 90 runs, 93 walks, an on-base percentage of .395, a slugging percentage of .468, 113 strikeouts, and 21 errors. Dick Allen was an offensive powerhouse, to say the least, and was a large reason why the 1971 Dodgers performed as well as they did.

Likewise, Willie Davis had another good season, hitting .309 with 33 doubles and 10 triples. Apart from Allen and Davis, the rest of the offense took a step back and were a middle-of-the-road team in the NL. As for the pitching staff, Sutton had a great year, going 17–12 with an ERA of 2.54. Newcomer Al Downing, acquired from the Brewers, had a 20–9 record with an ERA of 2.68. Overall, the Dodgers pitching staff had a slight improvement over the 1970 season.

However, for most of the year the team was not in contention. On June 1, they were 10½ games back of the division lead, and despite some good runs they were still eight games back on September 5. The Dodgers then proceeded to win eight in a row, including five against the Giants, to be only one game out of first place on September 14.

However, they then proceeded to drop four in a row, including two against the cellar-dweller Padres. In the end, the Dodgers could not quite overtake the Giants.

But they made it close. On the penultimate day of the season, the Dodgers were only one game behind. The Giants then proceeded to lose 4–1 against the Padres. Next, a win by the Dodgers at home against the Astros would have led to a tie at the top of the NL West. Taking the mound for the Dodgers was Downing. The Astros proceeded to hit him all over Dodger Stadium, as he gave up four runs in the first and only lasted 1⅓ innings. Conversely, Ken Forsch pitched a complete-game shutout, as the Astros won, 11–0. It was a demoralizing loss. While the Dodgers won on the final game of the season, the Giants also won and as such clinched the NL West crown.

Thus, the Dodgers once again finished in second place, this time one game behind the Giants. On a positive note, their record of 89–73 was their best since they won the NL in 1966. Nevertheless, the team had ample opportunity to win the NL West, but for whatever reason were simply unable to get the job done. Allen blamed it on the Dodger culture. As Michael Fallon recounted in *Dodgerland,* Allen stated, "The problem was all that Dodger Blue jive. [The organization puts] a lot of pressure on players to sign autographs and have their picture taken. They want you to visit with celebs in the clubhouse before games. Have a laugh with Don Rickles. Eat spaghetti with Sinatra . . . . It distracts from the team's mission to win ballgames."

Quite simply, in addition to be successful on the field, Walter and Peter O'Malley wanted the players to be part of the Los Angeles community. Dick Allen was paid to play baseball, not be part of the Dodgers' public relations. Nevertheless, the O'Malleys felt as though the two were intertwined. The Dodger players liked Allen as a teammate and person. As Bill Singer told Delsohn about Allen, "Most of the players loved him, but he was the kind of free spirit who would drive a manager nuts." Moreover, Alston never bothered to try to talk to Allen; Bobby

Valentine believed that Allen and Alston never actually talked. It was Campanis who went out and acquired Allen—a move that Alston was not in favor of. Allen told Valentine that "I'll lead this team in every category. Then I'll be traded when the year's over, because the old man [Alston] doesn't like me."

Peter O'Malley was not happy that Allen did not believe in doing PR, and Alston did not want him either. As such, it was not a surprise that, following the 1971 season, Allen was traded to the White Sox. In return the Dodgers acquired pitcher Tommy John and infielder Steve Huntz. Huntz never played a major-league game for the Dodgers, while John had a fine career and is now famous for the surgical procedure named in his honor. As for Allen in '72, he led the AL in home runs, RBIs, walks, on-base percentage, slugging percentage, and on-base percentage plus slugging (OPS) on the way to becoming the AL MVP. While Allen never recaptured the form in following seasons (largely due to injury), it is fair to say that if the trade never happened the Dodgers in 1972 would have been a much better side with him. Over time, the trade worked out better for the Dodgers than the White Sox, as Allen only lasted three seasons in Chicago, while John had six good seasons in Los Angeles. Nevertheless, Allen made a big difference to the Dodgers in 1971 and was sorely missed the following season.

## 1972–73: STRIKE, A LOCKOUT, AND BRIDESMAIDS

Throughout the years, there have been unofficial holdouts by players, such as those by Koufax, Drysdale, and Wills. In addition, the Detroit Tigers conducted a one-day strike in support of Ty Cobb in 1912. However, there had never been a work stoppage by all players. That changed in 1972. The players wanted an increase in their pensions, and the MLBPA asked for a 17 percent increase in the owners' contribution to the pension fund. The players were not asking for an excessive amount; the 17 percent increase was in line with inflation since the 1968 Basic Agreement. Rather than negotiate, the owners decided to play hardball and offered only an increase of $372,000 for three years. St. Louis Cardinals owner Gussie Busch stated, "We're not going to give them another goddamn cent. If they want to strike—let 'em."

While it was generally assumed that Miller was pushing for a strike, it was the players who had had enough of owners riding roughshod over them and wanted to strike. By a margin of 663–10, the players gave the MLBPA strike authorization. The MLBPA board matched the players resolve and voted 47–0, with one abstention, to begin the strike. Wes Parker, the Dodger player representative, was later removed from the post by his teammates for abstaining. As Parker told Leahy,

> I owed everything to the Dodgers organization. . . . That's why I didn't want to strike, because I knew how close I'd come to dying from the fear and discouragement I suffered in my home life. It was a miracle to me that I was even playing in the majors. Why would I strike against the team that gave me an opportunity to save my life? Mr. O'Malley and the organization had given me my chance. That literally saved me.

Several Dodger players were furious with Parker, as he put his own interests above what the rest of the team wanted. Despite

Parker's objections, on April 1, 1972, the first nationwide baseball strike began.

The media was frothing at the mouth in outrage at the players and especially Miller (a common occurrence from the moment Miller assumed the MLBPA leadership). However, despite the media's distaste for the strike, the players were united. The owners were not.

Within a week, the MLB's negotiator offered to increase the amount the owners would contribute by $400,000. In addition, three teams allowed the players to work out at their facilities. As the owners were not united in the slightest, a resolution came swiftly. Both sides agreed to a new agreement on April 13. However, bitter to the end, the owners, after agreeing to terms, demanded games be made up with the players playing for free. Not surprisingly, this was rejected by the players, and the owners agreed to players receiving their income for every game. As for the pension, the owners increased their contributions to the pension plan by $500,000 as well as increased health-care premiums. The owners' hard-line approach resulted in them losing $5.2 million in revenue. In contrast, the players lost $600,000 in salary. However, they received improved pensions and better health care, and, most importantly, the players signaled to the owners and MLB that they would no longer be pushed around.

As were the players, the Dodgers were busy in the offseason. On December 2, the Dodgers traded Doyle Alexander, Bob O'Brien, Sergio Robles, and Royle Stillman to the Baltimore Orioles. In return, the Dodgers received relief pitcher Pete Richert and outfielder Frank Robinson. While Richert had a good season for the Dodgers, appearing in 37 games with an ERA of 2.25, the real prize was Robinson. Even though Robinson would turn thirty-six during the upcoming season, he was a former Rookie of the Year, eleven-time All-Star (he would eventually be capped twelve times), and MVP with both the Reds and Orioles. In the previous season, he hit 28 home runs, walked 72 times, and had a batting average of .281. The Dodgers were hoping that Robinson would be the power hitter that the recently departed Allen was in the previous season.

Allen's departure also paved the way for Steve Garvey to spend more time at third base. Garvey, who was picked up by the Dodgers in their famed 1968 draft, made his major-league debut in 1969. While he only appeared in three games that year and 34 in 1970, he appeared in 81 in 1971. The team was slowly increasing his playing time, as the front office envisaged Garvey as an All-Star caliber player. In 1972, Garvey, like his previous seasons, had an average year with the bat, hitting only hit .269 with an OPS of .734. Garvey also had a major problem in the field, committing 28 errors. He had developed a case of the yips.

Garvey believed that a separated shoulder in college may have been the cause. Yet, as he told Delsohn, "It may have been partly psychological too. Because if I had to make a quick throw, if it was a quick play, boy, it would be on the money. Give me time and who knows where it would be going." The Dodgers would luck into a solution to Garvey's erratic throws the following season.

Once the 1972 season got underway, the Dodgers were on fire. They won seven of their first eight games, and nine of their first eleven. The team eventually went 11–4 in April and 15–12 in May. On June 1, the Dodgers had a 1½-game lead in the

NL West but by June 10 had slipped to a tie for first. Unfortunately for the LA and their legion of fans, the proverbial wheels began to fall off. By July 1, they were six games off the pace. Not helping matters was that Robinson hurt his hamstring during the month. In July he only hit .221 and a minuscule .175 in August. While Robinson rebounded strongly in September, the damage was already done.

Once again, while the pitching staff were their usual wonderful self (finishing with the best ERA in the NL), the offense was average at best. On the pitching side, Sutton had an outstanding year, going 19–9 with a career-best ERA of 2.08 and was an All-Star for the first time, while Osteen was his reliable self. He finished with a record of 20–9 with an ERA of 2.64. As for the offense, Willie Davis played well, hitting .289, and led the team in hits, doubles, triples, and home runs. The Dodgers still played well enough to finish with an 85–70 record but were 10½ games behind the Cincinnati Reds. The team was bridesmaids once again. Quite simply, the team was good, but not good enough.

In a sad note, time finally caught up with Maury Wills. While he had a good 1971 season, 1972 was one to forget. He played in 71 games and hit a measly .129 while only stealing one base. In April, Bill Russell became the Dodgers' starting shortstop. As Wills told Leahy, Russell

> just kind of took over the position and I was out. It happened quietly. But it was a lot easier for me to take my shortstop position from Don Zimmer in 1959 than to give up my own. I tried to do my best with the whole thing. I didn't want to do to Bill what some of the Brooklyn guys did to me when I took over. I tried to

give Bill what help I could. But it was hard. No matter what anyone else tells you, that's the way it is for players. That whole year hurt like hell.

Following the season, the team told Wills that his career as a Dodger was over. Rather than try to find another team, Wills retired from the game. Retirement was not a happy time for Wills, as he battled alcohol and cocaine addiction. Thankfully, he overcame his demons and has worked for the Dodgers for several years as an instructor. It is beyond dispute that without Wills the Dodgers would have not have been successful as they were. He was their offensive catalyst.

\* \* \*

There were changes afoot for the 1973 season that would have a profound impact on not only the Dodgers but also all of base-ball. The previous Basic Agreement had expired prior to the start of Spring Training. The owners seemingly had not learned anything from the 1972 strike and decided through the Player Relations Committee (PRC), which was created in the 1960s to deal with the MLBPA, to lock out the players until the sides could agree to terms. Once again, the owners were not united, and many teams simply ignored the PRC's directive. As such, while the lockout lasted twelve days, it had little to no impact. So, this lockout is barely remembered today.

In late February, an agreement was negotiated that led to an increase in the minimum salary, as well as increased meal money during Spring Training and for road games during the regular season. Once again, the MLBPA was successful in securing better terms for all players, while owner disunity doomed the lockout before it began. That the MLBPA was continually successful in securing victories for the players at the owners' expense would lead to further industrial action in the future.

There was another change in the offseason that would have a great impact upon the game, as the Dodgers traded Billy Grabarkewitz, Frank Robinson, Bill Singer, Mike Strahler, and Bobby Valentine to the California Angels for Andy Messersmith and Ken McMullen. At the time, it just seemed like a routine trade, but Messersmith would eventually be a catalyst for baseball players being granted limited free agency due to the actions of the Dodgers' front office. However, that was still to come. As for the 1973 season, the Dodgers were hoping that Messersmith would make their starting rotation even more formidable and help lead them to the postseason.

Things did not look too promising in that regard to start the season, as the Dodgers compiled an 11–11 record and were seven games out of first place by May 1. However, May was a great month for the team, as they were 19–8 to move within a half game of the division lead. June was to be even better, as they went 21–8 and finished with a 6½-game lead in the division.

The true highlight of June was the formation of the team's infield. At the start of the season, Alston had Bill Buckner playing at first, Lee Lacy at second, Bill Russell at short, with Ken McCullen at third. The below-average April led to changes upon changes, as Alston was searching for a winning formula. Despite the good month of May, things were still somewhat unsettled. However, June 13, 1973, will always be a great day for the Dodgers—even though they were massacred by the Phillies, 16–3. Alston had already turned to untested youngsters in the infield. Davey Lopes, who only played 11 games in 1972 as a twenty-seven-year-old rookie, had replaced Lacy at the second base, while the twenty-four-year-old Russell was entrenched at short and the twenty-five-year-old Ron Cey, who only played two games in 1971 and 11 games in 1972, was now the incumbent at third. Tom Paciorek was playing at first, but was injured. Steve Garvey took over for him as a defensive replacement, and the rest is history. Many people take credit for the move of Garvey to first, from his wife to Bill Buckner to Tommy Lasorda.

It is often assumed that Garvey became the incumbent first baseman on June 13, but this is mistaken. He next appeared as a pinch-hitter on June 15 and then did not play again until he was once again a pinch-hitter on June 23 in the first game of a doubleheader against the Reds. It was not until the second game of the doubleheader that Garvey played first base again. It was from there that Garvey became the incumbent first baseman, as Buckner did not play the outfield for the first time until June 24 of 1973. Nevertheless, what is most important is that the infield of Garvey, Lopes, Russell, and Cey would remain together for the next eight-and-a-half years. The length they were together is even more remarkable, considering that Garvey, Lopes, Russell, and Cey often did not get along. As Lopes told the *Los Angeles Times* in 2013, "I'm sure I was an ass. . . . I'm sure they were asses too, at times. But when push comes to shove and someone knocks them or something happens during a game, we were right there." Russell claimed, "We respected each other and knew each other's ability. . . . You knew all the intimate stuff—some of the stuff you probably shouldn't know." Likewise, former Dodger pitcher Mickey Hatcher noted, "There were times . . . when those guys hated each other. But when they got on the field they played together. They pulled for each other."

Regardless of whether the infield liked each other personally had no bearing on the field, as on June 23 the Dodgers led the NL West by 3½ games; by July 21, LA had a comfortable 7½-game lead. The team was not as consistent from that point forward, but on August 30 they still held first by 4 games.

Then once again the proverbial wheels fell off, as the Dodgers lost nine in a row and 12 out of 13. The Dodgers could not score runs, and when the offense did perform their pitching was woeful, such as an 11–8 loss to the Giants and 9–6 loss to the Padres. The 11–8 loss to the Giants was particularly heartbreaking because LA led 8–1 after the top of the seventh. The Giants then proceeded to score six runs in the bottom of the seventh. To cap off the nightmare, Bobby Bonds hit a walk-off grand slam off Jim Brewer to send the Giants fans and players into delirium. During the horrible stretch, not only did the Giants sweep the Dodgers in three games at Candlestick Park, but also the lowly Padres took three out of four games at Dodger Stadium. Finally, the now division-leading Reds defeated the Dodgers two games in a row at Riverfront Stadium to lead the division by five games. Unlike the Dodgers, the Reds did not suffer a monumental collapse and ended up winning the NL West crown by 3½ games. It was a very disappointing end of a season that started with so much promise. They finished with a 95–66 record, which would have easily won the NL East division, and in the wild-card era they would have made the postseason. Unfortunately they played in the NL West. As such, once again, while they were good, they were not quite good enough.

# 1974: OH, SO CLOSE

Recognizing that something had to be done if they were to once again make the postseason, the Dodgers front office decided that changes needed to be made. On December 6, the Dodgers traded Claude Osteen and a minor leaguer to the Houston Astros for outfielder Jim Wynn. While Osteen was coming off an All-Star season, he was in decline and had an average 1974 season with the Astros before being traded during the season to the Cardinals. In contrast, Wynn had an All-Star season, hitting .271 with 32 home runs and 108 walks while driving in 108 runs for the Dodgers, and finishing in the top five of NL MVP voting. It was a great trade for the Dodgers and a major factor in the team performing as well as they did. The reason for bringing in another outfielder was because, on the previous day, they traded away Willie Davis. Davis had a fine career for the Dodgers, yet was truly never recognized by the club for how good he was. However, like Osteen, Davis was beginning to decline. Thus, it was a major surprise that the Montreal Expos agreed to take Davis in exchange for pitcher Mike Marshall, whose specialty was the screwball.

Marshall, who was studying for his PhD in exercise physiology, believed that it was possible to pitch every day. While he did not quite do that, he came closer than almost any other pitcher. He appeared in 66 games in 1971, 65 in 1972, and 92 in 1973. In 1972, he finished in the top-four of Cy Young voting, while coming in second in 1973 while also finishing in the top five in MVP voting. He was a great player on the rise, so on the surface it was odd that Montreal agreed to trade him in a straight swap for Davis. But Marshall had a reputation for eccentricity and speaking his mind.

Marshall appeared in an astonishing 106 games, was the final Dodger pitcher in 83 games, notched 21 saves (he led the NL in all three of these categories), had an ERA of 2.42, was an All-Star, finished in the top three of NL MVP voting, and won the NL Cy Young Award. This was, in fact, the first time a reliever had won the Cy Young since the inception of the award in 1956. It was an outstanding season and an equally outstanding trade by the Dodger front office.

Indeed, the team's pitching staff had an equally impressive season, leading the NL in wins and ERA, with Messersmith leading the NL in wins (20), making the All-Star team, and finishing second in the Cy Young voting, while Sutton had a record of 19–9 and finished fourth in the voting. Tommy John had a great year as well, with a 13–3 record and an ERA of 2.59, before he injured his ulnar collateral ligament, which led him to miss the rest of the season. Later that year, John would receive a radical new surgery to fix his UCL. And while it was Dr. Frank Jobe who performed the surgery, the procedure would from then on be known as Tommy John surgery.

The Dodger offense also had a great year, leading the NL in runs, home runs, slugging percentage, and OPS. In addition to Wynn, Garvey had a monumental All-Star season—winning the selection as a write-in candidate.[12] Garvey had a batting average of .312, 200 hits, 32 doubles, 21 home runs, and 111 RBIs; he played Gold Glove defense at first and capped off the season by being named the NL MVP. Wynn and Garvey were ably supported by, among others, All-Star Cey and his 18 home runs and 97 RBIs; outfielder

---

12 In the entire history of the All-Star Game, only two players ever won selection through being a write-in. The first time this occurred was in 1970 when Atlanta Brave Rico Carty made the team; it was his only All-Star appearance.

Willie Crawford, who had the third-highest OPS for the Dodgers behind Wynn and Garvey; and Lopes, who stole 59 bases.

The Dodgers had a fast start, going 17–6 in April to lead the NL West by 3½ by the end of the month. By the end of May, the Dodgers were leading the division by 7. On July 10, they pulled away and were atop the NL West heap by 10½ games. However, a less-than-stellar run saw the lead slowly whittle away, and by September 14 their division lead had been reduced to only 1½ games. However, unlike in previous seasons, the Dodgers did not fold and eventually captured the NL West crown by four games with a 102–60 record over the Cincinnati Reds. Equally pleasing for the Dodgers was that the Giants had a simply awful season, going 72–90 and finishing 30 games behind Los Angeles. Following the team's fine year, Alston was awarded the NL Manager of the Year Award.

Facing LA in the NL Championship Series was the Pittsburgh Pirates. The Pirates had won the NL East over the Cardinals by 1½ games with a record of 88–74. The Dodgers were rightfully confident heading into the best-of-five series. Taking the mound in Game One at Three Rivers Stadium was Don Sutton; for the Pirates it was Jerry Reuss, who had a 16–11 record with an ERA of 3.50 for the regular season.

Reuss pitched a great game, going seven strong and only giving up one run after a bases-loaded walk to Lopes in the second. Unfortunately for Reuss and the Pirates, Sutton was even better. He pitched a complete-game shutout while only giving up four hits and a walk as the Dodgers took the first game, 3–0. Game Two was another good one for the Dodgers, as Messersmith put the team on his back with seven strong innings while only giving up two runs. He got help from Cey, who had two doubles and a home run while going 4-for-5, leading the Dodgers to a 5–2 victory.

The teams then headed to Los Angeles for Game Three, which did not go according to the home team's plans; the Pirates romped to a 7–0 victory after scoring five runs in the first. For LA, starting pitcher Doug Rau only lasted ⅔ of an inning while giving up three runs. However, any apprehension about the Pirates staging a comeback in the series evaporated very quickly by Game Four. In the bottom of the first, Wynn doubled to score Lopes. Following an uneventful second inning, Garvey homered in the third to score two. With Sutton pitching great, the game was effectively over. The Dodgers cruised to a 12–1 victory to capture the NL crown, once again heading to the World Series.

Facing the Dodgers in the World Series would be the two-time defending World Series Champion Oakland Athletics. In 1972 the A's defeated the Mets in seven and followed that up in 1973 by beating the Reds (also in seven). They had defeated the Orioles in four games to clinch their third straight AL title and were ready to face off against their Southern California counterparts. The A's were led by "Mr. October" and future Hall of Famer Reggie Jackson and their star starting pitcher James Augustus Hunter, more commonly known as Catfish Hunter. In 1974, on the way to winning the AL Cy Young Award, Hunter had a record of 25–12 with a 2.49 ERA. In addition to his Hall of Fame career, Catfish is also forever known as baseball's first free agent due to the A's breaching his contract after the 1974 season. Demonstrating how the lack of free agency artificially lowered wages in 1974, Hunter earned $100,000 playing for the A's. Following the breach of contract and an MLB panel ruling that the breach meant Hunter was a free agent, he signed a five-year contract with the Yankees worth $3.75 million. Hunter also received a signing bonus of $1 million.

Ken Holtzman took the mound for the A's in Game One of the Word Series at Dodger Stadium, while Messersmith was the Dodgers' starter. After a scoreless first inning, Jackson led off the top of the second with a home run to left-center. There was no more scoring until the top of the fifth when the A's scored again following a double, a wild pitch, and a sacrifice bunt. The Dodgers immediately got a run back in the bottom of the inning when Lopes scored from first on a single by Buckner. Unfortunately, the Dodgers literally threw their chances away in the top of the eighth following an errant throw from Ron Cey to first that allowed A's shortstop Bert Campaneris to score. The Dodgers had the tying run on the basepaths in the ninth following a home run by Wynn to cut the margin to one and a single to Garvey. However, Hunter struck out Joe Ferguson to end the game with a final of 3–2.

In Game Two, LA took an early lead, thanks to a single from catcher Steve Yeager in the second to drive home Cey. With Sutton dominating on the mound, the Dodgers increased their lead in the sixth with a two-run homer from Joe Ferguson. The score remained 3–0 until the top of the ninth. With Sutton looking for a complete-game shutout, he hit a batter and gave up a double to the first two batters he faced. This led Alston to bring in Mike Marshall. However, Joe Rudi singled on a line drive to score two, making it a one-run game. Marshall then struck out Gene Tenace, which led to A's manager Al Dark sending in Herb Washington to pinch-run for Rudi while having Ángel Mangual pinch-hit. Washington was then picked off, and Marshall struck out Mangual to close the game and tie the Series at one.

Game Three was played at the Oakland–Alameda County Coliseum in front of 49,347 rabid fans. In another incredibly close contest, the A's defeated the Dodgers 3–2. However, the real story came after the game which arguably doomed any chance the Dodgers had at winning the World Series. Bill Buckner was quoted after the game of saying, "I definitely think we have a better ballclub. . . . The A's have only a couple of players that could play on our club. Reggie Jackson is outstanding. Sal Bando and Joe Rudi are good, and they have a good pitching staff. Other than that . . . if we played them 162 times we'd beat them 100."

There is a fine line between confidence, arrogance, and just outright stupidity. While Buckner may well have been confident in his team, his comments did nothing to help them. Instead, he gave the A's ample ammunition. In Game Four, the A's jumped out to an early lead in the bottom of the third, thanks to a home run from pitcher Ken Holtzman.[13] LA came back in the top of the fourth on a triple to Russell, which drove in Garvey and Ferguson. However, in the sixth, partly due to an error on a pickoff attempt that led to an error and three walks (one intentional), the A's scored four runs, and the content was over. The A's defeated the Dodgers, 5–2, to take a three games to one lead.

Stupidity and possible arrogance came to the forefront in Game Five. In a despicable act, during the bottom of the seventh inning and with the scored tied at two, a "fan" threw a whiskey bottle at Buckner, hitting him in the head. The game was delayed while Buckner was attended to. If the same thing happened today, it is overwhelmingly likely that Buckner

---

13 In 620 career at-bats (both regular and postseason), Holtzman had three home runs, with his shot in Game Four being his only playoff dinger.

would be forced to leave the game due to the possibility of a concussion. However, in 1974, it would have seemed weak for Buckner to leave, and as such he "toughed" it out. On the mound for the Dodgers was Mike Marshall, who refused to warm up by throwing practice pitches after the delay, despite his teammates' objections. Facing Marshall was Joe Rudi. As Rudi told *SFGate* in 2004, "Standing there for all that time without throwing any pitches makes it difficult to throw a screwball because your arm isn't really warmed up . . . I figured he's got to throw a fastball." And a fastball Marshall did throw, which Rudi promptly hit into the stands for a home run. Maybe Marshall did not need any warm-up pitches. To this day, he claims he was warmed up, and maybe he was, but Rudi was waiting on a fastball.

Possible stupidity and arrogance further came to the forefront in the top of the eighth. Buckner led off the inning with a single to the outfield. The center fielder, Bill North, then committed an error, which allowed Buckner to advance to second—but Buckner kept going and was thrown out trying to reach third. As the old baseball adage goes, never make the first or last out at third. At that point in the game, they were only down by one run; Buckner was the tying run. Hitting behind Buckner were Wynn, Garvey, and Ferguson—all three were capable of cashing him in from second. Whether Buckner was confident, arrogant, stupid, or still feeling the effects of being hit in the head with a whiskey bottle is impossible to ascertain, but Buckner making the out at third was the death knell for the Dodgers' World Series hopes. The A's defeated the Dodgers, 3–2, to capture their third-straight World Series crown in five games. As for the Dodgers, they came oh, so close; indeed, no game was a blowout, and three of their losses were by one run, but they were not quite good enough.

## 1975–76: TURMOIL ON AND OFF THE FIELD

After coming so close to World Series victory, the Dodgers naturally had high expectations coming into the 1975 season. And it looked like those expectations could indeed be fulfilled following a 15–8 record in April. On May 22, the team had a 5½-game division lead. However, a poor finish to the month saw their lead cut to 1½ games, and the wheels truly fell off the season. The Dodgers just went into a slow freefall, and while they ended up second in the division, the Big Red Machine won the NL West by 20 games. The Reds then went on to beat the Red Sox in the World Series.

Cincinnati had an outstanding year, while injuries to Marshall and Wynn, among others, curtailed the season for LA. Also not helping was the turmoil around Steve Garvey. Thanks to his good looks and image as an all-American boy, Garvey was very popular with the fans and advertisers. He did not drink or smoke, and it was claimed that he looked down upon those players that did. On June 15, the *Sun-Telegram* ran a story by Betty Cuniberti in which numerous Dodger players, both anonymously and by name, severely criticized Garvey. Maybe the most benign comment was from one anonymous player, who told Cuniberti that "Steve Garvey doesn't have a friend on this team."

Following the story, the players called a team meeting. After the meeting, Lopes claimed that "the other eight starters look at baseball as a game. Garvey thinks of it more as a business. That's fine with me. It's just not my bag." Cey also went on the record after the meeting, stating that "I don't mind what Steve does. If he wants to go out of his way to be the clean-cut kid, that's fine—so long as he doesn't interfere with my style. Sometimes he has interfered." He added that "basically everyone knows he's a public relations man." Such comments were not exactly repairing any burnt bridges. Lopes later told Steve Delsohn in *True Blue* that "Steve had his own agenda. He wanted to be Mr. Dodger. And there was some bullshit involved, to be honest with you. There was a lot of favoritism from the Dodgers. Special favors were given to Steve, special favors to his wife, Cyndy." However, Lopes goes on to note that "I think you get caught up in the atmosphere. You're in Hollywood, you forget who you are, what you do, and you just get carried away with the whole scene." In other words, things get blown out of proportion, but, under the LA spotlight, even the littlest things can cause resentment and jealousy.

Now considering the year the Big Red Machine had, it is doubtful that the Dodgers would have captured the NL West crown, but all the distractions had a negative effect on the team. They were not like the A's who would brawl with each other and immediately make amends. The infighting, at least in 1975, was a detriment to the team.

In that regard, many players in both leagues believed they were not getting the respect they deserved. They wanted free agency, as they *knew* following Catfish Hunter being granted free agency and dramatically increasing in his salary that they were being grossly underpaid. To try to achieve free agency, Miller instructed the players in 1975 to play on the last year of their contracts without signing new ones—effectively playing the year on the reserve clause. By the end of the season, only Andy Messersmith and Dave McNally had not signed new contracts. This led the MLBPA to file a grievance dispute on the players' behalf, seeking free agency. All Messersmith wanted was a no-trade clause in his contract. The Dodger front office, in their infinite wisdom, continually refused his request. This led to Messersmith seeking free agency. After the grievance was filed, the Dodgers did indeed offer Messersmith a no-trade clause in his contract—but at that point it was too late. Messersmith, like McNally, sought free agency. As such, their grievances went to arbitration. The owners' representative voted for the players not being granted free agency; the players' representative voted for free agency. The deciding vote would be cast by the independent arbitrator, Peter Seitz. He wanted the two sides to compromise. The players were willing to do so, but the owners stood hard.

On December 23, 1975, Seitz made his ruling in favor of the players. Baseball players now could potentially become free agents. As with Curt Flood, several so-called fans were hostile toward Messersmith and McNally. Such "fans" would obviously prefer a game where the players are vastly underpaid. Messersmith later noted, "I came out as the dirty dog. I always had a good energy rapport with most of the fans. After that incident, the energy was 95, 100 percent negative. That was a real hard thing for me. I just wasn't ready for it." In April 1976, Messersmith signed a three-year contract with the Braves for $1 million. The reason why Messersmith signed so late is after the ruling, and failing to come to an agreement with the MLBPA over the issue of free agency, the owners locked out the players before the beginning of Spring Training.

Eventually, due to the owners' resolve once again being tested by the solidarity of the players, and with Walter O'Malley leading the way, the owners called an end to the lockout without an agreement being reached. On July 12, the two sides finally reached a compromise: In addition to an increased minimum salary and owner contribution to the players' pension fund, there still would be a reserve clause. However, it would only apply for the first six years a player is with a team. After those six years, a player would become a free agent. The modification of the reserve clause was a great benefit to the players. Their salaries increased, and teams began offering players multiyear contracts. Thus, an increasing number of players had increased economic security.

As for the 1976 Dodger season, the infighting and disappointment continued as the team was good, but once again not quite good enough. It was also the end of an era. One of the "highlights," if one could call it that, occurred on April 25 when two protestors ran onto the field at Dodger Stadium, interrupting a game between the Dodgers and the Cubs, and attempted to set fire to an American flag. Cubs center fielder Rick Monday charged the pair and grabbed the flag from one of the protestors. Monday was instantly hailed as an American hero. In 2016, Monday told *Vice Sports*, "What they were doing was wrong, and I wanted them off the field. . . . I did not want them to be able to desecrate an American flag that some of my buddies lost their lives for, representing the rights and freedoms that you and I enjoy." At the time, he also claimed,

Those of us in Major League Baseball and those of us American citizens are not going to let people use our flag or the game of baseball to make any type of demonstration as was tried. . . . If they don't want to do anything constructive to help this country become even a better country to live in and participate in, then also one of the rights that is available to them is that our borders are not guarded and they are free to leave. God bless America.

In fact, the two protestors were not antiwar protestors, hippies, communists, or anything like it. One protestor was identified as William Errol Thomas, and the second "protester" was his eleven-year-old son. William, a Native American, was allegedly protesting the treatment of his people. In addition, he was attempting to draw "attention to what he claims is his wife's imprisonment against her will in a Missouri mental institution." In the end, Monday was portrayed as a hero for protecting the flag, but not a single journalist interviewed Thomas or even looked into whether his wife was indeed being held against her will.

As for the season itself, in a positive for the Dodgers and more so for baseball as a whole, Tommy John returned from the surgery named after him and finished the season with a 10–10 record with an ERA of 3.09. That John could play again was due to his dedication and hard work, *and* the groundbreaking surgery performed by Frank Jobe. Following the season, John deservedly won the NL Comeback Player of the Year Award.

The Dodgers had a very good season, going 92–70. Unfortunately, the Reds were just that much better, going 102–60 to win the NL West. The Reds then proceeded to sweep the Phillies in the NLCS and then swept the Yankees to capture the World Series. The Reds were just that good. However, rather than accept this, there was infighting within the Dodgers— much of it centered on Alston.

Alston, who had begun managing the Dodgers back in Brooklyn in 1954, was on his usual yearly contract. However, an increasing number of people in both the organization and media were hoping that Alston would retire and allow Tommy Lasorda to take over managerial duties. There was a fear that Lasorda, who bled Dodger blue like no other, would eventually tire of waiting in the wings and decide to manage another team. In a *Los Angeles Times* article on September 19, 1976, one unnamed veteran stated,

> I flatly believe that Walt does not deserve to be rehired. He has made too many mistakes in strategy, and he has become too stereotyped. We're not aggressive; we don't intimidate anyone. We make fundamental mistakes and they're allowed to go uncorrected. . . . He's become more hardened and calloused to his own players. We're all just numbers. The other day, before the first game of the series with the Reds, he had a clubhouse meeting and told us we were not as good as Cincinnati, that the Reds were simply the better team. Maybe it's the truth but what point is there in saying it, how does it help our confidence?

Of course, not all players felt this way. In the same article, another unnamed Dodger player defended Alston. However, the proverbial writing was on the wall—Alston's days were numbered.

On September 27, Alston announced that he would be stepping down as Dodgers' manager, effective immediately. Under Alston, the Dodgers had won seven NL pennants (1955, 1956, 1959, 1963, 1965, 1966, and 1974) and captured the World Series crown four times (1955, 1959, 1963, and 1965). Based on those numbers, Alston was a more-than-worthy recipient to be inducted into the National Baseball Hall of Fame.

However, his departure did leave a sour taste. Considering that there were only four games remaining until the end of the season, it lends credence to the theory that Alston jumped before he was pushed. Whether the O'Malleys let Alston know that if he did not retire he would not have his contract renewed or he'd simply had enough will never truly be known. But what is certain was that a new manager was needed.

At the press conference announcing his retirement, Alston stated, "We used to have 24 or 25 farm clubs. It would take six or seven years to reach the majors. A player had to beat out a dozen guys to do it. He was appreciative of what he had. Now they get a free ride through college and a bonus even before they've swung at a major league curve. They expect it to be that easy for them all the way." That a major league manager was so dismissive of the current players clearly highlighted the Dodgers' need of a new person running the team. There was only one true candidate for the position. On September 28, the team announced that Tommy Lasorda would be the new manager of the Los Angeles Dodgers.

## 1977: THE FIRST TIME IS A TRAGEDY

Thomas Charles Lasorda was not a good major leaguer. He pitched for the Brooklyn Dodgers in 1955 and 1956, appearing in just eight games. His final season as a major leaguer was in 1956; he appeared in 18 games for the Kansas City Athletics. For his career, he had a 0–4 record and posted an ERA of 6.48. Following the end of his playing days, Lasorda remained in baseball in a number of roles before becoming a minor-league manager for the Dodgers where a number of future starters played under him. Lasorda eventually worked his way up to third-base coach for the Dodgers beginning in 1973.

Following Alston's retirement, while Dodger first-base coach and former player Jim Gilliam also put his hand up for the position,

Lasorda was always destined to be the team's next manager. At the press conference announcing his appointment, Lasorda said, "I think that when someone wakes up and finds that when he has inherited a position vacated by the greatest manager in baseball history, it's like waking up to find you have inherited the Hope Diamond." That he took over from Alston must have been particularly sweet for Lasorda, as he believed that when he was trying to break into the big leagues Alston never gave him a fair chance to succeed. He also claims that Alston never liked him. Thus, Lasorda had even more motivation to succeed as the Dodgers' manager and, in time, became *the* iconic figure of the franchise.

A story from Vin Scully in Lasorda's biography *Tommy Lasorda: My Way* sums up the person Lasorda is:

> The first time I ever heard the name Tommy Lasorda was in Vero Beach. . . . I was talking to Buzzie Bavasi, the GM of the Dodgers. We were chatting and he said, "Oh, I've got to leave. I have to stop a kid from killing himself. There's a kid who has bet me that he would pitch batting practice to every player in camp." In those days, we had 26 farm teams, so if you were going to pitch batting practice, with free agents, we're talking 600, 700 players. I asked what his name was, and he said, "Tommy Lasorda. He's a left-hander on the Montreal roster." That was the first time I heard his name, and I realized that whoever it was had to . . . [have] a terrific spirit to even think he could do such an undertaking. To pitch batting practice to 600 guys would kill you, but not Tommy.

Lasorda was a players' manager who did not care if the guys joked around, made fun of him, and the like. However, the players had to respect his rules and, above all else, bleed Dodger blue. In *Dodgerland*, author Michael Fallon recounted a story when Don Sutton, who never liked playing under Lasorda (as he preferred Alston) and who the Dodgers were allegedly trying to trade during Spring Training, went against the rules Lasorda set:

> Early on in Lasorda's reign, Sutton went against one of Lasorda's few pregame rules—that pitchers had to shag fly balls during batting practice. Sutton's custom was to use this time to run, so that's what he continued doing. One day in San Francisco during batting practice, Lasorda observed that Sutton and Doug Rau were running together. "Why do you do this to me?" Lasorda asked Rau, a player who had played under him throughout the Minor Leagues. "You've been like a son to me." Rau's response: "Sutton made me do it." Lasorda then summoned Sutton. Sutton bluntly told his manager he would continue to run during batting practice. And Lasorda locked the office door. "Fine, you want to change the rule, we'll change it right here," he said to Sutton. "Let's fight right here, you and me. If I beat you, the rule stays. If you beat me, I'll change it.

Sutton decided it was not a good look all round if he got into a fight with his manger and agreed to the rule.

Before Spring Training had even gotten underway, Lasorda attempted to put his stamp on the team by announcing that the starting lineup was already decided and that they would play together throughout the preseason. For the media used to reporting on who would make the team throughout the often monotony of Spring Training, such a pronouncement was like fingernails scraping down a chalkboard. However, for a majority of the players, Sutton being a notable exception, they enjoyed the enthusiasm Lasorda brought—as much as players can possibly enjoy the drudgery that is Spring Training before the real grind of the season begins.

The loud and bombastic Lasorda also had an influence on the Dodgers off the field. Lasorda was close friends with Frank Sinatra. As he recounts in his book, he met Sinatra "at a restaurant in Chicago [in 1973], and he said to me, 'You should be the Dodgers' manager.' I said, 'One day, God willing.' And he said, 'When you do become manager, I'll come sing the national anthem at your first game.'" And on April 7, 1977, on Lasorda's first day managing the Dodgers in the new season, sure enough Ol' Blue Eyes duly sang the National Anthem to a jam-packed Dodger Stadium. And to make the day even better for the Dodgers faithful and Lasorda himself, on the back of a complete game from Sutton, the Dodgers defeated the Giants, 5–1.

The Dodgers followed that up by winning the second game of the series, 8–2. They then proceeded to drop the next two games. This would be the last time they would be at .500 for the entire year. The team had an incredible first month under Lasorda, going 17–3 to lead the NL West by 7½ games. While it would have been impossible to be that successful for the rest of the season, and despite some hiccups along the way, the Dodgers' hold on first-place was never truly challenged. They eventually compiled a 98–64 record and easily captured the NL West crown by 10 games from the Cincinnati Reds.

Going into the final game of the season, three Dodgers had hit 30 or more home runs: Garvey hit 33; Reggie Smith, who led the league in on-base percentage, hit 32; and Cey hit 30. Stuck on 29 was Dusty Baker. After failing to hit a home run in his first two at-bats, the crowd at Dodger Stadium prayed and pleaded to the gods. Their prayers were duly rewarded when Baker connected on a 1-2 pitch to launch the ball over the left-field wall for his 30th home run of the season. This was the first time in major league history that a team had four players to hit 30 or more home runs in a single season. Even though the Dodgers lost to the Astros, 6–3, it was a great end to the first season under Lasorda.

Waiting in the NLCS was the Philadelphia Phillies, who had had an even better year than LA, going 101–61. Prior to the commencement of the series, there was trash talk from both sides. Sutton began it by claiming in a *Los Angeles Times* article that the Dodger pitchers were better than their counterparts. In addition, he said Los Angeles

> has more pitching depth, better defense, more guys capable of delivering offensively, and a more consistent offense. I don't mean to take anything away from the Philadelphia offense, but as for big guns you're really only talking about Greg Luzinski and Mike Schmidt. They'll have to hit a lot of solo home runs to beat us. By contrast, we have a handful of guys who can break it open with one swing. I think we have an advantage in offense as well as in pitching. It's just awfully tough to stop us completely.

The Phillies responded through manager Danny Ozark, who claimed that he was happy to face the Dodgers rather than the Reds. He said the Dodgers are "not the toughest, because Cincinnati knocked the beans out of us. We haven't won a game in Cincinnati in, I think, nine games. We played .500 against the Dodgers this year. So if you ask me which I'd rather play again, I'll take the .500 club."

Game One was held at Dodger Stadium, but it was the home team that battled nerves. Tommy John could not make it out of the fifth inning, giving up four runs. The Dodgers got one back in the fifth before giving up another run in the sixth. Momentum seemed to have shifted the Dodgers way in the seventh, as with one swing of the bat Cey leveled the score with a grand slam. However, things unraveled pretty quickly in the top of the ninth as Elias Sosa gave up two runs on three hits and a balk. The home team went quietly in the bottom of the ninth as the Phillies' drew first blood, winning 7–5. The visiting players were ecstatic with winning, and some even went as far as almost guaranteeing that the series was as good as over.

However, the Dodgers convincingly won the second game of the series, 7–1, thanks to a grand slam by Baker in the bottom of the fourth and a complete game from Sutton. The series then headed to Veterans Stadium in Philadelphia for the pivotal Game Three. The Dodgers quickly jumped out to a 2–0 lead in the top of the second after RBIs from Baker and Steve Yeager, but the Phillies scored three runs in the bottom of the inning due to three bases-loaded walks. The Dodgers tied the game in the fourth on a single from Baker, but the Phillies fought back and scored two runs in the bottom of the eighth. Trailing, LA's chances were seemingly over thanks to two quick outs to start the ninth. Pinch-hitter Vic Davalillo then singled via a bunt and was promptly cashed in by a double from pinch hitter Manny Mota. They were on a roll, and singles by Lopes and Russell gave the Dodgers a 6–5 victory in front of shell-shocked Phillies players and fans.

The momentum continued into Game Four the following day. Once again, the Dodgers scored two runs in the top of the second, this time due to a Baker home run. While the Phillies got one back in the fourth, the Dodgers scored twice in the top of the fifth. With Tommy John pitching magnificently, the Dodgers cruised to victory in both the game and the series. The players were ecstatic, as was Lasorda, but the manager was also angry. As recounted by Fallon, as the players were celebrating Lasorda shouted, "All anyone has talked about during the playoffs . . . is that the Dodgers couldn't win here at the Vet. . . . Everyone in the country thought this Philadelphia club was better than ours. But we showed them on the field who's the greatest ballclub in the league."

Lasorda was loud and bombastic, but on this occasion he was right. After dropping the first game at home, many in the media—as well as Phillies' players—wrote the Dodgers off. It was a testament to Lasorda and the players that they took three straight, including two on the road, to win the series in convincing manner. The Dodgers' opponents in the World Series were their old nemesis: the New York Yankees. The Yankees had defeated the Kanas City Royals three games to two in the ALCS. In the deciding fifth game, the Yankees trailed 3–2 after eight innings, but scored three runs in the ninth to defeat the Royals, 5–3, and head to another World Series.

In Game One of the World Series at Yankee Stadium, the Dodgers scored two in the first after an RBI triple by Bill Russell and a sacrifice fly by Ron Cey. The Yankees pulled one back in the bottom of the inning.

In the top of the sixth, Garvey was called out at home even though he appeared to beat the tag. Home-plate umpire Nestor Chylak was badly out of position and almost certainly had to guess whether Garvey was out. The decision was to prove costly, as the Yankees tied the game in the bottom of the inning and then took the lead in the eighth, thanks to a walk to second baseman Willie Randolph and a double by catcher Thurman Munson.

However, as in the Philadelphia series, the Dodgers never-say-die approach paid dividends, as pinch hitter Lee Lacy drove in Baker in the ninth to tie the game. The scores remained tied until the bottom of the 12th when, following a double by Randolph and an intentional walk to Munson, Dodger pitcher Rick Rhoden faced Paul Blair. Blair had previously broken Dodger-faithful hearts eleven years earlier when playing for the Baltimore Orioles in their sweep of the Dodgers in the 1966 World Series. Blair failed to bunt the runners over twice. As such, he was given the green light to swing away, and on a 2-2 count he drove in the winning run for the Yankees and once again broke the hearts of the Dodger faithful.

In Game Two, the Dodgers once again jumped to an early lead by scoring two in the first, one in the second, and another two in the third. While the Yankees got a run back in fourth, the game was already out of reach. For good measure, the Dodgers scored again in the ninth as they romped to a 6–1 victory. For LA, Burt Hooton pitched one of the best games of his life, throwing a complete game while only giving up one run on five hits and a walk. Such a performance was exactly what the team needed as they returned to Los Angeles with the Series tied up. This was key, as there was infighting within the Yankees clubhouse. Reggie Jackson had told the media after the game that he could not believe Yankee manager Billy Martin decided to start Catfish Hunter, considering that he had not pitched since early September due to injury. Martin did not take the high road, instead blasting Jackson. As recounted by Fallon in *Dodgerland*, Martin told the press that "If I'm going to back that ass

[Jackson] . . . why doesn't he back me? I didn't knock him when he messed up that play the other night." It did not end there, as Martin continued: "This isn't a one-way street. He has a lot of growing up to do. He's having enough trouble in the outfield without second-guessing the manager."

The press then sought out Yankee captain Munson for comment, who rightfully stated that "I do think it's unfortunate that at a time when we have a chance to win the championship, there's a guy out there trying to second-guess the manager." He then proceeded to pour more fuel on the fire by claiming that "I used to know what was going on around here but I stopped mixing drinks a long time ago. I've got only five more games at the most to worry about all this crap." However, like the A's in the 1974 World Series, the infighting seemed to inspire the Yankees.

In Game Three, in front of 55,992 fans at Dodger Stadium, the Yankees jumped all over Tommy John in the first inning, scoring three runs. The Dodgers leveled the scores in the bottom of the third by virtue of a three-run home run from Baker. But the Yankees were not to be denied, scoring in the fourth and the fifth, holding on to a 5–3 victory. The Dodgers tried to console themselves by claiming that very few of the Yankees hits were hit hard, but it does not matter, as they're all line drives in the box score.

In Game Four, the Yankees once again got to the Dodgers starting pitcher early, this time scoring three runs in the top of the second against Doug Rau. Indeed, Rau did not retire a batter in the second inning, with Lasorda replacing him with Rick Rhoden. Lasorda was wired for the game for ABC Television. When he got to the mound to replace Rau, the pitcher told Lasorda he wanted to stay in the game. This led to Lasorda going on a foul-mouthed tirade against the pitcher—all clearly heard on national television.

The Dodgers pulled two back in the bottom of the third, thanks to a Lopes' home run, but in the end, Yankees' pitcher Ron Guidry was just too good. The Bronx Bombers won, 4–2, to take a three game to one lead. In Game Five, the Yankees were never in the contest, as the Dodgers thumped them, 10–4, with Sutton pitching a complete game and collecting his second win in the Series. Then came Game Six at Yankee Stadium.

LA scored two runs in the first, due to a triple from Garvey, but the Yankees answered in the bottom of the second thanks to a two-run home run from first baseman Chris Chambliss. Reggie Smith restored the lead in the third thanks to a solo home run, but the rest of the game belonged to Mr. October, Reggie Jackson. In the bottom of the fourth, he hit the first pitch from Burt Hooton for a two-run home run. In the bottom of the fifth he hit the first pitch—this time from Elias Sosa—for another two-run home run. And in the bottom of the eighth he *again* hit the first pitch he saw—now from Charlie Hough—for a solo home run. The Yankees won the game, 8–4, and captured the World Series. Reggie Jackson single-handedly destroyed the Dodgers' hopes and tied a record with Babe Ruth for the most home runs in a World Series game; Ruth did it in 1926 and 1928. As he told the *New York Times*, "Perhaps for one night . . . I reached back and achieved that level of the overrated superstar. Babe Ruth was great. I'm just lucky." Only if we all could have such luck. As for the Dodgers, it was a bitter end to a very promising season. Unfortunately for the players, Lasorda, and the fans, history repeated itself the following year.

# 1978: THE SECOND TIME IS A FARCE

Even though they lost the 1977 World Series, the Dodgers were full of confidence heading into the '78 season. Indeed, Lasorda said that the second-best thing to happen to the Dodgers was to lose the World Series; obviously the best thing would have been to win it all. Fallon noted that Lasorda said, "This is a young team that has the ability to be better than it was last year . . . that can be more productive in each of the next several years . . . . The players know they can win. They know what it takes to reach the World Series and they want to do it again."

Considering the success Lasorda and the players achieved the previous season, one would expect ownership to do whatever it took to improve for the upcoming year. However, ownership decided to put profit over winning. Dodger GM Al Campanis made it known during Spring Training that the traveling roster would not be the maximum allowed of 25 players, but rather 24. Campanis was forced into this because ownership wanted to keep costs down. In many ways it is mind-boggling that the O'Malleys would hinder the chances of the team. If the Dodgers had no chance to contend for the NL West, one could potentially justify such a decision. But the Dodgers were not only contenders for the NL West but had a very good chance to return to the World Series—and even win it.

Nevertheless, they started the season strong, winning their first four games and going 13–7 for the month of April. The momentum did not continue into May, as the team only went 14–13, but LA still led the NL West by 3½ games. But May of 1978 would be remembered more for a curious, on the surface, trade of Glenn Burke to the A's with the Dodgers receiving Bill North in return.

It is fair to say that Burke never lived up to his potential and perhaps Burke's greatest contribution to the Dodgers and society was arguably inventing the high five. However, North was coming off an injury-plagued season, and his best years were behind him. It was not just the media and fans who could not understand why Burke was traded; many of his teammates were somewhat perplexed. Former Dodger beat writer Lyle Spencer remembered, "I was shocked that he was traded . . . I walked into the clubhouse . . . and guys were visibly distraught over the trade, and that told me that my sense of how important he was to them internally was accurate. I even remember a few players crying when they found out about it . . . which is stunning." Lopes later claimed, "You don't break up, disrupt a team going as well as it was going to make changes. I didn't feel it was going to make us a better ball club. Billy North was not going to make us, at that time, any better of a ballclub. Probably not the real reason why things happened." Or as Baker said, "I think the Dodgers knew; I think that's why they traded Glenn."

What the Dodgers knew is that Burke was gay. Also very problematic for Burke was he was friends with Lasorda's son, Tommy Lasorda Jr., who was gay and a sometimes cross-dresser. For all his positives, Lasorda was in denial over his son's sexual orientation. It is almost certain that Burke was traded because he was gay and was friends with Tommy Lasorda Jr. Burke was never given a true chance with the A's, with A's manager Billy Martin often calling Burke a faggot, among other insults. Burke was out of baseball by 1980. He eventually turned to drugs to try to fill the void in his life and developed full-blown AIDS. Glenn Burke died in 1995. He was forty-two. Thus, every year on April 20, the so-called National High Five Day, do not remember the Burke who invented the high five, but the Burke who was persecuted because he was gay.

The trade of Burke, however, was not the only controversy for the year. Even though the Dodgers played well in both June and July, having an identical 17–12 record for each month, there was a perception that the team played better the previous year. And perception often becomes reality. Dodger players seemingly always had to answer questions from the media about their "lackluster" season. Such questions were sure to annoy the players, especially considering that the season was going reasonably well. The tension within the team boiled over in mid-August.

Pitcher Don Sutton gave an interview to the *Washington Post* talking about how great a player Reggie Smith was. Now there is nothing controversial about that, but he took that opportunity to criticize Garvey:

> All you hear about on our team is Steve Garvey, the All-American boy. Well, the best player on this team for the last two years—and we all know it is—is Reggie Smith. As Reggie goes, so goes us. . . . [Yet] Reggie doesn't go out and publicize himself. He doesn't smile at the right people or say the right things. He tells the truth, even if it sometimes alienates people. Reggie's not a facade or a Madison Avenue image. He's a real person.

Garvey was obviously not happy with the slight and, over breakfast with Lasorda on August 20, he asked his manager how he should handle the situation. Considering neither Sutton nor Garvey were the most popular players in the dressing room, he believed the players letting off steam would help the clubhouse. As such, as recounted by Bill Plaschke in *I Live for This!*:

*Baseball's Last True Believer*, Lasorda told Garvey that it was up to him what he wanted to do, "but if it was me, and somebody said those things in the paper about me? The first time I saw him, I would deck him." It would not be the first time that a manager orchestrated a clubhouse fight in an attempt to forge unity, but such an approach could easily backfire.

Following Lasorda's advice, Garvey sought out Sutton later that day. As with every fight in the locker room, there are different stories about what actually happened. But what is certain is that Garvey and Sutton got into a brawl and had to be separated by teammates. Both had scratch marks and bruises on their faces. After the incident, Sutton told Lasorda he wanted to hold a press conference where he planned to blast Garvey. Lasorda told him that such an approach would not be in the best interest of the team and Sutton himself. Nevertheless, a few days later, Sutton held a press conference. Instead of criticizing Garvey, Sutton apologized for his actions. He said,

> For the last few days . . . I have thought of nothing else, and I've tried over and over to figure out why this all had to happen. The only possible reason I can find is that my life isn't being lived according to what I know, as a human being and a Christian, to be right. If it were, then there would not have been an article in which I would offend any of my teammates.

Lasorda's ploy worked, and there were no more issues between Garvey and Sutton. There is a perception that following the fight the Dodgers went on a roll and became more unified. However, while they may well have been more unified, the reality is that they were playing well both before and after the fight. On the day of the fight, the Dodgers had a two-game lead in the division. By the end of the month, they still had a two-game lead.

The team had a solid month of September, going 16–12. They also benefited from the Giants' only going 14–13 in August and 12–16 in September. And the Reds were also struggling, as they went 10–18 in August. Even though they went on a tear in September, it was not enough, as the Dodgers cruised to the NL West crown. Despite the turmoil of trading Burke, the perception that they were more focused the previous year, and the clubhouse fight between Sutton and Garvey, the reality was that the Dodgers were headed to the playoffs once again. But unfortunately for the Dodgers and their fans, history was about it repeat itself.

First up for the Dodgers was the National League Championship Series and a rematch with the Philadelphia Phillies. And like the previous season, there was trash talking prior to Game One, with the Phillies manager declaring they would sweep the series. There is a fine line between confidence, arrogance, and stupidity. However, there was a slight deviation, as in 1977 the Phillies won Game One, which was held at Dodger Stadium. This time, Game One was held at Veterans Stadium in Philadelphia. Nevertheless, history did repeat itself in the sense that the home team lost the opener. The Dodgers cruised to a 9–5 victory, thanks to home runs from Garvey (a three-run shot in the third and a solo in the ninth), Lopes (a two-run shot in the fourth), and Steve Yeager (a solo shot in the sixth). It was a perfect start for the Dodgers, which continued into Game Two. Tommy John and his surgically repaired arm put on a clinic, as he only gave up four hits and two walks on the way to a complete-game shutout, with the Dodgers defeating the Phillies 4–0 in front of a shell-shocked 60,642 at Veterans Stadium.

The series then reverted back to Los Angeles. And with Sutton taking the mound and having never lost a playoff game, the 55,043 in attendance expected to witness the Dodgers clinching the NLCS and heading to the World Series. However, the celebrations would have to wait a day—at least—as Sutton could not get out of the sixth inning, giving up seven runs (four earned), as the Phillies defeated the Dodgers, 9–4.

This brings us to Game Four. The Dodgers scored first, thanks to a double from Cey and an RBI single by Baker in the second. The Phillies scored in the third, thanks to a two-run home run from left fielder Greg Luzinski. Solo home runs by Cey in the fourth and Garvey in the sixth put the Dodgers back in front, 3–2. Once again, though, the Phillies came back thanks to pinch-hitter Bake McBride, tying the game with a home run in the seventh. The game remained scoreless heading to extra innings. After Los Angeles held the Phillies scoreless, Cey walked with two outs. Next up was Baker, who drove the first pitch he saw into center field. It should have been an easy out but, inexplicably, the Phillies multi–Gold Glove winner Garry Maddox misjudged the ball, allowing Baker to reach on an error and Cey to move to second. This allowed Bill Russell to drive in Cey and send the Dodgers to their second straight World Series appearance. Maddox was understandably distraught following the game. As Fallon noted, he told reporters, "I don't think it was a tough play at all . . . It was very routine. It was a line drive right at me that should have been caught. I missed it. Nothing distracted me. This is probably something I'll never forget the rest of my life." Phillies manager Danny Ozark claimed after the game that "It seems like all the bad things happen to the good guys."

## THE DODGERS

As in 1977, the Dodgers defeated the Phillies in four games and were set to face the Yankees who, just like in the 1977 season, defeated the Royals in the ALCS. Although in this case the Yankees only needed four games to clinch victory rather than the five games it took the previous season.

The Dodgers were favorites heading into the World Series. Not only did they have home-field advantage, but also a number of Yankee players were battling injuries, with second baseman Willie Randolph unable to play in the World Series. His replacement was rookie Brian Doyle, who hit a measly .192 (10-for-52, all singles) during the regular season. Doyle and Fred Stanley (regular season OPS of .606) shared second-base duties. Thus, understandably, the Dodgers were confident in bringing a world championship back to Los Angeles for the first time since 1965.

And such confidence seemed well founded following Game One. The Yankees were never in the contest, as the Dodgers crushed them, 11–5. Baker led off the second inning with a solo home run, and Lopes added a two-run shot later in the inning (as well as adding a three-run home run in the fourth). And on the mound, Tommy John had a decent outing, giving up five runs (three earned), but they came when the contest was already out of reach. Quite simply, the Dodgers and their fans could not have hoped for a better start to the Series. Following the game, Lopes told reporters, "When I'm in this kind of groove . . . I feel I can hit anyone at any time and anywhere. . . . Tonight, I was relaxed. I've probably never been more relaxed. I'm relaxed because I'm very confident that we're the best team until the Yankees prove otherwise."

The confidence seemed well placed following Game Two. The Yankees jumped to an early 2–0 lead, in the third, thanks to a double from "Mr. October" himself, Reggie Jackson. The Dodgers got one back in the fourth following singles from Garvey and Russell, with Cey plating the run with another single. The sixth inning was the turning point. After Hooton gave up a leadoff single, he got the next three batters out. In the bottom half, Lopes led off the inning with a single. After Russell failed to move Lopes over on a bunt, popping out, Reggie Smith singled to right field, allowing Lopes to advance to third. Garvey was unable to cash in the run after fouling out to the catcher, which brought Cey to the plate with two outs. On a 2-0 count, he deposited a ball into deep left field for a three-run home run and a 4–2 Dodger lead. The Yankees would get one back in the seventh, thanks to an RBI by Jackson. After a scoreless eighth, the Yankees got two men on with only one out. However, Lasorda brought on reliever Bob Welch, who quickly took care of Munson. Up next for the Yankees was the Dodger killer, Mr. October; to say that fans were on the edge of their seats would be an understatement. On a nine-pitch at-bat and with a full count, Welch struck out Jackson and gave the Dodgers a 2–0 lead in the World Series. As recounted by Mitchell, following the game, Welch said that on the final pitch Jackson "just missed it. . . . He missed it just enough. The first pitch I threw him was the one he really had a chance to hit, that was the one." As for Cey's home run, he said that Smith told him that he would hit one out of the park: Smith "told me that as soon as Hunter got out of a jam . . . he just knew Catfish would make a mistake. He told me he just knew. . . . It's one of those things that happens maybe once or twice in a season. It's just a feeling, an impulse, an instinct. It's hard to explain unless you've played the game." The Dodgers' confidence was running high, as it should have been.

The Series then headed to New York for three crucial games. If the Dodgers could even win one game they would be in a prime position to capture another World Series crown. Taking the mound was Sutton; for the Yankees it was Ron Guidry, who went 25–3 with an ERA of 1.74 (both led the AL). Guidry was a worthy recipient of the Cy Young Award.

The Yankees scored a run in the first and second, with the Dodgers getting a run back in the third. There was no more scoring until the bottom of the seventh when the Yankees plated three to blow the game wide open. The Dodgers went quietly in the eighth and ninth, with Guidry throwing a complete game.

Then came the pivotal fourth game, which remained scoreless until the top of the fifth. After Bill North grounded out, Yeager doubled, and Lopes walked. Bill Russell then struck out swinging, which brought Reggie Smith to the plate. And on a 1-0 pitch, he launched the ball into deep right field for a three-run home run. And with Tommy John pitching well, the Dodgers had every reason to be confident. However, things fell apart from the Dodgers in the bottom of the sixth. After striking out Paul Blair, John allowed a single to Roy White and a walk to Munson. Jackson then singled in a run for the team's first score, with Lou Piniella up next. Piniella then hit a ball to Bill Russell for what should have been an easy double play. Russell quickly stepped on second to force an out and then threw to first. The ball was close to Jackson who, illegally, stuck out his hip, and the ball went into right field, allowing another run to score as the umpire did not call player interference. The Dodger players were irate, and the play messed with their heads. They were still leading 3–2 but seemingly could not get the play out of their minds.

After John gave up a single to Blair to start the eighth, the Dodgers brought in Terry Forster. After Blair advanced to second on a sacrifice Munson brought him in with a double to tie the game. After a scoreless ninth and with two outs in the bottom of the 10th, Piniella singled in the winning run. The Dodgers were distraught, and the Yankees were ecstatic. Jackson's hip was seemingly the difference-maker. In his autobiography, *Becoming Mr. October*, Jackson recalled the play:

> "I saw the ball coming toward me, and I thought, *I'm going to get hit in . . . a highly sensitive area.* So I moved just a little. I could've just hit the dirt. I could've jumped all the way to one side or another. But I thought, *I'm in my right-of-way. I'm in the baseline. I'm going to be out anyway, so why not just stand there and play stupid?* I thought, *I'm out anyway, so it's not so bad if I stay here and let it hit me.*

Decades later, Cey said,

> The interference issue with Reggie Jackson was the one that pulled the rug right out from under us and that's still my biggest nightmare in baseball. . . . If the call is made properly and if they huddled together like they should have, we would have walked off the field with a 3–1 lead. We end up losing that game. The next day we were flat, deflated. And so I feel legitimately that '78 was the one that got away and it's still hard to talk about.

Whether the Dodgers were indeed flat the following day for Game Five is open to debate. They opened the scoring in the first, thanks to a single and stolen base from Lopes and an RBI single from Smith and added to their lead in the third with a single by Lopes and an RBI double by Russell. Thus, after the top of the third, the Dodgers were leading 2–0. Unfortunately, then the proverbial wheels fell off. Hooton could not get out of the inning for the Dodgers, giving up four runs. Reliever Lance

Rautzhan then gave up three runs in the bottom of the fourth, and the game was well and truly over. The Yankees stormed to a 12–2 victory and led the World Series three games to two.

Even though they were trailing, Game Six and, if required, Game Seven would be held in Los Angeles. The starting pitcher for the Dodgers was Sutton, who was having a less-than-stellar post-season, while Catfish Hunter would be starting for the Yankees. The game could not have started any better for the home team, as Lopes hit a leadoff home run in the bottom of the first. Unfortunately, the lead did not last long, as the Yankees scored three runs in the top of the second, thanks to three hits and a walk. Though Lopes cut the deficit to one in the bottom of the third with an RBI single, the Dodgers would not score again and fell further behind when the Yankees scored two in the sixth. And to cap off the miserable day, Mr. October hit a two-run home run on the first ball he saw in the top of the seventh. The Yankees defeated the Dodgers, 7–2, and captured the World Series four games to two—the same margin as the previous year. The 1978 World Series was the one the Dodgers let get away. If it was indeed Reggie Jackson's hip and the no-call in Game Four that led to the Dodgers squandering their chances—and judging from the comments from Cey it may well have been—one can safely call it a travesty. As such, history repeated itself; the 1977 loss to the Yankees in the World Series was a tragedy, and the 1978 World Series loss was a farce.

## 1979: A SAD END TO THE DECADE

Even with the loss in the World Series, one would have confidently assumed that the Dodgers would be contenders the following year. This was especially true as the position players remained virtually unchanged. In a slight upgrade, Derrel

Thomas replaced Bill North as the starting center fielder with North moving to the Giants, and Joe Ferguson got more regular playing time. Quite simply, the lineup looked as good as ever. The pitching side of things was a different matter. Tommy John wanted a long-term contract, but the Dodgers were not interested. Fallon notes that John's agent Bob Cohen told the media,

> We repeatedly attempted to sit down with the Dodgers last winter. . . . We tried to say, "Hey, Tommy's two-year contract is up this year, he can become a free agent when the season ends, he wants to sign here again, let's get a new contract out of the way so it's off everyone's mind." Nothing. April. May. June. They didn't really sit down with us until July. . . . Now, of course, what we want isn't what we wanted four or five months ago.

More than one commentator claimed that the Dodgers refusal to sign John to a long-term contract was a case of penny-pinching. As a result, John filed for free agency and eventually signed with the Yankees. John went on to have two very good seasons before injury slowed him down in 1981 and 1982. He eventually retired in 1989. Considering that John's career was considered over in 1974, his longevity is due to his dedication, hard work, and of course the pioneering surgery done by Dr. Frank Jobe.

As for the season itself, the offense led the league in home runs and was in the top-three in on-base percentage and slugging. However, the pitching staff had a below-average year, finishing seventh in ERA. The loss of John particularly hurt, but it was compounded by Don Sutton performing below his usual high standards and Dou Rau succumbing to injury in the second half of the season. In a bright spot, Rick Sutcliffe went 17–10 with an ERA of 3.46. At the end of the year, Sutcliffe won the Rookie of the Year Award. Overall, the Dodgers were never in contention and finished with a losing record of 79–83 for third in the NL West. It was an all-around disappointing season.

Writing in *Sports Illustrated*, Ron Fimrite summed up the plight of the 1979 Dodgers in a preview of the upcoming 1980 season:

> The Dodgers, the class of this virtually classless society, were beset by every conceivable misfortune last year. Their best relief pitcher, left hander Terry Forster, was felled by a recurring arm ailment and was finished for the season by August. Their centerfielder, Rick Monday, played only 12 games before succumbing to an injury to his left Achilles tendon. Their pitching phenom and 1978 World Series hero, Bob Welch, had a sore right elbow, which was bad enough. Then, after the season, he entered a rehabilitation center for alcoholics. Starting Pitcher Doug Rau was finished for the season and possibly forever by a torn left rotator cuff. Don Sutton, holder of many Dodger pitching records, remained in a season-long funk and demanded to be traded. And star Right fielder Reggie Smith had knee, neck, ankle and ego hurts and finally joined Sutton in Funk City. Actually, that is where most of the Dodgers spent the season. A team that had once represented itself as the soul of suburban affability, Los Angeles snarled and grumbled as churlishly last year as such curmudgeonly clubs of the past decade as the Yankees and the A's.

To top off the Dodger misfortune in 1979 was the death of team owner Walter O'Malley. On August 9, O'Malley finally succumbed to cancer that he had been battling for a number of years. While he would remain hated in Brooklyn and New York, O'Malley had the vision to move the team to Los Angeles. Of course, O'Malley was a businessman first and foremost, and the lure of the greenback facilitated the move. And a team in Los Angeles was inevitable. Nevertheless, O'Malley took the risk and was duly rewarded. For Dodger players, while they may have respected the man, many often wondered whether they were respected in return. I have highlighted throughout the 1960s a number of Dodger players who had to battle tooth and nail to get even a fraction of what they deserved. It was not until the increased strength of the MLBPA in the 1970s and limited free agency that the players began to be fairly rewarded for their efforts. As for the 1970s as a whole, the Dodgers played some very good baseball and had some mediocre seasons. There was a change in manager, infighting, and continued World Series heartbreak.

# 5

# 1980S: WORLD CHAMPIONS ONCE AGAIN

THERE WAS ONLY one goal in mind for the Dodger organization for the 1980s, just as there was for any privately run company: make money. But on the field, the overriding goal was to once again win the World Series. And in that regard, the 1980s would end up being much more successful for the Dodgers than the 1970s and its World Series heartbreak.

The offseason was an interesting time for the team, and Lasorda in particular. On February 17, both Lasorda and former Dodger and current Giant coach Jim Lefebvre were at KNBC-TV studios to be interviewed separately for a TV show. Lefebvre, who spent his entire playing career with the Dodgers, was the 1965 Rookie of the Year. He was the team's first-base coach in 1979 and was fired by Lasorda at season's end. Following Lasorda's interview he saw Lefebvre and told him that he wanted the two to talk privately. The conversation got heated, and Lefebvre decked Lasorda, which left the Dodger manager's face bloody. Lefebvre then appeared on the interview program. He took a diplomatic line by stating,

> It was in the best interests of Tommy, his coaching staff, the Dodgers, and Jim Lefebvre for me to step down. . . . There have been a lot of newspaper reports that came out that said there's a lot of bitterness between myself and the Dodgers or Tommy. All I can say is that a lot of it has been blown completely out of proportion. Baseball is a business, and if you can't get along on the staff or whatever then you've got to make changes and I realize that.

Considering that Lefebvre and Lasorda had just gotten into a heated argument and Lefebvre decked Lasorda, irrespective of who started the fight, it is fair to say that some bitterness still remained.

As for the Dodger players, considering the less-than-stellar 1979 season the team needed to make acquisitions in the offseason. While other teams, the Yankees in particular, took full advantage of players being granted limited free agency and signed anyone whom they believed could help their ballclub, the Dodgers generally preferred to rely on their farm system and not spend the necessary outlay to acquire big-name talent. Two of the highly sought after free agents were future Hall of Famers Nolan Ryan and Joe Morgan. While the former California Angel and Texas native made it known that he was looking to return home, Ryan may have been tempted by a big-money offer from the Dodgers. The team did not make such an offer, and he signed with the Houston Astros. The Dodgers had a much greater chance to sign Morgan, but they did not offer him a contract in the same ballpark of what he was worth. They were content with the same offense, minor changes aside, as they had in previous years. As such, Morgan eventually signed with the Astros. Thus, Houston made their formidable team even stronger. While Ryan only had an average season, by his standards, Morgan had a fine season; according to Baseball-refernce.com, he was worth 3.6 Wins Above Replacement (WAR) and was the fifth-best player for the Astros. In contrast, for the Dodgers, Lopes's best years were behind him. He was worth only one win above replacement—the seventeenth-best player for the Dodgers. Certainly WAR should not be taken as gospel. Nevertheless, while Lopes had a slightly higher batting average, Morgan had a higher on-base percentage, slugging percentage, and stolen-base total (admittedly, only one more), and he played better defense. Quite simply, Morgan had a much better season than Lopes. A Dodger side with Morgan as the starting second baseman with Lopes coming off the bench would have been a vastly improved team, as would a Dodger side with just Morgan. All things being equal, either lineup would have resulted in more victories. And considering how the season ended, deciding to go with the status quo and not sign big-name free agents cost them.

The Dodgers, however, did acquire free agents. They signed starting pitcher Dave Goltz to a six-year contract worth $3 million. Campanis, in a statement impossible to believe, claimed that Goltz was the best free agent on the market. Goltz was a good middle-of-the-rotation pitcher, but nothing more. The team also signed reliever Don Stanhouse to a five-year contract worth $2.1 million. To say that these pickups were wise choices would greatly miss the mark. Stanhouse had numerous injures in his one and only season with the Dodgers and only appeared in 21 games. He was released in April 1981. As for Goltz, he had two below-average seasons in LA before being released during the 1982 season.

While Goltz and Stanhouse did not deliver what the Dodgers were expecting of them, Pedro Guerrero was beginning to blossom. Originally signed by the Cleveland Indians as a short-stop in 1972, the teenager from the Dominican Republic was traded to the Dodgers in 1974. The team's solid infield delayed Guerrero's ascent to the majors, but he was eventually called up for a handful of games in 1978 and appeared in 25 the following season. In two stints with the big-league club in 1980, Guerrero played six positions with most of his time spent at either second or center. He outperformed the incumbent Lopes at second and rookie Rudy Law in center. Guerrero seemed to be adverse to walks but hit .322 with a slugging percentage of .497 while playing adequate defense.

There were also some pitching bright sports. Sutton went 13–5 and led the NL with a 2.20 ERA. After performing poorly (by his standards) in his first season with LA in 1979, Jerry Reuss rebounded in 1980 with an 18–6 record, making the All-Star team, leading the league in shutouts, and finishing second in Cy Young voting. He also threw a no-hitter on June 27 against the Giants at Candlestick Park. After retiring the first two batters, a throwing error by Russell allowed Giant right fielder Jack Clark to reach base. Reuss would retire the next twenty-five batters on his way to a no-hitter. It was a sublime performance, and only Russell's error separated Reuss from a perfect game. Following the game Reuss told the media, "I just threw a no hitter! . . . What could be a bigger thrill! I haven't pitched in a World Series yet." That thrill would be in his future. Lasorda was also ecstatic with the performance, saying, "In all of the years I have been managing, I've never had a pitcher pitch a no-hit, no-run game. It really was a thrill for me to sit there and watch him. He was awesome."

But there was one pitcher above all that grabbed the spotlight. Fernando Valenzuela was discovered by a Dodger scout in 1978 when Valenzuela, who was only seventeen, was pitching in the Mexican Central League. The Dodger scout, Mike Brito, begged Campanis to sign Valenzuela. However, Campanis was put off because the kid wasn't a flamethrower, was less than 6-foot, and, to put it mildly, had a less-than-athletic body. As a result, Campanis refused to sign him. Brito refused to give up and eventually convinced Campanis to take a look at Valenzuela the following year. Campanis was duly impressed and immediately wanted to sign him, but the young pitcher was now also on the Yankees' radar. As such, a bidding war ensued with the Dodgers eventually acquiring him after agreeing to pay Valenzuela's Mexican team $120,000. They could have signed Valenzuela in 1978 for *a lot* less than that.

Valenzuela pitched decently in his first few games in Single A, but the team wanted him to work on another pitch during the off-season. They enlisted Dodger pitcher Bobby Castillo to try to teach him the screwball. Castillo told the *Los Angeles Times*, "He didn't speak English and I didn't speak Spanish that well . . . but we did communicate. He caught on quickly. It was like it was meant for him." Valenzuela had a different recollection:

> The first half [in 1980], it wasn't going that well. . . . I said, 'I don't want to throw it anymore. I want to go back to what I do.' They told me, 'No. We don't care about your record. We don't care how many games you win. We want you to keep practicing it.' By the second half, it was a lot better. By then, I had good rotation on it and good control.

By mastering the screwball and being able to throw it at different speeds with the same arm action, Valenzuela became the Dodgers' best prospect and one of the top up-and-comers in baseball.

Given how well he was doing in the minors, there was considerable discussion on whether he should join the big-league club during the season. The Dodgers eventually called him up when rosters expanded in September, and he made his major-league debut on September 15, giving up a hit and two unearned runs in a blowout loss to the Braves.

Valenzuela's debut coincided with the Dodgers sputtering toward the finish line and handing the NL West to the Astros. Valenzuela pitched well in relief, not giving up another run, unearned or otherwise. The Astros had a three-game division lead with three games reaming against the Dodgers in Los Angeles. In the first game, on October 3, LA won in ten innings, thanks to a walk-off home run by Joe Ferguson. Valenzuela pitched two innings of scoreless relief and got the win. On October 4, the Dodgers triumphed again, this time 2–1, with Jerry Reuss pitching a complete game and outdueling Nolan Ryan. Thus, if the Dodgers won the last game of the season, it would force a one-game playoff to decide the NL West winner. The third and final game of the season didn't start off well, as the Astros led 3–0 after four innings. The Dodgers got a run back in the fifth and seventh and, in the bottom of the eighth, Cey blasted a two-run home run to give the Dodgers a lead, 4–3. They would hold on for the victory.

The sweep meant that the teams would play the following day to decide the NL West winner. The pitching match-up would be Houston's Joe Niekro against Dave Goltz. There was some talk that Valenzuela should start, but considering that he had yet to do so at the major-league level and had pitched the previous day, he was never seriously considered. In saying this, it is unlikely that Valenzuela could have performed as poorly as Goltz. The Astros ended up defeating the Dodgers, 7–1, with Niekro pitching a complete game. In contrast, Goltz only lasted three innings, giving up four runs (two earned) on eight hits, while Rick Sutcliffe's horrible season ended on a particular low as he gave up three runs in a third of an inning. One of the few positives was Valenzuela, who pitched two scoreless innings while only giving up a hit.

Thus, the Dodgers finished with a record of 92–71. While that was a vast improvement compared to the previous year, one cannot help but wonder what could have been. All things being equal, if the Dodgers signed Morgan, it is highly likely the Astros would have been sitting atop the NL West. The same could be said if Valenzuela was brought up earlier. Or if Guerrero had increased playing time. Or if the Dodgers did not sign Goltz and/or Stanhouse. Looking back, the 1980 season was one of lost opportunities.

## 1981: FERNANDOMANIA, STRIKES, AND WORLD SERIES CHAMPIONS

Following the less-than-successful foray into the free agent market the previous winter, one would assume that the front office would learn from their mistakes . . . and they did. The lesson they learned was not to splurge on mediocre talent. But they were seemingly scared off from the free agent market in general. While they made offers to three free agents, including future Dodger manager Dave Roberts, the offers were well below what other teams were willing to pay. As such, it was not a surprise that they didn't sign a single free agent. The front office was satisfied with the players they had. There were, of course, still changes to be made. The most notable was that, after fifteen years with the team, Don Sutton had elected for free agency. Quite simply, once Lasorda took over as Dodger manager, Sutton was never as happy as he was playing under Alston. Sutton was a very good pitcher that arguably never truly appreciated in Los Angeles. Indeed, he holds the Dodger pitching records for the most wins, strikeouts, shutouts, games, and games started. He was truly a great Dodger and eventually a worthy member of the Hall of Fame. Sutton signed with the Astros, which made the Dodgers' chances of winning the division all the more difficult.

Going into the season, the majority of the starting pitchers were either recovering from injuries or ill. This meant that the projected fifth man in the rotation, the player a team hopes can provide adequate to an occasional good start at best, would be the team's Opening Day starter. That man was Fernando Valenzuela.

Despite only being twenty years old and still technically a rookie, Valenzuela was indeed *the* man on Opening Day as the Dodgers gained some modicum of revenge against the Astros. The Dodgers won, 2–0, thanks to RBIs for Cey and Guerrero and moreover a complete-game shutout from Valenzuela in which he only gave up five hits. It was the start of a great run for the Dodgers, as they went 14–5 in April and 19–10 in May. By the end of May they held a 5½-game lead in the division. While the team was playing well, Valenzuela stood above all others. Valenzuela won his first eight starts. In those starts he only gave up four earned runs, while pitching seven complete games (in the other game he threw nine innings as the Dodgers won in ten), and five shutouts.

The adulation awarded to Valenzuela by the fans was soon labeled by the media as "Fernandomania." And it was running wild. Baseball fans could not get enough of him. Moreover, the Dodgers traditionally had difficulty drawing Mexican and Latino fans to their home games. That all changed because of Valenzuela. The number of Mexican radio stations broadcasting Dodger games increased from three to seventeen, and in Latin America as a whole from twenty to forty. The Dodgers' Spanish-language announcer Jaime Jarrin estimated that, before Valenzuela approximately, 8 to 10 percent of fans at Dodger Stadium were Latinos. By the mid-1980s it was approximately 30 percent, and by the mid-2000s it was above 40 percent. It was because of Valenzuela that the Dodgers continue to have a strong Latino fan base to this day. The team reaped the benefits as 11 out of 12 home starts by Valenzuela sold out. Likewise, in 1981 and 1982, Valenzuela's starts on the road drew an extra thirteen thousand fans compared to other Dodger starters. It is hard to disagree with Jarrin when he said, "I truly believe that there is no other player in major league history who created more new fans than Fernando Valenzuela. Sandy Koufax, Don Drysdale, Joe DiMaggio, even Babe Ruth did not. Fernando turned so many people from Mexico, Central America, South America into fans. He created interest in baseball among people who did not care about baseball."

Valenzuela was thankful for the support: "Having all the people from the Hispanic community, and really all the communities in Los Angeles, that gave me such a lift. . . Knowing that the people are there waiting to see what could happen next, that's one of the things that I always enjoyed. People didn't expect anything, but to be able to see the emotion and the excitement when I had a great game, that's all I could ever ask for."

The start to the season by Valenzuela was not sustainable. Nevertheless, he finished with a record of 13–7 and an ERA of 2.48. He led the NL in games started, innings pitched, complete games, strikeouts, and shutouts. Valenzuela made the All-Star team, won Rookie of the Year, was in the top five for the MVP award, and won the Cy Young Award. Following his Cy Young victory, the media asked whether he knew who Cy Young was. As recounted by Vic Wilson in an article in the *National Pastime*, Valenzuela responded, "I do not know who he was, but a trophy carries his name, so he must be someone very special to baseball."

Valenzuela was on a tear, as were the Dodgers after strong performances in April and May. June did not go according to plan, though, as the Dodgers lost six of their first nine games. Their record now sat at 36–21, and their lead in the NL West was cut to half a game over the Reds. The season was then interrupted by a player strike.

The 1981 stoppage was largely in part to free agency compensation. The owners wanted compensation for losing free agents, while the MLBPA argued that any form of compensation would go against the purpose of free agency. With the sides unable to reach a compromise, the players walked off the job on June 12. The strike lasted for 50 days with a total of 713 games being abandoned. Even though the owners had strike insurances from Lloyds of London, they lost approximately $72 million due to the strike, with the players losing approximately $28 million. The strike was not an outright success for either side as both eventually had to compromise. However, once again, the players were united while the owners were not. This allowed the players to achieve gains they would not have otherwise obtained.

When the season resumed, MLB decided on a split season. All teams that led their respective divisions prior to the strike would be automatically granted a playoff spot. In the first round of playoffs they would play against the team that finished first in the second-half of the season. This was great news for the Dodgers, as they were assured a playoff spot. It was even better considering how they played in the second half of the season, as they went 27–26. The Astros won the second half of the season by half a game over the Reds. Thus, even though the Reds had the best record for the full season—not only in the NL West but all of baseball—they missed out on the playoffs. The Dodgers would take on the Astros in the NL Division Series.

There was one Astro who should have been looking forward to facing his old side—namely, Don Sutton. During the season, there were quite a few negative comments directed between Sutton and the Dodgers, including claims that the pitcher tampered with the baseball during games. Of course many pitchers tampered with the ball during games, so this was not a breaking story.

Sutton was having a good first season with the Astros. Even though his record was only 11–9, his ERA was a solid 2.61 (which was ninth-best in the NL, and third best on the Astros). Sutton, like the rest of the pitching staff, suffered from a lack of run support. Despite an impressive season, he would not get an opportunity to pitch in the playoffs. During a game against the Dodgers on October 2, Sutton attempted to bunt against Reuss. He was unsuccessful, with the ball hitting him on the right kneecap, shattering it. Sutton was out for the season. Following the game Sutton said his injury "is going to cost me a chance at something I looked forward to, the playoffs and the World Series. But there's nothing I can do about it." Reuss said he did not deliberately attempt to hit Sutton, claiming the pitch was "just a fastball that ran on him." For his part, Sutton stated he did not know whether he was targeted: "The ball was way inside; I had no chance." It was a sad end to the season for Sutton. In a positive, the surgery to repair his kneecap, performed by Dr. Frank Jobe, was a success, and he was able to pitch in the major leagues for another seven years. In 1988, at the age of forty-three, Sutton rejoined the Dodgers, though retired during the season. He was inducted into the National Baseball Hall of Fame in 1998.

It initially seemed as though the Astros wouldn't need Sutton for the series, as the Dodger infield was beset by injuries. In a preview of Game One, the *Washington Post* stated,

> Dodger-Astro series really is a showdown between two decimated teams. . . . The Dodgers are in worse shape. Their long-running, stand-pat infield finally has fallen apart from ceaseless use. Shortstop Bill Russell, nursing three injuries, returned to the lineup on Sunday. Dave Lopes will try to play for the first time in weeks in the playoff opener. Ron Cey still hasn't taken batting practice after suffering a broken forearm. He might be back by the league championship series. Once-great Reggie Smith now is a pinch hitter.

In Game One, Valenzuela faced off against the legendary Nolan Ryan. Valenzuela only gave up one run in eight innings of work, but Ryan matched him by only giving up one run as well. The game was decided in the bottom of the ninth. With Dave Stewart pitching for the Dodgers, he gave up a two-run home run to catcher Alan Ashby as the Astros walked it off, winning 3–1. Game Two was also a pitching duel, with Reuss pitching nine innings of no-run ball. He was matched by Joe Niekro, who pitched eight no-run innings. The game was scoreless going into the bottom of the 11th, when Stewart gave up singles to

Phil Garner and Tony Scott, the latter sending Garner to third. The winning run was cashed in by pinch hitter Danny Walling. The Astros had taken the first two games of the series, and the Dodger batters were dormant. It seemed only a matter of time before Houston would clinch the series.

The Dodger batters, however, woke up in Game Three, scoring three runs in the first inning as they powered to a 6–1 victory. In Game Four, a solo home run by Pedro Guerrero opened the scoring in the bottom of the fifth, while LA added another run in the seventh. Valenzuela entered the ninth looking for a complete-game shutout. He was masterful up to that point, only giving up two hits, but then ran into some trouble. After retiring the first batter, he allowed a double to Terry Puhl. Lasorda later commented that there was not a chance he would have replaced Valenzuela. He learned his lesson from Game One when he took Valenzuela out for Stewart, who promptly lost the game. The Dodgers hopes were resting on Valenzuela's twenty-year-old shoulders. While he retired the next batter, with two outs the Astros got one back, thanks to a single to Tony Scott to cut the margin to one. Valenzuela, however, got the final out, and with it the Dodgers had tied the series at two.

With the fifth and final game of the series also being held at Dodger Stadium, the home team was confident—and their confidence was well founded even with Ryan pitching for the Astros. After a scoreless five innings, the Dodgers lit up the scoreboard in the sixth, thanks to a walk, three singles, and an error, as the home team took a 3–0 lead. With Reuss pitching brilliantly, the game was as good as over. He went the distance for the complete-game shutout, as the Dodgers won 4–0. They would now face the Montreal Expos in the NLCS, who had defeated the Phillies in five games. It was the Expos first and only playoff berth in their history.

While they progressed, the Dodgers were hoping that their offense would significantly improve in the championship series. In the Divisional Series, Garvey played fantastically; he went 7-for-19 with a triple and two home runs. Apart from him, every other batter had a very poor series, with only Bill Russell (who was coming off a below-average year) hitting better than he did during the regular season. As a whole, the Dodgers hit .198 in the NLDS, and their slugging percentage was only .302. Yet they managed to win the on the backs of their starting pitchers, particularly Reuss and Valenzuela. It would be wrong to say that the Dodgers hit a lot better in the NLCS; there was, however, some improvement.

Indeed, in Game One of the NLCS, the Dodger batters came alive for a relatively easy 5–1 victory at Dodger Stadium. Hooton pitched a strong 7⅓ innings for the Dodgers, while Guerrero and Mike Scioscia hit back-to-back home runs in the eighth. More importantly, Cey returned from injury and went 2-for-4 with a run and an RBI. The victory should not have come as a surprise considering the Expos had lost their previous 19 games at Dodger Stadium. The Expos, however, finally broke that losing streak in Game Two. On the back of a masterful pitching display from Ray Burris, the Expos won 3–0 with Valenzuela taking the loss.

The series then headed for Montreal and almost arctic conditions. Prior to the game, Lasorda was angry after reading an article that stated that his players would not be able to handle the cold. As such, as Rick Monday told Jonah Keri,

> "I don't want anyone wearing their jackets!" Tommy told us. So, we're introduced, we don't have our jackets, we're on the third-base line and they proceed to introduce all

but two people even in attendance for the game. They introduced everybody, and all the while the boys from Hollywood are standing there, shivering. And we're thinking, "Whose great idea is this?! It's cold!"

Despite showing how "tough" they were, the Dodgers lost the game 4–1; the Expos were on the brink of a World Series berth.

In Game Four, the score was tied at one after seven innings. In the top of the eighth, Garvey broke the game wide open with a two-run home run. LA then tacked on four more in the ninth, and what had been a tight contest was blown open as the Dodgers won, 7–1.

The Expos were still favored to advance, as the deciding Game Five would be played in Montreal on Monday, October 19. The game was meant to be played the previous day but was postponed due to snow and freezing conditions. The conditions on October 19 were not much better, but the game went ahead. Valenzuela started, while Burris was on the mound for Montreal. The Expos scored one in the first before the Dodgers tied the game in the fifth, thanks to a sacrifice groundout by Valenzuela. The scored remained tied entering the ninth. Then up to the plate stepped Rick Monday to face Steve Rogers. Rogers had last appeared in Game Three, pitching a complete game as the Expos triumphed. But Rogers had not made a relief appearance in three years. Rogers told Keri that the Expos

sent me down to warm up in a spot I wasn't necessarily expecting. I was fine physically, but my adrenaline was pumping too hard. I didn't control it and I was over-throwing the sinker. Mechanically, I lost the angle. I just took the bad mechanics from the bullpen out to the mound.

I was going to have a throw day on either the second or third day, so I mean, I could have thrown five innings if they needed it. Physically and mentally at least, I was fine.

While Monday never had the career envisaged by the Dodgers when they signed him in 1977, he still had some good seasons with the team. By 1981, he largely came off the bench, appearing in 66 games. He performed with aplomb, hitting .315 with an OBP of .423 and a slugging percentage of .608. But he was not having the best playoffs, only going 5-for-22, all singles.

But on October 19, in what Expo fans will always remember as "Blue Monday," Monday hit a 3-1 sinker that did not sink out of the park to give the Dodgers a 2–1 lead. The Expos, however, had a chance in the bottom of the inning. With two outs, Valenzuela issued back-to-back walks. Lasorda, who had previously decided against pulling his ace, brought in Bob Welch to face Jerry White. On the first pitch White saw, he grounded out to short to end the game. The Dodgers were heading back to the World Series, while the Expo players, fans, and city were devastated. Expos left fielder Tim Raines told Keri that

the Monday home run, it was probably one of the . . . I wouldn't say the worst thing that ever happened to me, but it was pretty hard to take. And then the last out was a groundball, bang-bang to first base. And I'll never forget this: Warren Cromartie and myself were sitting on the bench, because everybody else had left. Just sitting there. "What the hell, these guys beat us." We sat on the bench after it was over and I was like, "I can't believe we're not going." I could not believe we weren't going to the World Series. We won [Game Three], all we needed was to win one game. We just couldn't win that one game. . . . We probably had the best team in baseball. No, we did have the best team in baseball that year. We'd have kicked the Yankees' ass that year. If the Dodgers beat them, we'd have probably swept them. We had the team.

The Expos may have indeed been *the* team, and the playoffs may not necessarily result in the best team winning a series, but in the end the Dodgers came out victorious. And they had a chance to prevent history from mocking them; the Dodgers' opponent would *again* be the New York Yankees.

The Yankees had progressed to the World Series by defeating the Milwaukee Brewers in five games in the Divisional Series and then sweeping the Athletics in the ALCS. The Yankees, unlike the Dodgers, were well rested coming into the Series. Because of this, along with their home-field advantage and history against the Dodgers, the Yankees were rightly installed as favorites heading into Game One.

That billing was seemingly justified, as the Yankees jumped out to a 5–0 lead after four innings. LA managed to make things interesting by scoring a run in the fifth and two in the eighth, but it wouldn't be enough, as they dropped the first game, 5–3. The Yankees followed this up by defeating the Dodgers the next day, 3–0, with Tommy John pitching seven strong innings for the Bronx Bombers. History did indeed seem to be repeating itself. The Dodgers hitters were largely dormant, and momentum favored the Yankees.

Game Three in Los Angeles was the battle of rookies: Valenzuela against AL Rookie of the Year Dave Righetti. In 2010, Valenzuela told ESPN writer Tony Jackson: "I just tried to treat it like a normal game. . . . That wasn't easy, but we had a lot of veteran players who still thought we were going to win.

I think listening to them, guys I respected like Dusty Baker and Steve Garvey and Steve Yeager, gave me a lot more confidence." The hope was that his confidence would have been lifted following the first inning. as Cey hit a three-run home run to give the Dodgers an early lead. However, the Yankees got two back in the second and took the lead in the third, thanks to a two-run home run to Rick Cerone. Valenzuela later recounted to ESPN that he "had control problems, and it got me into trouble. . . . I walked a lot of hitters in that game." Indeed, Valenzuela claims that Lasorda wanted to take him out of the game at this point, but he convinced the manager otherwise. Lasorda had a different take, telling Jackson that

> everybody thought I was going to take him out . . . . A lot of people wanted me to take him out. But I knew him. He loved to pitch out of jams. He used to pitch like he didn't know we had a bullpen. He didn't like to come out of games. A lot of guys, when they get in trouble, they're looking down there for help. But not him.

To his credit, even though Valenzuela did not have his best stuff, he dug deep and willed himself on. The offense also picked him up, scoring three runs in the bottom of the fifth—largely thanks to a two-run double from Guerrero. After four straight scoreless innings, Valenzuela got into trouble in the eighth, due to singles from Aurelio Rodriguez and Larry Milbourne to start the inning. Lasorda, however, kept Valenzuela in the game. A double play, thanks to a poor bunt from Bobby Murcer, and a groundout by Randolph, ended the threat, and Valenzuela made light work of the Yankees in the ninth. Scully summed it up best: "It wasn't Fernando's best performance; it was his finest performance."

The Dodgers come-from-behind win in Game Three seemed moot due to their horrendous start in Game Four, as the Yanks scored two in the first, one in the second, and one in the third to take a quick 4–0 lead. Dodger starter Bob Welch did not even record an out in the game before being replaced by Goltz—who only lasted three innings. The Dodgers, working to keep the game competitive, pulled two back in the third and one in the fifth to cut the lead to one. The Yankees then proceeded to score two in the top of the sixth, but the Dodgers responded with three in the bottom of the inning, thanks in part to a two-run home run from pinch hitter Jay Johnstone and a crucial error from Reggie Jackson which tied the game at 6–6.

The Dodgers took their first lead of the game in the seventh when Steve Yeager hit a sacrifice fly to bring in Dusty Baker, and Davey Lopes singled down the third-base line to bring in Rick Monday. While the Yankees got one back the following inning, thanks to "Mr. October" himself, the Dodgers held on for an 8–7 victory and leveled the Series at two games apiece.

In contrast to Game Four, Game Five was a pitching duel between Ron Guidry and Jerry Reuss. The Yankees scored in the top of the second, helped in part by an error from Lopes. Lopes ended up having three errors on the day and six for the series. The Yankees had the lead until the bottom of the seventh when Guerrero and Yeager hit back-to-back home runs to give the Dodgers the lead. That was the end of the scoring, and the Dodgers held on to win 2–1; they were now one win away from winning it all. There was, however, a scary moment.

In the eighth inning, Yankees pitcher Goose Gossage accidently beaned Cey straight in the helmet with a fastball. Cey collapsed in a heap. Gossage told the *New York Times,* "Nobody wants to hurt anybody. . . . You want to win at every expense. But not that expense." Cey suffered a concussion but, as was the norm, he played in the next game. To his credit, after the game Gossage and Yankee manager Bob Lemon checked to make sure Cey was fine. As Gossage told the media, "I just wanted to make sure he was all right. . . . If he'd hit me in the face with a line drive, he'd be in to see me."

Cey was not the only person getting hit that day. In the middle of the night Yankee owner George Steinbrenner called a news conference, arriving with a cast on his left hand. He claimed to have gotten into a fight with two Dodgers fans in an elevator at the Hyatt-Wilshire Hotel in Los Angeles where the Yankees were staying. Steinbrenner said,

> I was coming down the elevator to have dinner. . . . There were two people, one in the elevator and one holding the door. One had a beer in his hand. Then he said some things about New York City and the people who live there. The next thing I knew he hit me. I'm getting too old for that. I don't condone that sort of thing. I get tired once in a while of people knocking New York. The fight was started not by me.

Despite battling two men who were supposedly in their twenties, Steinbrenner claimed he fought them off. He stated that, "There are two guys in this town looking for their teeth and two guys who will probably sue me." However, the fans did not sue Steinbrenner, there were no arrests, and indeed they have never been identified. Considering this, more than one person believes that Steinbrenner broke his hand in a fit of rage after the Yankees lost to the Dodgers.

Considering how Game Six went for the Yankees, it was a mild surprise that Steinbrenner did not break his other hand. The game was meant to be played on October 27 but was postponed to the following day due to rain. The postponement helped Cey, who was still feeling the effects of the concussion. He told the press on October 27 that "I felt good this morning and I was optimistic about playing, but this afternoon changed my mind. . . . There was some dizziness and lightheadedness. I was not in good shape." Even though he should not have, Cey ended up starting the next day.

The Yankees opened the scoring in the third, thanks to a solo home run by Willie Randolph, but the Dodgers immediately came back and leveled the score in the fourth—which was as close as the game would stay.

Led by a RBI single by Cey and a two-run RBI triple by Guerrero in the fifth and RBIs by Bill Russell, Derrel Thomas, and Guerrero in the sixth, the Dodgers took a commanding 8–1 lead. Cey was pinch-run for in the sixth due to him not being fully recovered from the concussion. And with that the Dodgers destroyed the Yankees with a final score of 9–2. Not only were the Dodgers world champions for the first time since 1965, but also they had gotten back at the Yankees for two Series wins over them in 1977 and '78.

Not surprisingly, the Dodger players were ecstatic, especially as they had triumphed over the Yankees. Lopes told *Sports Illustrated*, "You don't know how sweet it is to beat New York in New York. . . . We wanted the Yankees. If somebody has kicked your butt twice, you want the chance to kick his." Russell summed up the feelings of the Dodger infield: "It was a silent feeling that this might be our last chance. We didn't mention it, but it was there. I'm glad it was against the Yankees. Not that we felt we owed them one, but it was just nice. Of course, we're too old to win it. We're over the hill. We've only been doing it for eight years. I think we dispelled any doubts." The team did dispel any doubts, but at the same time it was an end of an era.

## 1982–83: TIME FOR CHANGE

In *Sports Illustrated*, Ron Fimrite wrote about the party the Dodgers threw for the players to celebrate their World Series victory:

> "Old Brooklyn hero Roy Campanella told everyone how proud he was of them. "Fellas, there's nothing like playing on a winner," he said. For laughs, a belly dancer was turned loose to bedevil Lasorda. And as the afternoon wore on, the sun, which had shone brilliantly on the green field below, dropped behind the stadium rim so that there were only shadows outside. There were shadows inside as well. For many of the Dodgers, their moment in the sun will be all too brief. As Campanis said that afternoon, quoting The Bard, "Uneasy lies the head that wears a crown."

The front office was relatively happy to start the 1982 season with only a few changes compared to the previous year's squad. After a fine 5½ seasons, the seven-time All-Star Reggie Smith left to join the Giants. (Smith would retire at the end of the season.) In bigger news, the Dodgers traded Davey Lopes to the Athletics for Lance Hudson. The Dodger infield was no more. The group had played together for 8½ years—a streak that is unlikely to ever be surpassed. While Hudson never appeared in a game for the Dodgers nor made the majors, Lopes would go on and play another six years in the big leagues. While his best years were behind him, coming off the bench (assuming he would have accepted such a role) would have greatly improved the team. Lopes's replacement was the twenty-two-year-old Steve Sax. Sax had appeared in 31 games the previous season as a replacement for an injured Lopes, performing quite well. Sax did even better in 1982, hitting .282, stealing 49 bases, making the All-Star team, and earning the NL Rookie of the Year. As for other changes, the Dodgers again did not engage in the free agent market after their less-than-successful foray a couple of seasons back.

And such an approach seemed foolhardy early in the season. The team had a losing month in April, going 10–11, and was 6 games behind the division-leading Atlanta Braves. While they were only three games back by the end of May, their playoff chances seemed to be over by July 28 as they were 10 games behind the Braves.

Not helping the mindset of the players throughout the season was the criticism of their performance from management. The front office suggested that it may be time to bring up some minor leaguers and see how they would perform. Baker told *Sports Illustrated*, "I didn't understand how everyone could give up on us so quickly with such a long season ahead. . . . It makes you aware of what the future may hold." Likewise, Cey said,

All that nonsense about making a move here and a move there was upsetting to players who had proved they were winners. You got the feeling that half the club wasn't even here yet, that we couldn't take the team picture without [Greg] Brock and [Candy] Maldonado [two triple-A Albuquerque flashes]. It affected me personally, and I know it affected others. I don't care how old you are if you can still do the job. I don't know of many teams this successful who've had to face this dilemma. It's almost as if they're saying nothing is good enough. There was a lot going on here that didn't need to be going on. When they finally decided to leave us alone, we got back to playing baseball.

Moreover, the Braves totally collapsed, at one point losing 20 of 21 games. Their collapse was so bad that the Dodgers actually led the NL West on August 10. They then proceeded to throw away the division by going on an eight-game losing streak in mid-September. Most frustrating for the players and fans was that in those eight games, six of them were decided by one run with three being lost in extra innings. Helping them was that the rest of the division also played poorly, and they were only one game behind with three games remaining. The Dodgers, Braves, and Giants all had a chance to win the division. The Braves had three games with the Padres, while the Giants and Dodgers went head-to-head in San Francisco. The Braves won their first two games against the Padres. Likewise, the Dodgers won the first two games against the Giants, hence eliminating San Francisco from contention. On the final day of the season, the Padres defeated the Braves, 5–1. If the Dodgers were to win, there would have been a one-game playoff.

Taking the mound for the Dodgers was Fernando Valenzuela. While his numbers weren't as stellar as the previous year, he still had a fine season and was chasing his 20th win. With the score tied at two entering the seventh inning, the Dodgers loaded the bases with one out, but Bill Russell struck out with the pitcher's spot up next. In a fateful decision, Lasorda decided to pinch-hit for Valenzuela. Unfortunately, Jorge Orta grounded out to second base to end the top half of the inning.

Replacing Valenzuela was Tom Niedenfuer, who immediately gave up a single to Bob Brenly and a double to Champ Summers, giving the Giants runners on second and third with no outs. Niedenfuer got the next batter to strike out, and then Lasorda brought in Terry Forster, who got the second out on a strikeout. But Joe Morgan was next up and hit a three-run home run to give the Giants the lead. And for those who think that players of yesteryear did not showboat like today, Morgan cele- brated as he rounded the bases. Giant second baseman Duane Kuiper noted, "I still remember watching Joe between first and second base. . . . He raised his right arm as if to say, 'If we're not going to win it, you're not either.'" The Giants wound up winning, 5–3, and condemned the Dodgers to second place.

It was later revealed that a miscommunication was the reason why the Dodgers pinch-hit for Valenzuela. Prior to the pitcher's potential at-bat, pitching coach Ron Perranoski asked Valenzuela how he felt. Valenzuela touched his left shoulder; his pitching arm. Perranoski took this to mean he was hurt, but Valenzuela said his gesture meant he was running out of gas. In 1999, talking to *SFGate,* Perranoski said, "Knowing the type of competitor he was and became, I wish we could have communicated more. . . . He was tired, but OK. When it happened, there was a lot of second-guessing, but the situation was unknown at the time. We never let on why we pinch-hit for him." Quite simply, with their season on the line it's shocking that such a mix-up could have happened. That may well have been the difference between forcing a playoff and the despair of lost postseason chances.

The Dodgers failing to make the playoffs led to major orga- nization changes in the offseason. Garvey wanted to sign a new deal prior to the start of the 1982 season. However, the front office made it clear that they would not discuss a new contract until July. This led him to wonder whether they really wanted him to be a Dodger for life. After debuting in 1969 with LA and continuing through 1982, Garvey left the Dodgers and signed as a free agent with the San Diego Padres. While he had a decent

1983 in San Diego after two less-than-stelllar seasons with LA, Garvey thereafter faded. He retired following the 1987 season after being limited to only 27 games. Garvey's replacement with the Dodgers was rookie Greg Brock, who was hyped to the moon by the front office. The team thought very highly of Brock and expected him to have a distinguished career. However, he never lived up to those heights in five seasons with the club and was traded to the Brewers in December 1986. If Garvey had remained with the Dodgers, it would have made the team a lot better than it was.

The other major offseason departure was Ron Cey, who was traded to the Cubs for minor-league pitchers Dan Cataline and Vance Lovelace. Cey had some decent years with the Cubs before retiring, like Garvey, following the 1987 season. In contrast, neither Cataline nor Lovelace ever played for the Dodgers. To cover the vacancy at third base, Pedro Guerrero moved from the outfield, with Mike Marshall becoming the everyday right fielder. Marshall had a decent season for the Dodgers; his OPS was the third highest on the team. It is fair to say that Guerrero was a less-than-adequate third baseman, as he readily admitted; he led the team with 31 errors. Lasorda once asked Guerrero what he was thinking when a he was on the field. Guerrero replied something along the lines of, "God, please don't let him hit the ball to me. . . . And God, don't let him hit it to Sax either." Guerrero, though, made up for his defensive shortcomings with his bat, leading the Dodgers in batting average, OBP, and slugging percentage.

As for Sax, his offensive numbers were virtually identical compared to the previous season. However, he was a less-than-successful base stealer: he stole 56 bags but was caught a league-leading 30 times. Steve Sax and his brother, Dave, also became the first and only brothers to start a game for the Dodgers. However, Sax's 1983 season is best remembered, as Guerrero alludes, to his miscues at second. Sax committed 30 errors, most throwing to first. He developed a case of the "yips." By August 7 he had already racked up 25 errors, but after that he only committed five more in almost two months of play. Sax attributed the turnaround to a pep talk from Lasorda, and a talk from his father. In *Tommy Lasorda: My Way*, Sax said his father

> told me that what I was going through was horrible, but that one day I would wake up and it would all be over. . . . He told me that he went through the same thing when he played. I thought, *Wow, my invincible father went through this? If the toughest guy in the world could go through this, maybe I'm not so bad.* He told me that there was nothing wrong with me, it was just my confidence. I took that advice, and that was the last thing he ever told me.

Sax's father passed away two days after their conversation.

While Sax was struggling in the field, one of his teammates was suffering off of it. Steve Howe, the Dodgers closer, was going through some personal turmoil. The pitcher who had won and saved a game during the 1981 World Series had a cocaine problem. In November 1982, he checked himself into a drug rehab center in an attempt to get clean. The rehab did not work, as he was still using—so much so that he missed a game in May 1983 because he was high. Howe later went back to rehab. In an "enlightened" approach, MLB fined Howe one month's salary—the time he was away from the Dodgers. Once again, the rehab did not work, as in September of 1983 he missed a team flight. The Dodgers suspended Howe for the remainder of the season, and the league suspended him for the entirely of the 1984 season after testing positive for cocaine following the end of the 1983 season. MLB Commissioner Bowie Kuhn's reason for suspending Howe for the year was to preserve the image of baseball. Howe returned to the team in 1985 before being traded to the Twins and continued to play in the big leagues until 1996. Howe battled addiction for the rest of his life and tragically lost his life in a car accident in 2006. Howe was under the influence of methamphetamines at the time of the crash. He was only forty-eight.

Despite the turmoil throughout the season and trailing by 6½ games in early August, the team went on to compile a 91–71 record and win the division by three games. They had the best record in the NL despite their offense being near the bottom third of NL teams. As was the norm, the pitching staff was potent; indeed, they led the NL. Yet it was difficult to shake the feeling that they had over-performed; a few hot streaks made the difference. They played very good ball in April (14–6 for the month), May (18–8), and August (20–10), but were well below .500 for June, July, and September. Nevertheless, the players were confident going into the playoffs as they had beaten their opponents, the Phillies, 11 out of 12 games during the season. That confidence, however, was misplaced. The Phillies won Game One, 1–0, in Los Angeles, thanks to a first-inning home run from Mike Schmidt. The Dodgers came back in Game Two, taking it 4–1. However, the Phillies dominated Games Three and Four, winning each game 7–2 and ending the Dodgers' season.

Thus, on the surface, the 1983 season was a good one for the Dodgers, as they once again won the NL West. Yet the less-than-happy departures of Cey and Garvey, their replacements failing to perform to expectations, Sax's throwing yips and more so the loss of his father, and the drug problems of Howe made the 1983 season one to forget.

## 1984–87: SOME GOOD, A LOT NOT SO GOOD

Considering that the Dodgers were defending NL West champions and had the best record in the NL, there was a good feeling all around that the team would have another good season in 1984. And, once again, the front office was happy to rely on the players they had while promoting rookies. One player the front office no longer had was Dusty Baker; he was a free agent and signed with the rival Giants. One could not help but get the impression the ownership simply did not want to spend the necessary money to acquire free agents—players that could have made the team a lot better. However, ownership was happy on occasions to spend money to keep their homegrown players that were in their prime. In February 1984, Pedro Guerrero signed a five-year, $7 million contract. It was the largest contract ever given out by the organization.

Dodger management's decision to go with their usual approach seemed wise considering that the team got off to a good start, having a 17–8 record in April. But April and September were their only winning months, as they finished with a record of 79–83 in fourth place in the NL West, 13 games behind the Padres. Once again the pitching staff had a fine season, and once again the offense was seemingly nonexistent. A series of injuries did not help the team either. This included pitcher and future long-serving Dodger pitching coach Rick Honeycutt, who hurt his shoulder after trying hurdle a chain barrier in the Dodger Stadium carpark. With him that day was relief pitcher Tom

Niedenfuer. Niedenfuer also missed time with injury after swallowing his tongue due to excruciating pain from a kidney stone. Luckily scout Charlie Metro was close by and performed CPR on Niedenfuer, who had stopped breathing, saving his life.

There was one bright spot in the season, though, well apart from Metro saving Niedenfuer's life: Orel Hershiser. Hershiser was far from a can't-miss prospect, as he was a 17th-round pick in the 1979 draft. Very few players drafted that late ever make it to the big leagues. Nevertheless, Hershiser worked his way through the minor-league system. It helped Hershiser that Lasorda believed in him. In *Tommy Lasorda: My Way*, Hershiser recalls a speech Lasorda gave to him back in Spring Training of 1982:

> I was pitching in an intra-squad game and struck out nine batters in a row. . . . Tommy pulled Dusty Baker off the bench because he wanted to see me pitch to a big-league hitter. I struck Dusty out—10 batters in a row. Two days later we are sitting in the stands watching another game and Tommy comes over to sit with me. He gave me a motivational speech, saying if I didn't make it to the big leagues he will have an investigation as to why not. That was the opening line, and it went on for six, seven minutes, but that was the first time that Tommy motivated me and told me I could be a big-leaguer. He probably gave that speech to 100 minor-leaguers, but it meant a lot to me. It still took me another two years, but I made it.

Hershiser made his major-league debut when rosters expanded in September 1983. He appeared as a reliever in eight games and performed reasonably well. And in 1984 he made the Dodgers' Opening Day roster.

In 1984, just like the previous season, Hershiser started off in the bullpen. But by the end of May the Dodgers began transitioning him into the starting rotation. He eventually appeared in 45 games, had a record of 11–8 with an ERA of 2.66, led the NL in shutouts with four, and finished third in the NL Rookie of the Year voting. It was a fine rookie season from the player known as "Bulldog." However, the season did not start out so promising. Hershiser recalled,

> I started the year going 2–2 with a 6.20 ERA. . . . I was trying to hang on for dear life in my first full season in the big leagues. I couldn't maintain any consistency or get anything going. I might get a guy or two out, but then I'd get too fine, too careful, and walk somebody. I'd get even more careful, and before you knew it someone had doubled up the alley. I'd be yanked, aired out for not doing what I was being paid to do, and then I'd sit, wondering what was happening to my brief career.

What turned Hershiser's season around? It was Lasorda giving Hershiser the Bulldog nickname. Lasorda said he told Hershiser,

> I never saw a pitcher pitch as negatively as you. . . . You were afraid to throw the ball over the plate. You were saying to yourself, *I better not throw the ball there or he is going to hit it.* Instead, you should have been saying to yourself that you are going to throw the ball there and he ain't going to hit it! . . . And furthermore, I don't like your first name, Orel. If I bring you in tonight to pitch to Dale Murphy and the PA announces, "Now pitching for the Dodgers, number 55, Orel Hershiser," Murphy is

going to think hitting against you is going to be easy. . . .
From now on your name is Bulldog! You are going to act
like a bulldog. You are going to pitch like a bulldog. And
you are going to walk around like a bulldog!

The Bulldog was even better in 1985. Hershiser led the Dodgers
with a record of 19–3 and an ERA of 2.03, finishing third in
voting for the Cy Young Award. It was a wonderful performance
and helped the Dodgers win another NL West pennant. That
they made the postseason would have been a major surprise to
pundits and fans after how they had started the season.

In the month of April, the Dodgers went 11–10. They were
even worse in May, going 12–14. While they played quite a bit
better in June, they were still 5½ games out of first place near
the end of the month. Fueling the team's improved performance
was Pedro Guerrero. The Dodgers finally realized the Guerrero
was a better outfielder than third baseman. (He played his last
game at third on May 31.) At the time, his OPS was .756. By
the end of June, his OPS was .949. For the season, Guerrero
led the NL in OBP at .422 and slugging at .577. He finished
third in MVP voting. His move to the outfield seemed to fuel
the entire offense. While a long way from being the best hitting
team in the NL, there was a stark improvement compared to
previous years. And the pitching staff, as usual, was great. Hershiser, Valenzuela, Reuss, and Welch led the staff to once again
being the best in the NL. In many way, as Glenn Stout argues in
*Dodgers*, the usual superlative pitching made the Dodgers seem
better than they were. While the offense would occasionally go
on hot streaks, the pitching staff, just like in the mid-1960s with
Koufax and Drysdale, "kept the cracks from showing."

\* \* \*

The 1985 season will also be remembered for the infamous strike, which took place during the middle of the season. It only lasted two days, and while 25 games were lost, they were replayed. The reason the strike was so short is largely because Peter Ueberroth did not want a work stoppage under his reign as MLB commissioner. At the start of the strike, he demanded the head of the Player Relations Committee to finalize a deal with the MLBPA within 24 hours. Moreover, Ueberroth announced a deal between MLBPA and the Players Association before it was approved by the owners on the PRC and the rest of the owners. Both sides accepted concessions.

Once the strike was over, the Dodger pitching staff did such a good job that they easily won the NL West and ended up with a record of 95–67. Facing them in the NLCS would be the Cardinals, who had the best record in baseball at 101–61. With the Dodgers having home-field advantage, as they had a winning record against the Cardinals, they were quietly confident heading into the series.

And that confidence led them to winning the first two games of the series. They won Game One by a margin of 4–1, with Valenzuela picking up the win. In Game Two, they were dominant again, winning 8–2 with Hershiser pitching a complete game. In Game Three, with the series now in St. Louis, the Cardinals jumped on Welch early—scoring two in the first and two in the second, knocking him out of the game in the third. The Dodgers were never in the contest, losing 4–2. And in Game Four, the Dodgers were blown out, 12–2, with the Cardinals scoring nine runs in the second.

With the series tied at two apiece, Game Five would prove to be a closer contest. The Cardinals scored two in the first off of Valenzuela, who settled down after the rough inning, and the Dodgers tied the contest in the fourth, thanks to a two-run home run from third baseman Bill Madlock. The score remained tied until the ninth. Following eight innings of work, in which he had thrown 132 pitches, Valenzuela was replaced with Tom Niedenfuer by Lasorda. It was the correct decision, but oftentimes in baseball the right decision can backfire. With one out, switch-hitter Ozzie Smith (batting lefty) blasted a home run to deep right field to walk it off for the Cardinals and bring them within one game of going to the World Series. Prior to that, Smith only had 13 home runs and none from the left side. Baseball can be wonderful and cruel at the same time, depending on which side you're on. Then came the fateful Game Six at Dodger Stadium.

The Dodgers scored quickly, putting up a run in the first and second to take a 2–0 lead. The Cardinals got one back in the third, but the Dodgers scored two in the fifth, thanks to a sacrifice fly by Guerrero and a home run by Madlock.

On the mound for the Dodgers was Hershiser. He did not have his best stuff, and after only giving up one run in the third he ran into trouble in the seventh. He gave up two runs on three hits in the inning, only retiring one batter, and was replaced by Niedenfuer. The "Wizard" was up next, Smith tripled to bring in the game-tying run. The Dodgers retook the lead in the eighth when Marshall hit the first pitch he saw for a home run and sent Dodger fans into a frenzy. They were only three outs from forcing a deciding Game Seven.

Niedenfuer struck out the first Cardinal before giving up a single and a walk. He rebounded by getting Tom Herr to ground out, with the runners moving to second and third.

With first base open and two outs, Lasorda had the choice of walking Jack Clark. Clark was the lone Cardinals power threat and had hit 22 home runs for the year. The next best on the Cardinals was Andy Van Slyke with 13. Clark, who was a former Giant, had been having a good NLCS, albeit one with no extra-base hits. Before the series, Lasorda drummed it into the pitching staff to be wary of Clark, as he had the power to beat the Dodgers. Hitting behind him was Van Slyke, who was not having a good NLCS (batting a measly .100). Lasorda elected not to walk Clark. It was not the correct decision, as he hit the first pitch he saw, a fastball right down the middle, for a three-run home run to give the Cardinals a 7–5 lead. The Dodgers went quietly in the ninth, and the Cardinals were the NL Champions.

"I was surprised I got that fastball," Clark said. "I knew it was gone. . . . But I did not upper-cut it. I chopped down and actually missed it a little bit, but it had some backspin and stayed nice and straight." That he beat the Dodgers made it extra sweet for Clark: "There was a lot of payback for a lot of reasons . . . For all those years in Candlestick Park. Not only was it bad enough just having to play there, but the Dodgers kept whipping up on us every year. . . . I had one mission. To seek and destroy everyone on that team, from Fernando [Valenzuela] to Orel Hershiser. I wanted it all." Talking to the *Los Angeles Times* in 2010, Niedenfuer said, "It's a very proud feeling that your manager had enough confidence in you to be the guy he put in that situation. I wouldn't trade that for anything in the world because I loved being out there. But when it happened, all I can remember is . . . you let the team down." But Niedenfuer should not have been in that position. Nevertheless, Lasorda defended his decision. Following the game he said, "I thought about walking Clark for a second. . . . But then, you know what can happen when you get the bases loaded. Anything can happen. Besides, Tom's my man. He has been my man all season in that spot. And the last time up, he blew Clark away." He went on to claim, "If you want to second guess me, go ahead. . . . All I know is that I had to make the first guess, and when he hit that ball, it tore my heart out. This was one of the toughest losses in my life."

If prior to the NLCS Lasorda made no mention of not letting Clark beat the Dodgers, Lasorda would have a better argument for pitching to Clark. But he constantly reminded the pitchers about how dangerous Clark was. That makes Lasorda's decision all the more baffling—even more so as Niedenfuer was tiring. It was the wrong decision and one that may have well cost the Dodgers a place in the World Series.

\* \* \*

If the Dodgers had a good year in 1986 and made the postseason, Lasorda's decision to pitch to Clark, while not forgiven, would have faded into the background. Alas, the team did not have a good year at all. The season was pretty much doomed when, in the final Spring Training game before the regular season was to get underway, Pedro Guerrero ruptured a patella tendon in his knee sliding into third base. Following confirmation that he was out for most of the season, Guerrero told the media that "I hoped I wouldn't have to slide. I wasn't even sliding into second base on grounders earlier this spring. Too dangerous. I slid the day before the first time. . . . This time, I went because I thought I saw the hit-and-run sign. Just as I was going to slide, I saw Virgil (Braves catcher Ozzie Virgil) was trying to get the ball and wouldn't be throwing. My spikes got caught. As I fell, I reached for my knee. It was already getting bigger." Lasorda was outwardly optimistic about the Dodgers chances without Guerrero: "We can't let this affect us. We've got to believe whoever replaces Pete will do a good job. God delays, God doesn't deny. He just put up one stop sign."

As was the Dodger Way, the front office made no effort to trade for a suitable replacement, nor did it pursue any notable free agents in the offseason. In 1985 and 1986, the Dodgers were no different than other teams, as the owners colluded not to sign free agents in these years. In 1985, there were 62 free agents, but only five signed with new teams. In 1986, there were 33 free agents, but only four signed with new teams. The collusion drove salaries down and provided players with less job security, as a majority of free agents were forced to accept one-year deals. The MLBPA successfully proved that MLB had colluded against free agents; as a result, MLB had to pay over $280 million in damages.

As for the Dodgers, Guerrero did not return to the lineup until August 1 but only played in a few games before injuring himself again. He finally returned full-time in early September. By then the team was well out of contention. God obviously never lowered the stop sign.

In Guerrero's absence, the offense was one of the worst in the NL, with only Sax having an OPS above .800 among the starters. To go along with the dismal offense, the Dodgers committed the most errors in the NL. And their usual reliable pitching staff had an average year. One person to shine, though, was Valenzuela; he led the NL with 21 wins and 20 complete games. As well as making the All-Star team, he finished second in Cy Young voting and won a Gold Glove. Overall, the Dodgers finished in fifth place in the NL West with a record of 73–89—23 games behind the first-place Astros.

In a fitting somber note to the season, Bill Russell retired after 18 seasons with the ballclub. In his final season, as a thirty-seven year old, Russell appeared in 105 games, hitting .250. While arguably never receiving the plaudits compared to the rest of the infield, Russell was an integral part of many successful Dodger teams and was a great defensive shortstop. Russell still holds the record for the most games as a Los Angeles Dodger and is second behind Zachary Davis Wheat on the Dodger (Brooklyn and LA) all-time list. Following his retirement he stayed on in the organization as a coach for the big-league club in 1987.

*  *  *

Considering the dismal 1986 season, one would assume that the team would pursue big-name free agents—especially hitters. Of course, one would assume that only if one did not understand how the team's front office operated. Once again, the Dodgers did not pursue any good free agents, preferring to stick with their current roster, as well as the young up-and-coming rookies. And, predictably, the Dodgers had another awful season. The offense was somehow even worse than the previous year, despite Pedro Guerrero having a great season with an OPS of .955. Apart from catcher Orlando Mercado, who appeared in seven games, going 3-for-5 with one walk, no other Dodger had an OPS above .800. The Dodgers once again had the most errors in the NL, but at least the pitching staff had a better year; their ERA was second best in the NL.

Walter Alston managed the Brooklyn and Los Angeles Dodgers between 1954 and 1976. He led the team to four World Series triumphs.

Don Newcombe only played eleven games for the Los Angeles Dodgers, but he is still revered as a Brooklyn Dodger great and has been involved with the LA Dodgers behind the scenes for a number of years.

The LA Coliseum during the 1959 World Series. The Dodgers played their home games at the Coliseum from 1958 until 1961.

**SANDY KOUFAX**

PITCHER                    L.A. DODGERS

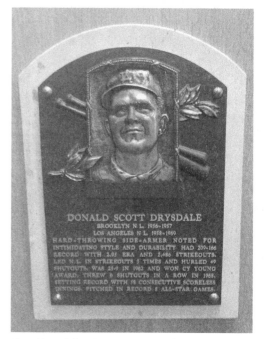

Sandy Koufax: NL MVP, three-time NL Cy Young Award winner, and a very worthy member of the Hall of Fame.

Don Drysdale: Cy Young Award winner, nine-time All-Star, and as with Koufax a proud member of the Hall of Fame.

Frank Howard battled personal issues, but had a fine career as a player and manager.

Maury Wills was a base-stealing machine and an offensive catalyst for the Dodgers.

Tommy Lasorda still bleeds Dodger blue and led the team to two World Series triumphs.

Davey Lopes was part of the legendary Dodger infield with Steve Garvey, Bill Russell, and Ron Cey.

The 1988 World Series trophy.

Manny Ramirez was one of the Dodger's best ever short-term signings, but his legacy will always be tarnished due to his use of performance enhancing drugs.

A birds-eye view of Dodger Stadium.

Clayton Kershaw is one of the greatest pitchers of all time, a future member of the Hall of Fame, but needs to lead the Dodgers to World Series glory to cement his legacy.

Eric Gagne and Kenley Jansen are the two best closers in Dodger history.

Juan Uribe returning to the dugout after hitting the game-winning home run in Game Four of the 2013 NLDS. Hanley Ramirez is ecstatic, but a fastball to his ribs in Game One of the NLCS potentially cost the Dodgers a World Series.

Yasiel Puig has all the talent in the world, but frustrates both opponents and his teammates.

Matt Kemp had a fine career as a Dodger. His 2011 season is one for the ages.

Corey Bellinger is another in the long-line of Dodger NL Rookie of the Year Award winners.

Zack Greinke had three outstanding seasons in Los Angeles and is a firm believer in good hygiene.

Corey Seager is well on his way to being an all-time Dodger great.

Justin Turner went from being an afterthought to one of the best players in baseball.

Orel Hershiser was instrumental in helping the Dodgers to World Series glory in 1988.

Fernando Valenzuela electrified the Los Angeles public as Fernandomania ran wild.

Vin Scully will always be the voice of the Los Angeles Dodgers.

They ended the season fourth in the NL West with a record of 73–89 (same as in 1986), 17 games behind the first-place Giants.

* * *

The 1987 season should have been a year to celebrate, as it was the fortieth anniversary of Jackie Robinson breaking the color barrier with the Brooklyn Dodgers. But the Dodgers were *again* dismal on the field. Unfortunately, what happened off the field was even worse.

Following an Opening Day loss to the Astros in Houston, Dodger GM Al Campanis appeared on *Nightline* to celebrate the anniversary of the color barrier being broken. Campanis was seemingly a good choice because, in addition to being the Dodgers GM, he played with Robinson in Triple-A in 1946 and the two even roomed together. The interview should have been good PR for the Dodgers and baseball in general. Unfortunately, it was anything but. Among other things, Campanis claimed that black people "may not have some of the necessities to be, let's say, a field manager, or perhaps a general manager." He continued, "Why are black men, or black people, not good swimmers? Because they don't have the buoyancy. . . . How many quarterbacks do you have? How many pitchers do you have that are black?"

Interviewer Ted Koppel asked Campanis during the commercial break whether he wanted to clarify his remarks. When the broadcast resumed, Campanis reiterated his beliefs that black people lacked certain "qualities." He said that some black people are "highly intelligent, but they may not have the desire to be in the front office. . . . I know that they have wanted to manage and some of them have managed, but they're outstanding athletes, very God-gifted, and they're very wonderful people, and that's all I can tell you about them."

Quite simply, what Campanis said on *Nightline* was indefensible. However, there were those that tried to defend him by claiming he was drunk, misunderstood, etc. But he was not drunk, and Campanis made it abundantly clear what he thought of black people. By all accounts, Campanis was not outwardly a racist or bigot, but his opinions had absolutely no place in society, let alone baseball. Following the interview, both Campanis and Peter O'Malley made public apologies. Amazingly, O'Malley made it clear that Campanis would remain as the Dodger's GM. However, there was immense public pressure to fire Campanis. As a result, O'Malley told Campanis he had to resign or be fired. Campanis resigned, with Fred Claire taking over as GM. Following the announcement, Lasorda broke down, claiming that Campanis made a mistake and did not know why he said what he did. He believed that he should not have been fired, but instead given a second chance. Speaking to Delsohn years after the interview, Lasorda sought to defend Campanis. He claimed, "They hung an innocent man. . . . I would never talk to Ted Koppel for what he did to Campanis. He shouldn't have let that happen. I don't care what he tells you, he should never have allowed that to happen." Campanis was not innocent in the slightest; he made it very clear what he thought. Moreover, Koppel almost implored Campanis to clarify his statements during a commercial break so as not to come across as a bigot. It is understandable that Lasorda would want to defend his friend, but the reality is Campanis dug his own grave and the Dodgers and baseball as a whole were better off that he was replaced as GM.

## 1988–89: "THE IMPOSSIBLE HAS HAPPENED"; IT COULD NOT HAPPEN AGAIN

The change of GM had a positive impact in one respect: Claire was allowed to sign free agents and engage in meaningful trades. The Dodger Way of relying almost exclusively on homegrown talent was no longer working in the era of free agency. As part of a three-team trade, the Dodgers sent Bob Welch and Matt Young to the A's and Jack Savage to the New York Mets. In return, they received shortstop Alfredo Griffin and relief pitcher Jay Howell from the A's and relief pitcher Jesse Orosco from the Mets. The Dodgers were not done; they signed several free agents, including forty-three-year-old Don Sutton. Of course, not all of the trades and signings bore fruit. For example, Sutton was let go during the middle of the season and retired. But that the Dodger front office actively sought to make the team better was an all-round benefit. Turnover was so great that, out of the twenty-four man Opening Day roster, thirteen players were not in the organization at the start of the 1987 season.

Despite changes to the roster, most pundits expected the Dodgers to be well off the pace in the NL West. This was despite them having the highest payroll in baseball. Writing in the *Los Angeles Times* after the team's Opening Day loss to the Giants, Jim Murray stated, "This team cost Dodger owner Peter O'Malley $17.5 million. Now, I can remember when you could buy a railroad for that. Or a coal mine. Or a Manhattan skyscraper. A small country. Peter got a whole bunch of .270 and .260 hitters for it."

As was, and in many cases still is, the norm for sportswriters, Murray derided the money the players were getting. He went on to claim, "Baseball is big on incentive clauses these days. Maybe owners should check into the possibility of *decentive* clauses. If you get $50,000 for making the All-Star team, winning the MVP, or just appearing in 150 games or being on the team by September, etc., maybe you should give back a few thousand for throwing to the wrong base, popping out with the bases loaded, or whipping a pickoff throw into center field. . . . On the basis of their play Monday, *decentive* would wind up with the Dodger outfield owing O'Malley money."

People were skeptical of the Dodgers' chances, even though they had signed a decent number of free agents. However, among the solid players they'd signed, they captured a superstar in Kirk Gibson. It was, in fact, because the owners colluded against free agents that the Dodgers were able to sign Gibson. An MLB arbitrator ruled that, due to the collusion, seven players, including Gibson, were now free agents, despite the players having contracts for the 1988 season. Gibson had signed a one-year deal with the Detroit Tigers for $1.3 million, but that contract was now null and void. The Dodgers signed Gibson to a three-year deal worth $4.5 million. Gibson had wanted to stay with the Tigers, but they were loath to pay him any more money. In response to Gibson signing with the Dodgers, Tigers owner Tom Monaghan ripped the player who had been with the team for nine years, claiming,

> I didn't like Gibson's grooming. I thought he was a disgrace to the Tiger uniform with his half beard, half stubble. I didn't like his long hair. . . . His best talents, hitting home runs against right-handed pitchers and stealing bases, are not worth a million-and-a-half dollars a year. . . . Which means the best he could do for the Tigers would be to serve as a designated hitter against a

right hander. He has one of the weakest arms in baseball for an outfielder and cannot field well. He was a liability in the outfield. We do not need to replace Kirk Gibson.

Whatever one thought of Gibson's baseball abilities, as Gibson pointed out, Monaghan did not care what he looked like when he helped the Tigers win the 1984 World Series. Moreover, a person such as Monaghan would most likely approve of the way Gibson played baseball—very, very serious and hard-nosed.

Such an approach quickly resulted in problems for the Dodgers' laid-back clubhouse, where practical jokes were the norm. During Spring Training, Guerrero put shaving foam on the clubhouse telephone. He told Gibson he had a call, and predictably Gibson got an earful of shaving foam. While Gibson laughed at the joke, he was not laughing a few days later. On March 3, Jesse Orosco placed eye black, which players use to help cut down on the glare from the sun, on the bill of Gibson's cap. Gibson put on the hat as he took the field and the eye-black ran down his face. While players on the Dodger benched laughed, Gibson was not one of them. He stormed off the field and left the stadium after the sixth inning. To say he was not amused is an understatement. He was furious and addressed the team the following day. As he recounted in his book, *Bottom of the Ninth*, he told his teammates,

What are we here for? We're here to be world champions. You know what? I've been a world champion. You don't become world champions by just stumbling into it. We're getting ready to enter the marathon race. We're going to see how much heart we have. If we haven't got heart, we haven't got a prayer. We've got to start challenging ourselves mentally—now, because it's going to get a lot worse than this. If I'm wrong, then I'm on the wrong team, the front office will move me, and you guys can go your own route. Now if anybody's got a problem with what I've said, tough. I'm standing right here. If you want me—one of you, all of you—I don't care. I will do anything to prove to you that I'm here to sacrifice in order to become world champions.

The folklore around the speech is that it set the tone for the season, but, while it may well have focused the team, the reality is if the season had gone differently, and if Gibson did not have the year he did and never hit the walk-off home run in Game One of the World Series, the speech would not have taken on the mythical status that it did.

There were other pressing issues for the team going into the season, such as what to do with the glut of outfielders. Gibson was assured to play left; John Shelby, who was signed by Claire during the 1987 season, was slotted in center; and another free agent signing, Mike Davis, was slotted in right. That left Guerrero and Mike Marshall without a position. Marshall was moved to first base, but Guerrero was moved back to third—the same position where he prayed the ball would not be hit to him. Despite being the best Dodger hitter for a number of years, Guerrero was not long for Los Angeles. The front office and an increasing number of players began to tire of his antics and love of partying. Also not helping was that he had been suspended for four days after throwing his bat at Mets' pitcher David Cone. Guerrero did so after Cone hit him with a pitch, and then he charged the mound, triggering a melee. It was not a fastball that hit Guerrero, but a curveball. This did not matter to Guerrero, as he said, "I don't care what he hit me with. . . . It was a curveball, so what? I just don't want to get hit. They have all the advantages, pitchers do.

They can hit the hitters and nothing happens." To call Guerrero's actions an overreaction is an understatement. Guerrero should not have charged the mound, let alone thrown his bat at the pitcher.

Guerrero was already on the proverbial thin ice with the Dodgers and some of his teammates. This came to a head after a loss to the Cardinals in St. Louis on July 19. The Dodgers had a big lead in the division, and the loss snapped a six-game winning streak. Nevertheless, Gibson hated to lose and was not happy in the clubhouse. What raised his ire even further was that Guerrero, who was on the disabled list, invited several Cardinal players into the team locker room. Gibson, who viewed the clubhouse as sacred, was furious and let Guerrero know all about it in no uncertain terms. While Gibson and Guerrero did not come to blows, the writing was on the wall. If Guerrero had been hitting as well as he had in previous seasons, the front office would have most likely overlooked his indiscretions and found a way for the two ballplayers to coexist. But he was not hitting well. His OPS was .785, well below his other seasons in Los Angeles, bar his rookie year. That, combined with Guerrero's inadequate defense at third, his longer-than-expected recovery from injury (in part due to him not being diligent in attending daily treatments), and the Dodgers' need for a left-handed starting pitcher led to Guerrero being traded on August 16 to the Cardinals for John Tudor. It was a sad end to a truly great Dodger.

The team's need for left-handed pitching was in large part due to Fernando Valenzuela succumbing to injury. Since becoming a starter, Valenzuela had pitched more than 250 innings in every season.[14] Such usage was almost certainly guaranteed to take its

---

14 Except for the strike-shortened 1981 season, where he still lead the NL with 192½ innings pitched.

toll. He was no longer the pitcher he once was, but still led the NL with complete games and pitched 251 innings in 1987. Valenzuela struggled at the start of the following season but was not bad by any means. However, it was clear that something was wrong. Showing the fickleness of certain fans, Valenzuela was booed at Dodger Stadium on May 17 against the Expos after giving up six runs in seven innings of work. The booing got worse on May 22, when he gave up five runs in 1⅔ innings against the Mets. Valenzuela's struggles continued, and his ERA was 4.39 after 4⅔ innings (giving up two runs) against the Astros at Dodger Stadium. His season was effectively over, and as he told the *Los Angeles Times* after the game,

> Right now, it feels weak. . . . It's not just the shoulder, it's the whole arm that feels weak. I don't know when I will throw again. It depends on what happens. I felt good when the game started. I knew this was a big game for us. But on the fastball to [Billy] Hatcher, the arm felt weak. I got the next batter [Ken Caminiti], but I knew my arm was weak. I thought I could get the next out, but I couldn't. I had to leave.

Valenzuela did not return to the lineup until September 26. Even with a two-month break, he did not look impressive, as he reached his 60-pitch limit in three innings while giving up two runs. His final appearance of the season came in relief on October 1, when he gave up one run in four innings while picking up a save. However, when the Dodger playoff roster was announced, Valenzuela's name was not on it. Lasorda did not believe that his ace had recovered enough to start and claimed it would not be fair to pitch him in relief. Valenzuela told the *Los Angeles Times* that he agreed with the decision, although his expression told another story: "I know those guys don't want to rush me. They know I like to play . . . but I never say I'm hurt. I'd love to play, but I'm not ready." He went on to claim, "I'm not ready to start, and my arm isn't good for the bullpen. . . . This gives me more time to rest." Unfortunately, Valenzuela's arm never truly recovered.

While Valenzuela did not have a good 1988, one Dodger pitcher had a career year: Orel Hershiser. Hershiser finished the year with a record of 23–8 and an ERA of 2.26; he led the league in wins, innings pitched (267), complete games (15), and shut-outs (eight). He was an All-Star, finished sixth in MVP voting, and won the Gold Glove and Cy Young Awards. It was a truly memorable year. What made it even more special was his scoreless-innings streak. On September 5, Hershiser pitched a complete-game shutout as the Dodgers beat the Braves in Atlanta, 3–0. In a particular highlight, Hershiser struck out seven-time All-Star, four-time Silver Slugger, and two-time NL MVP Dale Murphy four times. On September 10, the Dodgers defeated the Reds 5–0 with Hershiser giving up seven hits and three walks in nine innings of work. September 14 witnessed another complete-game shutout by Hershiser, as the Dodgers defeated the Braves 1–0. Murphy had a better game this time around, managing a hit, but still struck out twice. And on September 19, Hershiser once again pitched another complete-game shutout as the Dodgers won, 1–0, in Houston against the Astros. While the lack of offense may have bothered some pitchers, Hershiser was "happy" about the situation because he could not trade any runs for outs. He had to be at his absolute best.

On September 23, the Dodgers traveled to San Francisco with the Giants hoping to end the streak—and history repeated itself. As discussed earlier, Drysdale's scoreless-inning streak in 1968 was seemingly over when Drysdale hit Dick Dietz with a pitch with the bases loaded and none out. But umpire Harry Wendelstedt ruled that Dietz made no attempt to get out of the way of the pitch. Drysdale managed to get out of the inning unscathed, and the streak continued. For the Giants, the first time was a tragedy, the second time a farce. In the third inning, the Giants had runners at the corners with one out. Third baseman Ernie Riles hit a pitch to second, but the Dodgers were unable to turn the double play as Alfredo Griffin's throw under pressure, due to a hard slide from Brett Butler, was nowhere near first baseman Tracy Woodson. The streak was over . . . or was it? Second base umpire Bob Engel ruled both Riles and Butler were out, as Butler had interfered with Griffin. And with that, Hershiser's streak continued. As with the Drysdale controversy, if the scoreless-innings streak was not on the line it is extremely doubtful the umpire would have made the same call. The Giant players and manager were understandably livid. Butler later claimed that "I slid into second and I could touch the bag . . . and Bob Engel called me out. I said, 'Really?!' He said, 'You went out of your way to get him.' I said, 'But I could still touch the bag.' He said, 'No, no, no, you couldn't.'" As for Hershiser, he ran off the field screaming, "Dick Dietz revisited! Dick Dietz revisited!" He noted that most likely "Tommy Lasorda was the only one in the dugout who knew what I meant." Hershiser went on to shut out the Giants, leading the Dodgers to a 3–0 victory.

Hershiser had pitched 49 scoreless innings heading into his final regular-season game on September 28 against the Padres in San Diego. If he pitched nine scoreless innings, he would tie

Drysdale's mark of 58 innings. He needed the game to go into extra innings to break the mark. While he could have broken the record the following year, it was generally agreed that if that happened either an asterisk would be placed against Hershiser's record or a new record created. Hershiser was also aiming to tie Drysdale's record of six complete-game shutouts in a row. Hershiser held up his end of the bargain, pitching nine innings of shutout ball. The Dodger offense followed suit by failing to score against Padre starter Andy Hawkins in regulation. The game was headed for extras. Amazingly, Hershiser wanted out of the game. In 2015, he told Bill Plaschke in an article in the *Los Angeles Times*, "We had already clinched the division, the game meant nothing, and how cool would it be for two Dodgers to share the record? . . . I thought the situation was perfect, I wanted to be linked with Big D forever." Lasorda would have nothing of it and ordered Hershiser to pitch the 10th. In the bottom of the inning, Hershiser struck out Marvell Wynne, but he reached first on a wild pitch. He was then bunted over to second. Hershiser got Randy Ready to ground out to short, with Wynne moving to third. Garry Templeton followed with an intentional walk, and went to second on defensive indifference. With two outs and the record on the line, Hershiser faced pinch hitter Keith Moreland. On a 1-2 count, Hershiser got Moreland to fly out to right field. The scoreless-innings streak now belonged to Hershiser. Following the 10th inning, Lasorda replaced Hershiser with Jesse Orosco. As such, Drysdale still held the complete-game shutout streak—but Hershiser's scoreless innings streak was 59 innings. Thus, not only did he beat Drysdale's official record of 58 innings, he beat the *unofficial* record of 58⅔ innings. Hershiser credited the team for the record, telling Plaschke, "We just had a really good team, it wasn't about me, I was always just part of the whole. . . . What had happened to me during the streak just kept happening the rest of the season. . . . Guys would continually make great plays behind me. My record was as much of a team record as an individual record."

The 1988 Dodgers were indeed a good team, holding first place for the overwhelming majority of the season. They would run away with the division, finishing with a record of 94–67, seven games ahead of the second-place Reds. Indeed, Los Angeles only spent 15 days out of the division lead. In one respect, the doom and gloom spouted by Jim Murray after the Opening Day loss was wrong. The Dodgers did not have a bunch of .260 and .270 hitters—they were worse than that. Only six of the twenty position players who suited up for the Dodgers had a batting average above .260. The Dodgers were fifth in the NL in batting average, a miserable eleventh in OBP, and eighth in slugging. But one Dodger had a great year with the bat: Kirk Gibson. He led the Dodgers in runs scored, doubles, walks, home runs, batting average, OBP, and slugging. Gibson also stole 31 bases while only being caught four times. He was duly rewarded by winning the NL Silver Slugger Award and was voted the league's MVP.

While Gibson dominated the offense, the pitching staff was its usual great self. In addition to Hershiser, Tim Leary went 17–11 with a 2.91 ERA, and rookie Tim Belcher had a record of 12–6 with a 2.91 ERA as well. The bullpen was also a source of strength. Closer Jay Howell saved 21 games and posted a 2.08 ERA, while Alejandro Peña—who began his career in Los Angeles in 1981—saved 12 games with a 1.91 ERA. The Dodgers had the second-best pitching staff in the NL.

Facing the Dodgers in the NLCS was the team that led the NL in hitting and pitching: the New York Mets. Not only did the Mets dominate in the statistical categories, they also posted a 100-win season for the second time in three seasons, and had beaten the Dodgers in 10 of 11 contests throughout the season. In those 11 games, the Mets scored 49 runs compared to a lowly 18 for the Dodgers. Also favoring the Mets was that Gibson's body, specifically his left hamstring and right knee, were causing him great discomfort. As such, the Dodgers were rightfully underdogs heading into Game One of the NLCS—even with Hershiser taking the mound.

Hershiser was once again at his brilliant best and took a 2–0 lead into the ninth inning. But all good things must come to an end, and following a single by Gregg Jefferies and a groundout by Keith Hernandez to move the runner over, Hershiser threw two hanging curveballs to Darryl Strawberry, the latter of which was belted for a double to cut the lead to one. And then, in a head-scratching moment, Lasorda took Hershiser out of the game in a double switch with Howell taking the mound and batting in Gibson's spot in the lineup. Howell then proceeded to give up a walk to Kevin McReynolds. While Howell got Howard Johnson to strike out, Gary Carter followed with a double to center field to give the Mets a 3–2 lead. The Dodgers went quietly in the bottom of the ninth, and the Mets took the first game of the series. It was not the best start for the Dodgers, but help was on the horizon.

As previously noted, there is a fine line between confidence, arrogance, and outright stupidity. Prior to Game Two, Mets starter David Cone, who finished third in Cy Young voting behind Hershiser, in a ghostwritten column in the *Daily News*, claimed that "Orel [Hershiser] was lucky for eight innings." He went on to trash Howell:

> I'll tell you a secret: As soon as we got Orel out of the game, we knew we'd beat the Dodgers. Knew it even after Jay Howell had struck out HoJo. We saw Howell throwing curveball after curveball and we were thinking: *This is the Dodgers' idea of a stopper?* Our idea is Randy [Myers], a guy who can blow you away with his heat. Seeing Howell and his curveball reminded us of a high school pitcher.

It is fair to say that Cone crossed the line into outright stupidity. The column was even more mind-boggling considering that Cone was starting Game Two. The Dodger players were indignant with the column but were somewhat pacified following the game. Cone lasted only two innings in which he surrendered five runs. The Mets were never in the contest, as the Dodgers won 6–3 to even the series. For the Dodgers, Belcher went 8⅓ innings. He noted after the game, "That column really backfired on David Cone. . . . I can't believe he'd even agree to do it, much less to write what he did. I can't understand what was going through his mind."

The Dodgers were hoping to capitalize on the Cone column even more by winning Game Three. Taking the mound for the Dodgers was Hershiser on three days' rest. He started the game because it was postponed by a day due to a rainout. It should have arguably not gone ahead the following day as it was cold and windy, and the ground resembled a mud heap in parts. Even the Mets did not want to play, but television dictated the game go ahead. After three innings, the Dodgers led, 3–1, but the Mets rallied in the bottom of the sixth. Hernandez led off the inning with a single, and Darryl Strawberry followed suit. Hernandez was indecisive about trying to get to third; he eventually slipped and was tagged out at third (with Strawberry taking second). However, Kevin McReynolds then reached on an error, largely due to the deplorable conditions. While Hershiser got Howard Johnson to ground out, back-to-back singles by Gary Carter and Wally Backman, the latter barely leaving the infield, tied the game.

A bases-loaded walk by Mike Sharperson in the top of the eighth restored the Dodger lead, but, once again, the bullpen imploded, giving up five runs in the bottom of the innings as the Mets pulled out the win, 8–4. The inning was notable because the Mets complained to crew chief Harry Wendelstedt about something on Howell's glove. Wendelstedt checked Howell's glove and promptly threw Howell out of the game. Talking to the *Los Angeles Times* the following year, Howell said, "It was tough. . . . I felt all the way through it that what I was doing wasn't a federal offense. It was a holding penalty. I wasn't trying to hide anything. Pitchers have been doing it for 100 years in the game. Anybody who thinks they're not using pine tar is naive." Howell received support from Keith Hernandez, who argued, "I feel badly for him, because I don't think he was trying to make the ball do anything. He was just trying to get a grip on it. . . . If the Dodgers would lose their best reliever now, that just wouldn't be fair." Fair or not, Howell was suspended for three games, which was reduced to two on appeal. In a sad note, following the game, Howell got a phone call to inform him that his father-in-law had succumbed to cancer. Neither Howell nor his wife Alison had a chance to say goodbye.

Game Four was played the following day. As was the case in Game Three, the Dodgers jumped out to an early lead, thanks to a John Shelby single that drove in two in the first. The Mets then came back, scoring three in the fourth, thanks to back-to-back home runs from Strawberry and McReynolds and added another run in the sixth to take a 4–2 lead. The Dodgers were looking down the proverbial barrel as they faced Dwight Gooden in the top of the ninth, who was looking for a complete-game victory. Shelby walked to start the inning, and then Mike Scioscia, on the first pitch he saw, drilled a two-run home run. Scioscia was far from a power hitter, as he had hit only three home runs for the year and would only hit 68 in his 13-year major-league career. But in this game, he tied it with one swing of the bat. As Scioscia told the *Daily News* in 2013, "What I remember most is how quiet it got at Shea. It was really eerie. It was the first time I could ever remember running around the bases and hearing my spikes crunching as they hit the ground. And I'm thinking, *This is pretty cool but it's almost surreal.*"

After the Mets went down in order in the bottom of the ninth, the game headed for extra innings. The score remained tied until the top of the 12th when, on an 0-1 count, Gibson destroyed a sinker from Roger McDowell, sending it well beyond the center-field wall to give the Dodgers the lead. Gibson later told the *Los Angeles Times*, "You got to tell yourself that there are moments like this you dream about, and I wanted to have an impact on the game." Little did Gibson know that this home run was just a prelude of what was to come. The Mets rallied in the bottom of the inning to load the bases with one out, but Orosco got Strawberry to pop-up. In a surprise to those watching, Lasorda brought in Hershiser, who started the previous day in deplorable conditions, to get the last out. Facing Hershiser was McReynolds who, in addition to the home run earlier in the game, had doubled.

And on a 1-1 count, Hershiser got McReynolds to bloop a ball to center field, where Shelby made a running catch. The NLCS was now tied at two games apiece.

And Game Five continued the winning ways for the Dodgers. They put three runs up in the fourth inning, thanks to a two-run double from Rick Dempsey and another double from Griffin to drive in Dempsey. And the game was as good as over following a three-run home run from Gibson in the top of the fifth. While the Mets rallied for three in the fifth and the Dodgers' nerves got frayed, they held on to record a 7–4 victory, taking the series lead back to Los Angeles. It was not all positive for the Dodgers; Gibson had a recurrence of his hamstring injury to his left leg when trying to steal second in the top of the ninth. However, despite the injury, Gibson (perhaps foolishly) played the following day in Game Six (going 0-for-4). In a measure of revenge, Cone pitched a complete game as the Mets won, 5–1. The NLCS was heading for a series-deciding Game Seven.

And showing that the Mets had learned nothing, prior to the game, Mets manager Davey Johnson told the press that he could not believe that Hershiser pitched in relief for Game Five and, as Josh Suchon recounted in *Miracle Men*, Johnson claimed Hershiser was "going to have to be Superman. I don't expect him to have much stuff." When told of Johnson's comments, Hershiser replied to tell Johnson to grab a bat. Once again, there is a fine line between confidence, arrogance, and outright stupidity.

Hershiser struggled in the first inning, giving up a single and a walk, but got through unscathed. In the bottom of the inning, Gibson, who should not have been playing, put the Dodgers on the board with a sacrifice fly. Later in the game, he injured a ligament in his right knee—he was effectively playing with two bad legs. Nevertheless, the game was effectively over after the bottom of the second as the Dodgers piled on five runs to knock Mets starter Ron Darling out of the game. It was death by papercut: the Dodgers had four singles in the innings—two intentional walks—and the Mets committed two errors. As for Hershiser, he only pitched a complete-game shutout, as the Dodgers defeated the Mets, 6–0, to advance to the World Series. Not surprisingly, Hershiser was named NLCS MVP. In 2015, Hershiser reminisced about the game and the series to MLB.com:

> We got a little more fire because Davey Johnson then joined the media parade as far as ripping on us. . . . It was just so much fun to compete at the highest level on the biggest stage [in] really a David and Goliath situation, with the Mets as talented as they were and as much as they had beaten us. And to make it to Game Seven and to have that responsibility is the utmost thing you want to do as a competitor. You go out in the driveway as a little boy and you compete with your brothers or your neighborhood kids and you make these scenarios up.

The Mets vs. Dodgers may well have been a David and Goliath situation, but it paled into comparison to what was expected in the World Series. The Dodgers were set to face the A's, who had gone 104–58, won the AL West by 13 games, and had the best record in the majors. They swept the Red Sox in the ALCS and were waiting patiently for their opponent.

While the Dodgers arguably had a slightly better pitching staff, the A's hitters were, as a collective whole, a lot more potent. The A's were led by AL MVP Jose Canseco, who hit 42 home runs, had 124 RBIs, and had a slugging percentage of .569 for the season. Moreover, the Series was personal for a number of players, as

Tim Belcher, Mike Davis, Alfredo Griffin, and Jay Howell used to play for the Athletics, while Rick Honeycutt, Dave Stewart, Bob Welch, and Matt Young were former Dodgers.

What made it even more personal was the A's designated hitter, Don Baylor. Baylor, along with Stewart, stated that they wanted to play the Mets in the World Series because the Mets were the best team in the NL. There is nothing wrong with a person making such a claim, but Baylor crossed the line into outright stupidity as he ripped Howell. Saying he was tired of being diplomatic, Baylor said Howell

> couldn't save games over here [in Oakland], so they got rid of him. . . . We want him in the game, all right. He was right where he wanted to be in Games 4 and 5 in New York. He didn't want to be pitching with all those people screaming at him. He can't handle that. He couldn't handle it when he was in New York with the Yankees. I know; I played with him.[15]

A's manager Tony La Russa was not happy with Baylor speaking to the press. "To me, if anybody speaks for the club, it's the manager and not the players. And to me, speaking for the Oakland A's, our strategy—knowing how good Jay Howell is—is that we're going to try to keep him out of the game."

Nevertheless, if the Dodgers needed ammunition, Baylor provided it. Nobody expected the Dodgers to beat the Mets, the opposing team seemingly wanted to play the Mets, the A's players were disrespecting Dodger players, and the Dodgers would seemingly have to win without Gibson, as he could barely walk, let alone run.

---

15 The two played together in 1983 and 1984, as members of the New York Yankees.

It may have been David and Goliath once again, but the Dodgers were ready as ever to shock the world. Taking the mound for the Dodgers in Game One was Belcher, and opposing him was Stewart, who had been traded by the Dodgers to the Rangers and ended up in Oakland after a less-than-successful stint in Philadelphia. In Oakland, Stewart lived up to his promise, finishing third in the Cy Young in 1987 and fourth in 1988. But Game One started out well for the Dodgers, as Mickey Hatcher, who was having an average postseason, on an 0-1 count hit a fastball right down the middle to deep left field for a two-run home run. For those expecting Oakland to dominate, "order" was restored in the top of the second as Canseco destroyed a fastball from Belcher and deposited it into deep center field for a grand slam, the first of Canseco's career. Tim Leary replaced Belcher in the third and pitched three innings of scoreless ball. Indeed, the Athletics did not score another run for the game. In fact, they were shooting themselves in the foot, as they were only 1-for-11 with runners in scoring position. Unfortunately, while the Dodgers got one back in the sixth, thanks to an RBI single from Scioscia, they trailed 4–3 going into the bottom of the ninth. The Athletics called on Dennis Eckersley to replace Stewart. Eckersley had a stellar season, leading the AL in saves and finishing fifth in MVP voting and second in the Cy Young. He easily retired the first two Dodgers before issuing a walk to Mike Davis.

Lasorda then brought in Kirk Gibson as a pinch hitter. Gibson hobbled to the plate. Indeed, he should not have been out there, as he almost fell down swinging the bat. The only reason why he was hitting is because calling the game for a national audience was Vin Scully, who had said that Gibson would not be playing. This pissed off Gibson. As such, he started hitting balls off a tee and willed himself to pinch hit if needed, even though he could hardly stand. On a 2-2 count, Davis stole second. The count was now full. Scully told the viewing audience, "The tying run is on second base with two out. Now the Dodgers don't need the muscle of Gibson as much as a base hit." Now whether Gibson could even run to first was debatable. In the scouting report before the game, the Dodgers were told that in a 3-2 count Eckersley will throw a backdoor slider. And Eckersley did throw a backdoor slider. The result? As Scully so majestically put it, "High fly ball into right field, she is gone!" Scully, unlike a lot of commentators, knows when to stay silent and did not say another word for over a minute. He then said, "In a year that has been so improbable, the impossible has happened." Scully was silent once again before exclaiming, "And now the only question was, could he make it around the basepaths unassisted." Gibson made it around the basepaths, pumping his arm—an unforgettable moment for any Dodger fan. That would be Gibson's last plate appearance for the Series. Reflecting on the home run in 2016, Gibson claimed that "It was pretty quick. There's really no explanation. That's an ugly swing, against Dennis, who was dominant and a great competitor. I've watched it a few times. . . . In all honesty, Mike Davis stole second base, I was just trying to get a little blooper over the short-stop's head, and it went the other way. But it was a good result."

While the Dodgers were only up one game, the Gibson home run shell-shocked the Athletics. It was the defining moment in the World Series. Maybe if there was a rest day before Game Two the Athletics could have recovered, but there was not. Less than twenty-four hours later, the Athletics had to face a domi-nant Hershiser, who was pitching on what was becoming his accustomed three days' rest.

In the bottom of the third with one out, Hershiser and then Steve Sax reached on singles. Franklin Stubbs then followed with his own single to load the bases. In continuing with the trend, Mickey Hatcher followed with another single, cashing in Hershiser. This was followed by yet *another* single, this time from Mickey Hatcher, to drive in Sax. Then Mike Marshall stepped up to the plate. Now, while he did not hit a single, he did a bit better by launching a three-run home run to blow the game wide open. That was all the runs Hershiser needed as he pitched a complete-game shutout, giving up three hits and two walks while striking out eight to lead the team to a 6–0 win. To cap off Hershiser's day, he went 3-for-4 at the plate and drove in a run in the sixth. It was a memorable performance. Despite the Dodgers' dominance, the A's were still confident. Following the game, A's left fielder Dave Parker told the media, "Nobody believed it was going to be easy. . . . I haven't seen anything exceptional from the Dodgers. . . . We're still going to win. We're going to win the World Series. We're going to get back to Oakland and kick their *bleep*." And to cap it off, when asked who he thought was the best pitcher in the majors, Parker, while admitting that Hershiser pitched a complete game, replied, "If you want to know who I think is the best pitcher, it's [Houston's] Mike Scott." That was just pouring fuel on a raging inferno. However, the Athletics came back to win Game Three in Oakland. With the scores tied at one apiece in the bottom of the ninth, Mark McGwire hit a pitch from Howell out of the park to give the Athletics a 2–1 walk-off victory. It was rapidly turning into a postseason to forget for Howell. Redemption, though, was on its way.

In the Game Four pregame show, NBC commentator Bob Costas gave the Dodgers even *more* ammunition. As Lasorda recounted,

> We're in the clubhouse watching the pregame show on TV, and Costas comes on and says the Dodgers will be the worst team ever put on the field to play in a World Series game. . . . My players went wild. They started screaming and yelling. They were yelling, "Kill Costas. Kill Costas." He got our players fired up to show everyone they can play, they can win, no matter who we put out there. My guys were ready.

Game Four was a rematch of the Game One starters, Belcher for the Dodgers and Stewart for the Athletics. And as in Game One, the Dodgers scored two runs in the first inning, this time due to a passed ball allowing Sax to score and a groundout from Shelby. In the bottom of the inning, Canseco got a run back for the A's on a sacrifice groundout. Shoddy defense allowed the Dodgers to score in the third due to an error, which allowed Stubbs to score. The Dodgers, however, were the walking wounded. Apart from Gibson, Marshall, and pitcher John Tudor struggling with injuries, Scioscia injured his knee on a failed hit-and-run attempt in the fourth. He was replaced by Rick Dempsey behind the plate in the bottom of the inning. With the score 3–1 favoring the Dodgers, the Athletics got one back in the bottom of the sixth. A groundout by Tracy Woodson restored the Dodgers' two-run lead in the seventh, but once again the Athletics got a run back in the bottom of the inning. This led to Lasorda replacing Belcher with Howell. The Oakland crowd was ecstatic, sardonically cheering Howell. After walking Canseco, Parker hit a liner to

Griffin who somehow dropped the ball. The bases were loaded, with two outs and McGwire at the plate. Howell was staring down the barrel of infamy. He threw a fastball down the middle of the plate, but it had enough movement to jam McGwire. He popped it up, and the threat was over. Howell would go on to pitch the eighth and ninth innings. With two outs in the bottom of the ninth and a runner on the first with the Athletics trailing by one run, Howell faced Parker. Undoubtedly, Parker's comments about his abilities and resolve were in the back of Howell's mind. Parker swung at the first pitch he saw and hit a foul pop fly down the third base line where it was caught by Jeff Hamilton. Howell achieved redemption; he recorded the last seven outs to record a save and put the Dodgers on the verge of World Series triumph.

Following the game, Howell said, "People are going to say a lot of things, but I don't feel it's very healthy or productive to say things back, particularly if you know that those things are wrong. . . . Why fuel fire? Why dwell on negatives?" Howell noted that following the loss in the previous game, "A lot of guys on the team came over to me and told me not to worry about it. . . . Kirk Gibson came over and told me that I had been doing it all year for them and that I was the man and that I shouldn't even think about it. I know I believe all that, but it's nice to hear."

What was also nice to hear was that Hershiser would be starting Game Five. And what was even better is that, once again, the Dodgers scored two runs in the first inning, this time via a two-run home run from Hatcher. The Athletics cut the margin to one after the third, but, once again, the Dodgers rallied, scoring two runs in the top of the fourth, thanks to a two-run home run by Mike Davis. Davis had an awful year for the Dodgers and was largely considered a free agent bust, but on the biggest stage he came through and, like Howell, redeemed himself. That was more than enough for Hershiser. While he was not at his peak, he only gave up two runs on four hits and four walks while striking out nine as the Dodgers won Game Five, 6–2. The Los Angeles Dodgers were once again World Series champions. No one—not even some Dodger players—could believe it. "It wasn't supposed to happen," Howell said. "People weren't supposed to write this. I think we are as overwhelmed as anyone by this. We didn't think we'd beat the [New York] Mets in the playoffs, and we weren't sure about the A's."

Lasorda claimed, "This is, without a doubt, the greatest accomplishment of a team who didn't have the greatest talent. This was greater, for me, than 1981. Because we didn't have that talent, but we had guys who wanted to play and who had that desire. I've said it all along, this is a team of destiny." Lasorda may well have been right. Hershiser and Gibson were superstars, but it was the so-called lesser lights that shone—maybe none more so than Hatcher. In twelve years in the majors, Hatcher had only hit 38 home runs. During the 1988 regular season he only hit *one*. Yet in the World Series, he hit two and led the Dodgers with a .368 batting average. As Gibson said about Hatcher, he "exemplifies what this team is all about. . . . This team has always believed in itself. I got hurt, and the team accepted that I would be out. And Mickey steps in and fills my role and I filled his. We had a team approach that kept us together." Likewise, Davis only had one hit in seven at-bats in the World Series, although he did walk four times. The hit was a two-run home run in the deciding game. The 1988 Dodgers, just like the 1959 Dodgers, may not have been the best team in the majors, but they *were* World Series champions.

* * *

Of course, it is unlikely for lighting to strike twice or any other cliché one wants to use, but the 1989 Dodgers were a shell of the 1988 team. The front office tried to improve the team signing thirty-four-year-old Willie Randolph and thirty-three year old and future member of the Hall of Fame Eddie Murray. The team learned that signing free agents can work out great, as was the case with Gibson. However, generally, signing free agents already well into their thirties is a big risk and can also be a colossal waste of money. Neither Murray nor Randolph would have good years. Moreover, Steve Sax departed to the Yankees via free agency, Fernando Valenzuela never recaptured his previous magic, John Tudor missed most of the year through injury, and Kirk Gibson only played in 71 games. Overall, the offense, which was not that good in 1988, was even worse in 1989, ranked dead last in the NL. Of course, the pitching staff had another great year. Apart from wins, the staff was ranked best in the NL, along with the lowest ERA in the majors. Belcher led the NL in complete games and shutouts, and Howell saved 28 games and was voted an All-Star.

As for Hershiser, prior to the season he signed a three-year $7.9 million deal to stay with the Dodgers. At a news conference to announce the deal, Hershiser said, "Deep down, this is what I wanted. . . . Now I can concentrate on baseball. I won't have to worry about free agency." And he had a fine year; his ERA was only .05 higher than in 1988, and he had 15 wins (compared to 23 in 1988). He also led the NL in losses with 15 (eight in 1988). Despite pitching well, he won his 14th game on August 8 and did not win again until October 1.[16] To get the win on the final day of the season, Hershiser threw 161 pitches in 11 innings, as he finally won 3–1 against the Braves in Atlanta in front of an announced crowd of 4,840. Dodgers GM Claire told the *New York Times*, "We've had outstanding pitching, but we've struggled offensively. . . . Orel has been the highlight—or lowlight—of that."

Indeed, despite being a better side than the 1988 team on paper, the 1989 team contended until the end of May but began to steadily slip in the standings. A particular lowlight stands out: On June 2, the Dodgers lost to the Astros, 5–4. The score was tied after six innings and neither team could score for the next 15 innings. The Dodgers used nine pitchers—including Hershiser, who pitched seven innings in relief. In the bottom of the 21st inning, Lasorda turned to third baseman Jeff Hamilton. The Dodgers escaped the inning unscathed, with Hamilton striking out Billy Hatcher looking. In the bottom of the 22nd inning, Lasorda had a choice of Hamilton or Valenzuela, with the latter having pitched the previous day. Lasorda stuck with Hamilton. And with two outs in the bottom of the inning, Hamilton gave up the winning run. While the Dodger players were not happy with the result, they were happy the game was over. The same could be said for the season.

The Dodgers finished with a losing record, going 77–83, "good" enough for fourth place, 14 games behind the Giants.

---

16 Thus showing why pitching wins and losses are often a meaningless statistic when determining how well a player pitched.

If there was any solace for Dodger fans it is that the Athletics swept the Giants in the World Series.

Thus, while the 1980s did not end on the best note, two World Series titles made the decade one to remember. Unfortunately, the Dodgers have yet to recapture those heights or even do as well as the 1970s. The 1990s, as they would find out, would be a particular low time for the mighty franchise.

# 6

# 1990S: PLAYER CHANGES, OWNERSHIP CHANGE, AND BEWILDERMENT

IN 1990, THE Dodgers celebrated their 100th anniversary—first with Brooklyn and then Los Angeles, playing in the National League. For almost their entire existence, the Dodgers were a conservative franchise, relying on the players they had in their system. Yet the success of free agent Kirk Gibson, who helped win the Dodgers a World Series, led O'Malley and Claire to chase the proverbial dragon. If the current crop of players were not good enough to win a divisional title, let alone a World Series, a new crop of players was the answer. Such an approach would doom the Dodgers for most of the decade. A conservative approach may well have been outdated by the 1990s, but a winner-take-all mentality every year was certainly not the answer.

# 1990–94: ALSO-RANS, A COLLAPSE, AND UNWELCOME HISTORY

In a prelude for what was to come, the owners locked the players out during Spring Training, as the two sides could not reach a new agreement to replace the expiring 1985 Collective Bargaining Agreement. The owners were attempting to limit the amount players could earn and impose a salary cap. Eventually, after 32 days the lockout was lifted, and a new contract was signed. It was similar in scope to the 1985 agreement, but the players won back some concessions they agreed to in the previous contract. The contract was a victory for the MLBPA and the players. However, the owners had enough of the MLBPA getting the best of them. As such, the 1994–95 industrial dispute was inevitable.

As for the Dodgers, they were searching for a winning lineup. They traded for Juan Samuel from the Mets, and in return sent Mike Marshall and Alejandro Peña to Queens. LA signed free agent Hubie Brooks to play the outfield, and after trading for starting pitcher Mike Morgan and left fielder Kal Daniels (in part for Tim Leary) during the 1989 season, the lineup looked the strongest it had in a number of years. Morgan and Samuel had decent seasons, Brooks played as well as expected, while Daniels and Murray were the standouts on a much-improved offense.

Yet while the Dodgers were in contention for parts of the season and played well in July and August, the reality is that they were always unlikely to make the postseason. Injuries, once again, cost them dearly. Kirk Gibson was limited to 89 games and had one of the worst seasons of his career. The season-killer was that Orel Hershiser only played in four games before succumbing to a season-ending shoulder injury. The Dodgers finished with a record of 86–76, five games behind the NL West champion Cincinnati Reds.

There were, of course, individual highlights. Ramon Martinez, who began his career with the Dodgers in 1988, went 20–6 with an ERA of 2.92 while leading the NL with 12 complete games. He was an All-Star and finished second in the Cy Young voting behind Pittsburgh's Doug Drabek. And on June 4 against the Braves at Dodger Stadium, Martinez pitched a complete-game shutout. He only allowed three hits and a walk, while striking out an astonishing 18 Braves. The only inning where Martinez did not record a strikeout was in the ninth. The 18 strikeouts was a record jointly held by Sandy Koufax, who did it on two occasions. Martinez told the *Los Angeles Times*, "Tonight in the bullpen before the game, I feel it. I have everything. Fastball, changeup, everything. I feel relaxed and I just go throw. That's all I do is throw."

One Dodger who did not have a good season was Fernando Valenzuela. He had the dubious distinction of leading the NL in earned runs, and his ERA for the season (4.59) was easily the worst of his career up to that point. Quite simply, Valenzuela was not the same pitcher he once was. Overuse had obviously destroyed his pitching arm. However, on June 29, in a magical performance, Valenzuela turned back the clock and pitched a complete-game shutout, as the Dodgers defeated the Cardinals, 6–0. Valenzuela struck out seven, issued three walks, and did not allow a hit. In the bottom of the ninth, with one out and a runner on first, Valenzuela induced former Dodger Pedro Guerrero into a game-ending double play to secure the no-hitter. The game was one of beauty. What made it even more special was that former Dodger Dave Stewart threw a no-hitter earlier that day (the first time there were two no-hitters on the same day), and Valenzuela's effort was the first no-hitter ever thrown in the major leagues by a Mexican player. Reflecting on his performance in 2015 to ESPN Deportes, Valenzuela noted,

> I think it is something very special, because these kind of games don't come around very often. June 29, 1990, was my chance to throw a no-hitter, and I think that leaves great memories because it wasn't just my achievement, it was the whole teams'. Because to throw a no-hitter, you need support from the offense, you need them to make runs. You also need to play well on defense. There were several plays where the team helped to prevent a hit and keep the game on track toward a no-hitter. I think everything came together with the team, my teammates rose to the occasion and we finally did it. It's a nice memory, as the chance to be involved in those kind of games isn't something that happens every day.

It was arguably Valenzuela's last fond memory in a Dodger uniform.

\* \* \*

With only a few days remaining during Spring Training in 1991, the Dodgers put Fernando Valenzuela on waivers. After no team claimed him, Valenzuela became a free agent. Valenzuela had not performed well during Spring Training—his ERA was 7.88. In isolation, Spring Training numbers are often meaningless, but Valenzuela had been struggling for a long time. In his last six starts of the 1990 season, he posted an ERA of 8.40. Despite all of this, the timing of the release left a lot to be desired and seemed to be more of a cost-cutting exercise. Because it was so late in Spring Training, almost all teams had already settled on their rosters. Moreover, Valenzuela noted,

> I think they already decided before this spring that I would not be on the team. . . . They told me after last season that I was not in the Dodger plans, then later they said, 'No, don't take that in the wrong way; we are just trying to make some decisions.' Then in the end, they changed their mind and decided to sign me. I'm not sure why.

Valenzuela mused that perhaps the only reason why he was kept around was to play an exhibition game with the Dodgers in Monterrey, Mexico, during Spring Training. Once that occurred, he was no longer needed. Peter O'Malley vehemently denied that this was the case: "That Mexican trip was not in cement until well after we had offered Fernando a contract. His signing had nothing to do with that." Whatever the reason, it was a sad end to Valenzuela's time with the Dodgers.

As with Valenzuela, another Los Angeles legend was moving on; after three injury-plagued seasons, Kirk Gibson left to join the Royals. Gibson only had one good season with the Dodgers, but what a season it was. He was worth his contract and then some. The 1988 World Series victory would have never happened without Gibson.

As Valenzuela's and Gibson's time with the Dodgers was ending, another player's career with Los Angeles was beginning. In November 1990, the Dodgers signed superstar free agent Darryl Strawberry. Baseball wise, it was a great move. Strawberry was a former Rookie of the Year, two-time Silver Slugger, two-time top-three finisher in MVP voting, seven-time All-Star, and not even twenty-nine when he signed with the Dodgers. At a press conference to announce the signing, Lasorda said, "I'd compare it to Bruce McNall's signing of Wayne Gretzky for the [Los Angeles] Kings. Darryl Strawberry is one of the outstanding players in baseball, and his willingness to play center field shows you what kind of person he is." Strawberry, who grew up in Los Angeles, stated, "I didn't want to fly all over the country and get in a bidding war. I wanted to be with a winner, which the Dodgers have always been. I wanted to come home." The Dodgers signed Strawberry to a five-year contract although, prophetically, Claire said they would have preferred a shorter duration.

While Strawberry was great on the field, off the field was another matter. Strawberry had battled alcohol addiction, including entering rehab, and was previously arrested for domestic violence against his wife. Further, stories of drug abuse circulated. And the Mets manager and GM were happy to see Strawberry go.

With a slow start to the season, it seemed Strawberry would be another free agent bust. However, by the middle of July, Strawberry started to hit and eventually had a very fine year. Somewhat surprisingly, even though he struggled and Hershiser did not come back from his shoulder injury until the end of May, the Dodgers played solid baseball. They were in contention for the first two months, and, at the time, Strawberry started to hit, and the team had a 5-game lead in the division. Indeed, at the All-Star break, the Dodgers were the best team in baseball—at least their record was. They were good, but not that good. But they ended up having a lackluster July, going .500, and played even worse in August, before going 20–8 in September.

There was just one problem: the Atlanta Braves did not just catch fire, they went nuclear. In their last 76 games of the season, the Braces won 55. Despite this, the Dodgers still led the Division by one game heading into October.

On October 1, the Dodgers defeated the Padres, 3–1, to retain their one-game lead—and then things fell apart. The following day, the Braves beat the Reds, and the Dodgers lost, evening the teams at the top of the division. The Dodgers headed to San Francisco for a three-game series against the Giants to close out the season, while the Braves played the Astros in Atlanta. The teams both won their series openers, but while the Braves won the second game, the Dodgers went meekly, losing 4–0, and ended any chance of a postseason berth. It was a disappointing end to the season. Following the game, Lasorda told the *Los Angeles Times*, "It's like walking down the street and finding $1,000 in an envelope. . . . You keep walking and walking, you go about 15 blocks, then when you get to your doorstep, somebody taps you on the shoulder. 'Buddy,' he says, 'you've got my money.'" As poetic as that response was, the best one was from the Giants' Will Clark; he asked, "Do I feel sorry for the Dodgers? . . . Ha, ha, ha, ha, ha, ha, ha . . ." Such a laugh was apropos for what was coming.

In November, Strawberry went on record stating that the Dodgers should trade outfielder Kal Daniels. He claimed, "I don't want to deal with what we dealt with last year, a guy like Kal, a player who doesn't want to play. . . . Trade Kal. If he doesn't want to play, get him out of here. And you can quote me on that." He went on to state that "somebody has to finally say something about him, and I'll be the guy. . . . I'm talking about us needing somebody who is determined to play with injuries, somebody who won't get kicked out of a game in the first inning in the pennant race, somebody who always wants to be in there. . . . When it comes to winning, you can't have players who do some of the stuff that Kal did. Others agree with me. Of course they do."

While Daniels did have an average year, and was on the decline, he did appear in 137 games. Whether Strawberry was indeed talking for the rest of the team is debatable, but what was beyond debate is that Strawberry was hoping that the Dodgers would sign his high school teammate Eric Davis who would, in effect, replace for Daniels. When he was on the field, Davis was a fine player, but was also injury prone. Still, on December 1, the Dodgers traded for Davis as part of a four-player deal that sent Tim Belcher to Cincinnati. Strawberry and Davis were ecstatic. But there were other changes in store.

Looking for that winning lineup, the front office sought additional change. Alfredo Griffin, Eddie Murray, and Juan Samuel were let go. Eric Karros was earmarked to take over at first for the departing Murray. He had a solid rookie season, earning NL Rookie of the Year honors. Lenny Harris moved from third to second, with Dave Hansen taking over at third. Neither of them had good years with the bat. And to replace the departed Griffin, twenty-three-year-old José Offerman took over at short. Offerman had a much better year with the bat compared to how Griffin performed in the previous season. In the field, however, was another matter. While Griffin was a good defensive shortstop, Offerman was prone to mental lapses. In the 1992 season he made a whopping 42 errors. Indeed, Lasorda thought Offerman was not a good shortstop, yet his bat kept him in the lineup. It is likely that the front office told Lasorda to play Offerman.

Bill James claims that "there is reason to believe that Lasorda, left to his own devices, would never have played Offerman at short or Guerrero at third. The Dodgers sometimes make those decisions in the front office and tell the manager to live with them."

The 1992 Dodgers simply could not hit, field, or even pitch. Orel Hershiser played a full season, but was declining from his peak, and Ramon Martinez had a down year. Kevin Gross, who was signed in 1991, and Tom Candiotti, who was signed in the offseason, had decent years but were let down by the offense and defense. Of course a down year for the Dodger pitching staff meant they were more middle-of-the-road. A down year for the Dodger offense meant they were near dead last in almost all offensive categories.

As for the Strawberry-Daniels feud, the two coexisted for part of the season until the latter was traded to the Cubs for Mike Sodders.[17] Due to injuries, Davis only appeared in 76 games and posted career-worst in almost all offensive categories. And to cap it off, Strawberry was also injured for most of the year, appearing in just 43 games. He posted career-worst in *all* offensive categories. Off the field, he was still battling drug and alcohol abuse.

It was certainly a season to forget. The Dodgers finished the season with a 63–99 record, a mammoth 35 games out of first, and finished in dead last. Attendance declined dramatically, and their record was the worst in 87 years, when the 1905 Brooklyn Superbas went 48–104. In other words, it was the worst season ever, whether in Brooklyn or Los Angeles, for a team known as the Dodgers.

---

17  Sodders never played in the big leagues.

With all that said, there was still a highlight to the season. On August 17 at Dodger Stadium, Kevin Gross walked two, hit a batter, struck out six, and did not allow a hit, as he no-hit the Giants. It was the first no-hitter of the year. When he recorded the final out, Gross had tears in his eyes. "It makes up for a not-so-good year for the Dodgers and myself," Gross said. "It brought tears to my eyes, no doubt about it." It is understandable that Gross, who was never a star in his fifteen years in the majors, would be overcome with emotion. Such events are indeed rare, but the reality is that the no-hitter did not redeem the 1992 Dodgers.

It's not surprising, considering the horrid 1992 season, that the front office made changes for the upcoming season. Infielder Jody Reed was signed from the Red Sox to play second, and Tim Wallach, formerly of the Expos, was slotted into third. Offerman was still the starting shortstop and had a similar year with the bat, as well as a slightly better year in the field; while he committed 37 errors, he was more sure-handed. With Strawberry restricted to only 32 games due to injury, former Giant Cory Snyder became the everyday right fielder. And while Davis had a better year than his less-than-stellar 1992 campaign, the Dodgers traded him to the Tigers midyear for pitcher John DeSilva. DeSilva appeared in three games for the Dodgers in his one and only season in Los Angeles.

Overall, LA had a much better season than the previous year, although that was not hard to do. They went 81–81 and finished in fourth place in the NL West, 23 games behind the Braves. The Dodgers once again were near last in the NL in hitting, but their pitching was back to its usual standards.

The lowlight for the season was Strawberry. While struggling on the field, his life off the field was spiraling out of control. In

November, as fires were raging out of control in the Los Angeles hills, he said in a radio interview, "Let it burn. I don't live there anymore. Let it all burn down." Now while it was a bad joke, for the people affected by the fires it was no laughing matter. If that was the only controversy, such a "joke" could be forgotten. However, in September he was arrested for domestic violence after allegedly assaulting his girlfriend. As is usually the case in domestic-violence incidents, the alleged victim declined to press charges. Strawberry also noted that during the season he had contemplated suicide. He told the media,

> I thought, *What would it be like if I wasn't around anymore?* There wouldn't be any problems if I wasn't around. Then people wouldn't have anything else to say. I had been stressed out and in deep depression all year. The one thing I didn't want to have to do this season is go through everything again after going through it in '92. And that's what happened. It was a living nightmare.

Quite simply, Strawberry was a very troubled individual and needed help. Unfortunately for Strawberry, things would get worse the following season.

On the final Spring Training game before the start of the 1993 regular season, Strawberry failed to show because he went on an alcohol and drug bender. Strawberry called Dodgers GM Fred Claire that night to apologize. The following day he admitted to Claire that he had a substance-abuse problem. The Dodgers placed Strawberry on the disabled list and publicly announced his problem, with Strawberry checking himself to the Betty Ford Center in an attempt to get clean. Rather than have sympathy for what Strawberry was going through, Lasorda lashed out. On Opening Day he told the assembled press hungry for a quote,

First of all. . . . It's against the law. No. 2, it's harmful to your body. No. 3, all it will do is lead you down the path of destruction. How anybody could be dumb enough or weak enough to take [drugs] is something I cannot comprehend. I mean, it's crazy. There's a guy that is making a lot of money, he's got a lot of fame, he's got a family, and yet he puts something inside him knowingly, knowing that this thing can ruin his career, that it could ruin his entire life. To have the weakness to put it into his body is something I just don't understand. This is not a disease, like leukemia or cancer. It's a weakness.

Lasorda's response was similar in scope when Steve Howe was battling addiction. While Lasorda has always been antidrugs, it would have been much better for all concerned if he had simply wished Strawberry the best. There was a backlash against Lasorda for his comments, although to this day Lasorda claimed the public sided with him. Strawberry completed his rehab in early May. Claire stated that he called Strawberry during the rehab stint, but the staff "wouldn't put my calls through, but I left messages." As for Lasorda, he said he would have called, but incredibly, claimed "he did not know where Strawberry was." After completing rehab, Strawberry did not immediately rejoin the team. On May 24, the Dodgers released Strawberry. Strawberry eventually joined the Giants for the 1994 season before finishing his injury-ravaged career with the Yankees following the 1999 season. Strawberry is now an evangelical born-again Christian.

There was another lowlight in the 1993 season, although this one was the Dodgers' own doing. Ramon Martinez's younger brother, Pedro, who appeared in two games the previous season, got a greater opportunity in 1993 primarily appearing as a relief pitcher. He appeared in 65 games and finished ninth in Rookie of the Year balloting. However, Lasorda never had faith in Pedro because of his light build and height (5-foot-10). Lasorda also thought that Martinez would never be a front-line starter; he belonged in the bullpen. So when the Dodgers needed a second baseman after Reed signed with the Brewers as a free agent, they traded Pedro Martinez to the Expos for Delino DeShields. DeShields was an adequate second baseman and had an average three years in Los Angeles. The Expos would put Martinez into their starting rotation, and the rest is history. Martinez became one of the best pitchers of all time, and is rightfully a member of the Baseball Hall of Fame.

The trade of Martinez for DeShields is one of, if not the, worst trades in Dodger history. Writing in the *Los Angeles Times* in 2008, Ross Newhan noted that the Dodgers had traded away so many promising pitchers for limited returns: "The one Dodgers constant in each [ill-advised trade] was Manager Tom Lasorda, who has never been shy about offering an opinion and who often said that the Dodgers couldn't afford to operate a developmental camp in the major market that is Los Angeles." Another of the worst trades in Dodger history also involved a rookie on the 1992 team, although this one was not Lasorda's fault and was a few years away.

Lasorda was close friends, and a distant cousin, with Vince Piazza who lived in Pennsylvania. They were so close that Vince Piazza and his son Mike were allowed into the clubhouse after the Dodgers clinched the 1977 NLCS. Mike Piazza was the Dodgers bat boy when the Dodgers played in Philadelphia. Piazza was also becoming a decent ballplayer in high school. Nevertheless, he was not drafted. As such, Lasorda called in a favor and Mike Piazza spent a season sitting on the bench at the University of Miami. The following year he played for a community college as a first baseman. Following a suggestion and encouragement from Lasorda, Piazza made the transition to catcher. Still, his draft prospects were nonexistent. But as a favor to Lasorda, the Dodgers selected Piazza in the 62nd round, 1,390th overall. Then something miraculous happened: Piazza slowly but surely began to work his way up the minor-league ranks. And in 1992 he made his major-league debut for the Dodgers, appearing in 21 games. With Scioscia retiring at the end of the 1992 season, Piazza became the Dodgers everyday catcher in 1993. In addition to being more than competent behind the plate, Piazza was an offensive juggernaut. He finished with 35 home runs, 112 RBIs, and had an OPS of .932; the next best everyday player was Brett Butler: his OPS was .758. Piazza was an All-Star, finished ninth in MVP voting, won the Silver Slugger Award, and was named the NL Rookie of the Year. A favor to Lasorda ended up unearthing a future member of the Hall of Fame.

And 1994 was shaping up to be another great year for Piazza, as well as an improved year for the Dodgers. Piazza was ably supported from Butler, Tim Wallach, and rookie right fielder Raul Mondesi. Mondesi, who appeared in 42 games in 1992, was having a great season and was eventually rewarded with Rookie of the Year honors. On Thursday August 11, the Dodgers had a record of 58–56 to lead a mediocre NL West by 3½ games. The Dodgers benefited greatly when MLB decided to introduce a Central Division in both the AL and NL. The NL West only had four teams: the Dodgers, Giants, Padres, and Rockies. Both the NL East and NL Central had five teams. Then greed got in the way—not greed from the players, but from the owners.

Even though the owners opted out of the previous Collective Bargaining Agreement in December 1992, they did not present a new proposal to the MLBPA until July 1994. The owners wanted a seven-year contract, with the players receiving a maximum 50 percent of revenue; the elimination of salary arbitration; and a salary cap. The MLBPA estimated that the proposal would mean a reduction of player salaries of at least $1.5 billion over the life of the contract. Quite simply, the MLBPA had no choice but to reject the proposal. While the owners derided the amount of money the players were receiving, they happily shelled out the money when it suited them, such as new San Francisco owner Robert Lurie signing Barry Bonds to a then-record six-year $43 million contract. The owners and the players could not reach a compromise, and thus the longest strike in major-league history began. The strike continued into September, and, on the 14th of that month, Commissioner Bud Selig canceled the 1994 season. Both the players and, for the first time, the owners were unified, as such prolonging the conflict.

## 1995–96: SCABS, PLAYOFF BASEBALL, AND A CHANGING OF THE GUARD

The owners and MLB were willing to play the 1995 season with replacement players. This is how Spring Training began, but the Baltimore Orioles refused to do so. For the Orioles, this was partly due to the team wanting Carl Ripken Jr. to break the consecutive-games-played record. Likewise, coaches in some other teams, including the Detroit Tigers and Toronto Blue

Jays, refused to work with replacement players. The Dodgers, however, had no qualms about using replacement players.

The strike was eventually called off following a National Labor Relations Board ruling in favor of the players and a judicial ruling. A contract was signed in November 1996, over two years after the strike first began. Minimum salary increased by $41,000 to $150,000, and in a further win for the players there were no changes to salary arbitration and free agency. Even though it took until November 1996 for a new contract to be approved by both parties, baseball resumed under the terms of the previous Collective Bargaining Agreement. On April 25, 1995, the first regular-season games occurred since the strike.

And for the most part, the fans blamed the players for the abandonment of the 1994 season. For a substantial minority or even a majority of the fans, the players are interchangeable. All that matters is the team; nothing is more important than the team. They have a similar view as the organization. For the Dodger ownership and front office, the players *must* conform to what the team wants and they must be loyal, but the team does not have to be loyal to the players. Thus, when a player begins to decline, such as was the case with Valenzuela, he is simply let go or traded. Before the start of the 1995 season, the same thing happened with Hershiser. The Dodgers informed Hershiser in January that he would not be offered a new contract. His best years were indeed behind him, and the front office believed the pitcher was no longer worthy of a roster spot. Hershiser understood the decision but noted to the *New York Times*, "I think if the day comes when I don't go to spring training as a Dodger, it will be different to look down at my chest and not see that name. . . . I was born and raised a Dodger." In baseball, loyalty is not a two-way street.

However, in baseball, unlike in the NFL, NBA, and the NHL, the players are largely united. This is why their salaries have continued to rise. As such, unlike the other sports mentioned, there have been no crippling lockouts or strikes in recent years. If a player is disloyal, he is ostracized by his brethren. And in 1995, the replacement players who participated in Spring Training games were a target.

The Dodgers were having a good season; Piazza, Karros, and Mondesi were once again having fine years. And Ramon Martinez, rookie Ismael Valdéz, and closer Todd Worrell were the leading lights on the usual dominant pitching staff. Moreover, Hideo Nomo was signed from the Japanese league. An interesting fact is that no one in the Dodger organization had ever seen Nomo pitch in person; they only saw a short highlight reel. Nevertheless, Dodger GM Fred Claire stated that Nomo "has the type of ability that we believe is at a major-league level. . . . I think he has the ability to be a starting pitcher this year." Nomo was the first Japanese-born player to appear in the majors since Masanori Murakami, who played for the Giants in 1964 and 1965. As for Nomo, he did indeed have the ability he led the NL in strikeouts, was an All-Star, finished fourth in Cy Young voting, and won the Rookie of the Year. It was a magnificent first season for the Japanese pitcher.

Also magnificent was an occurrence that happened on July 14 at Dodger Stadium with Ramon Martinez on the mound. On his previous appearance at home, Martinez gave up eight runs on ten hits and two walks in 4⅔ innings. The Dodger faithful booed him as he walked off the mound. On July 14,

Dodger fans gave Martinez a standing ovation as he struck out eight, walked one, and did not give up a hit as he no-hit the Marlins on only 114 pitches. Martinez flirted with a perfect game, as the only blemish was a solitary walk after 7⅔ innings. Following the game, Martinez said, "I feel like a giant out there. . . . It was a great feeling. For many people, the guys, fans, and my family, I am very excited. It doesn't show, but that's the way I am."

In late August, an injury to Wallach put him on the shelf for a couple of weeks. Claire decided the best course of action was to call up a rookie from Triple-A, Mike Busch. Under normal circumstances there would be nothing wrong with such a decision. However, when the players were out on strike Busch played in Spring Training games. Mike Busch was a scab.

While it is claimed that MLBPA head Donald Fehr told players that it would be OK to play in Spring Training games that occurred in the mist of the strike, the reality is for every single player out on strike, replacement players were the lowest of the low. Thus, it was mind-boggling that Claire would call up a mediocre player like Busch, which was guaranteed to upset the rest of the Dodger players. The other players would not take the field with Busch during practice, kicked him out of the clubhouse, and were furious that he was even called up. As Butler said, "He's a scab, pure and simple . . . and there will be individuals who'll treat him as such. . . . Obviously, the players aren't happy with the decision that was made. There's a lot of pressure on everybody right now. Our focus is on trying to win a world championship, and distractions are not what we need right now." Indeed, following the announcement that Busch was called up, the Dodgers lost twice against the Mets.

Why did Claire do it? He claims that Busch was the best option, and his only obligation was to put out the best team. However, numerous players believed that Claire did it to show he was the boss, as the wounds of the strike were a long way from being healed. Whatever the reason, on August 30, Busch suited up for the Dodgers and pinch-hit. Even though he struck out on three pitches, he was cheered wildly by the fans before and after his at-bat. In contrast, Brett Butler, who was staunchly prounion, was booed by the Los Angeles fans. For these fans, and the ones who flooded the *Los Angeles Times* with pro-Busch letters, all they cared about was that there was baseball. They were blind to the fact that the player-owner struggles in professional sports mirrored the struggles many of them faced—or eventually would face—with their own employers. For these fans, they did not care at all about the players, they just cared that there was a team known as the Los Angeles Dodgers.

As the situation was spiraling out of control, the Dodgers held a press conference attended by Busch, Butler, and Karros. It was a sham of a press conference, as everyone could tell that the players were not happy with the current situation. But to their credit, they were professional about the situation and put winning above all else—even if it meant they had to play, practice, and share a clubhouse with Busch.

And the players were good enough to propel the Dodgers to a record of 78–66 and another NL West crown. But the reality was that while the Dodgers were a better side than the previous season, they were not *that* good. The team mainly took advantage of a weak NL West. Out of all the divisional winners, the Dodgers had the worst record. This was borne out in the playoffs, as the Braves handily defeated the wild-card-winning

Colorado Rockies three game to one in the other National League Divisional Series.[18]

As for the Dodgers, they were blown out by the Reds in Game One at Dodger Stadium, 7–2, and they lost Game Two, 5–4. The Reds completed the sweep in Game Three, destroying the Dodgers 10–1. It was a disappointing end to the season. There would be more of the same in 1996, albeit with some important changes.

* * *

The Dodgers were largely quiet in the offseason. The Offerman experiment at shortstop was deemed a failure, and he was traded to the Royals for Billy Brewer.[19] Offerman would have decent-to-good seasons with a number of teams before retiring following the 2005 season. Replacing Offerman would be thirty-four-year-old Greg Gagne. Gagne had an average season, albeit more defensively than with the bat. A plethora of Dodgers would play at third throughout the season, including thirty-one-year-old Mike Blowers, who was acquired from the Mariners for two prospects. As for the pitching staff, it remained virtually the same. The Dodger front office was, somewhat surprisingly, happy with what they had and sought to get average-to-good veteran players; one would assume big-name talent was seemingly off-limits due to the price of such players, even though Los Angeles was truly a major market. Indeed, attendance was once again on the way up after bottoming out during the disastrous 1992 season and

---

18 The Wild Card was introduced in 1994.

19 Brewer never played a game for Los Angeles and was traded midseason to the Yankees for Mike Judd. Judd would go on and appear in 16 games across four seasons for the Dodgers.

would be well over three million for the 1996 season. The Dodgers, as they had often done, would stand pat, with a few veterans and rookies thrown into the mix.

At least the front office had a knack of unearthing Rookie of the Year winners. In 1996, they did so again with outfielder Todd Hollandsworth. Hollandsworth, who appeared in 41 games the previous season, became the starting left fielder in 1996. He was a respectable player, the fourth-best offensive threat for the team behind Piazza, Mondesi, and Karros. Admittedly, Hollandsworth was not that great in the field, and arguably Edgar Rentería should have won the 1996 NL Rookie of the Year Award. Rentería had slightly weaker offensive numbers compared to Hollandsworth but was a much better defender.

The front office was also adept when it came to unearthing quality pitchers, Nomo being no exception. However, like most pitchers, Nomo did not have success at Coors Field. In his previous two starts at the ballpark his ERA was 11.18. But on September 17, on a rainy day at Coors Field in Denver, Nomo achieved something that was considered impossible. In a year when Coors Field broke the record for the most home runs allowed, Nomo allowed four walks, struck out eight, and did not give up a hit. Nomo pitched a no-hitter in the rarified air of Coors Field. The park, which opened in 1985, has yet to see another no-hitter through the 2019 season. It was simply a magnificent performance. On a side note, the largest crowd to witness a no-hitter was on that day in Denver; 50,066 saw history. It was the only no-hitter through 2019 to be viewed by more than fifty thousand people.

As for the season itself, as was seemingly customary, the offense was horrid—the worst in the NL. In contrast, the pitching was great—the best in the NL. The pitching was seemingly more than enough for the team, as with four games left in the season they led the NL West by 2½ games. A loss to the Giants and a win by the Padres cut the lead to two, with the two sides scheduled for a three-game series in Los Angeles to end the season—games that the Dodgers proceeded to lose, handing the NL West over to the Padres. They still made the playoffs as the wild-card winner, but it was not the best way to enter the postseason. Moreover, as wild-card winners the Dodgers had to face the best side in the NL: the Atlanta Braves. And history repeated itself, as they were once again swept (dropping seven games in a row, including regular and postseason). While they did not get blown out against the Padres and Braves, the already-dormant offense went into a full-fledged coma. And the pitching staff, no matter how good it was, could not be perfect. The Dodgers lost 2–1 (in 10 innings), 3–2, and 5–2 in the LDS. Thus, as in 1995, the season ended on a disappointing note. However, the 1996 season will be more remembered for what happened off the field.

* * *

While baseball can consume our lives, one must understand that the players, coaching staff, etc. are human; they have to deal with the same things that everybody may have to face. In that regard, two prominent Dodgers had major health scares during the 1996 season. Brett Butler, who had been with the Dodgers—apart from a brief stint with the Mets in 1995—since 1991, developed tonsil cancer that required surgery. He released a statement that read in part, "We have many friends in and out of baseball and this will come as a major shock. It is impossible to speak to all of them personally. My wife and I would ask for your prayers for us and our children at this difficult time. We're not sure where this road will lead us."

At the time, the surgery was thought to end his season, and maybe his career, but Butler returned to the starting lineup on September 6. Unlike when he was booed unmercifully the previous year during the Mike Busch controversy, this time the Dodger faithful gave him a standing ovation. Of course, the past was not forgotten, at least to Butler. He noted that, according to his doctors, stress may have been a factor, along with him previously chewing tobacco, in the cancer. Butler told *Sports Illustrated*, "It came with the pressure from the strike, the Dodgers not re-signing me [after 1994], my mother dying [in 1995, of brain cancer], getting traded from the Mets back to the Dodgers and the whole replacement-player thing." Butler would go on and play the reminder of the season, as well as appear in 107 games for the Dodgers in 1997. He retired at the end of the season after seventeen big-league seasons at the age of forty.

A bigger off-field incident was that Lasorda had a mild heart attack and on June 26 had to undergo angioplasty surgery. While the surgery was a success and the doctors said that Lasorda would be able to resume his managerial duties, there were rumblings that considering the stress of the job it would be better if Lasorda retired. There were also rumblings that it would be better for the Dodgers if Lasorda retired. During his recovery, former Dodger and now coach Bill Russell took over the managerial duties on an interim basis. Under Russell, the Dodgers went 14–16 when Lasorda dropped a bombshell. On June 29, Lasorda announced, despite the doctors clearing him to resume as manager, that he was stepping down and would move into the front office as the team's vice president and that Russell would continue leading the team. Lasorda said that he did not want to end up dying in a hotel room alone like what happened to Drysdale. He noted, "I got to thinking about my little 9-month-old granddaughter, and how I'd like to be around when she goes to school . . . . For me to get into a uniform again—as excitable as I am—I could not go down there without being the way I am." In response to a question about whether he was forced out, Lasorda vehemently denied it. "Some people might think that, hey, they asked me to do this. . . . No way. Peter said to me, 'You're the manager. If you want to put that uniform on Tuesday, you are the manager of this team.' I really appreciated that. That really made me feel good."

Even despite the denials, some claim to this day that Lasorda was pushed, but he has continually made it clear that it was his decision to retire.

Nevertheless, the Dodgers needed new blood to lead the club. While Lasorda never lost the clubhouse, only Karros and Piazza attended the press conference where he announced his retirement. Indeed, outfielder Billy Ashley actually went on record, noting,

> I think you can see a difference in this team already. . . . There's just a different attitude. It's calmer. It's a lot more relaxed. You don't have all of that yelling and screaming. It's tough playing for Tommy. It's like you're playing for two different things. It's like you're playing for the Dodgers and you're playing for Tommy, too. It's hard to explain, but it's just a different atmosphere.

Considering what would happen in 1997, Ashley's claim that things were calmer and more relaxed under Russell would turn out to be quite ironic indeed.

## 1997–99: TENSION, A CHANGE IN OWNERSHIP, AND A BEWILDERING TRADE

It was claimed that one of the team's problems was that there were too many different cliques in the locker room. What people were trying to claim is that as they had players from a number of different countries, and due to this could not work together as a cohesive unit. Of course, numerous teams throughout history have not been best buddies off the field yet still managed to perform on the field.

The Dodgers were no different. However, closer Todd Worrell felt it was a big enough problem to address the issue before the season. Worrell, of the belief that teams must be united, told his teammates as much during a players-only meeting. Yet he also felt the need to tell the media what was said:

> When you're not together, it detracts from what this game is all about. I don't expect the season to start and a light to go off and we're all lovey-dovey. You're not going to have all 25 guys getting along without any conflicts. But if you can work through that, and leave it off the field, we'll be all right. . . . I think it certainly makes it more difficult with the international flavor in here. . . . We have different cultures, different ways of living, and we don't always see eye to eye. But just like any relationship, it takes time and effort. That's what we have to work on around here.

Of course, talking to the press about a lack of unity and what was said in a closed-door meeting is not exactly the best way to bring people together.

It is certainly true that the clubhouse was splintered. Indeed, former Dodger Joe Black noted, "I stepped into that clubhouse last year, and I couldn't believe what I was seeing with all of those cliques. . . . It was never like that when we played, not even in the early days of integration." Yet the unity had less to do with the cultures and more between pitchers and hitters. The most glaring example was after Brett Butler held a players-only meeting to discuss the issue of unity. Eric Karros and Ismael Valdez got into a shoving match. During the meeting, Karros got pretty animated and called Valdez some choice words—not exactly the best way to build bridges. Once the meeting ended, Karros took a shower while Valdez got more heated. As Mike Piazza recounts in his book *Long Shot*, Valdez eventually confronted Karros outside the showers. Words and then shoves were exchanged. Karros was only wearing a towel that, not surprisingly, fell off during the physical confrontation. This led Billy Ashley to exclaim, "What are you going to do now, Eric? Hit him with your cock?"

The alleged lack of unity also occurred between Russell and the pitching staff as they believed he favored the hitters over them. Whether this was true or not is very debatable, but in June there were two high-profile incidents between manager Bill Russell and the pitching staff. On June 5, Russell and Valdez got into an altercation after Russell lifted the pitcher for a pinch-hitter. Russell shoved Valdez out of the dugout after Valdez showed his displeasure about being pulled from the game. And on June 8, following Pedro Astacio allowing a homer to give the Cardinals a 5–0 lead, Russell visited the mound and got into a very heated conversation with the pitcher. Astacio finished the inning and then proceeded to slam his glove in frustration on the bench, and another heated discussion with Russell ensued. Third-base coach Joey Amalfitano had to restrain Astacio, while first-base and hitting coach Reggie Smith was accidently hurt shepherding Astacio back to the clubhouse. Following the game, Astacio apologized. "I was just frustrated, and I knew I made a mistake. . . . It's not going to happen again, and that's all I have to say." While Valdez remained a Dodger, Astacio was traded to the Rockies on August 19 for former Dodger Eric Young.

The reality is that when the Dodgers performed badly, such as dropping 20 of 30 games in late May and June, the media and fans were quick to blame the lack of unity within the team. But when the Dodgers went on hot streaks, such as going 39–17 in July and August, all of a sudden there was nary a mention of clubhouse turmoil. Instead, it was claimed that the Dodgers were living up to what was expected; indeed, the majority of pundits predicted that the Dodgers would be one of the best teams in baseball.

On September 16, the Dodgers led the division by two with 11 games remaining in the season. It was then that they would once again throw away a NL West pennant. They handed the NL West to the Giants by losing five in a row, and six out of seven. It was another disappointing end to the season. Karros "predicted" such an outcome in June when he told *Sports Illustrated*, "You could spend every last dime on every world-renowned psychiatrist, and they couldn't figure out this team."

Yet for the disappointment of a wasted season, 1997 will always be remembered for what happened off the field. The so-called lack of unity of the clubhouse was news. But *the* news was the bombshell Peter O'Malley dropped on January 6: the Los Angeles Dodgers were for sale. There were rumors that O'Malley wanted out dating back for at least a year, and his announcement was the missing piece of the puzzle as to why the Dodgers had not been signing big-name free agents. At the press conference, O'Malley noted that the idea was on his mind for a while and "it finally occurred to me that this is the time [to sell]. . . . If you look at all sports, it's a high-risk business. Professional sports today is as high risk as the oil business. You need a broader base than an individual family to carry you through the storm." Without saying so, O'Malley was alluding to the escalating player salaries and the potential, although unfounded, of more industrial conflict.

In addition, O'Malley claimed he was selling the team in part due to the high estate taxes his family would have to pay if he died and still owned the team. Of course, since the O'Malley name was part and parcel of the team dating back to the Brooklyn Dodgers, there was much speculation about the "true" reason the longtime owner was getting out. This included his diminished power base at MLB. When Bowie Kuhn was commissioner, O'Malley had a lot of sway. But with Bud Selig now in charge, there were a lot of owners with more power than O'Malley. Another possible reason was that O'Malley wanted to bring an NFL team back to Los Angeles and build a stadium at Chavez Ravine, but he was beyond furious with local politicians for not supporting his vision. And with his declining power in baseball, the estate tax, and the escalating player salaries, O'Malley simply had enough.

While there was sadness within the fan base about O'Malley selling, it had the potential to be the best thing for the team, the players, and the fans. A major market team like the Los Angeles Dodgers were spending like a midmarket team. In 1995, the team only had the seventeenth largest payroll, the twelfth in 1996, and the eighth in 1997. Of course, money does not necessarily buy championships, but it is a good start—especially in the era of free agency. O'Malley simply did not want to spend the money to secure the players that were needed to not simply compete for the NL West pennant but to win a World Series.

There was immediate speculation about potential bidders, but soon a front-runner would emerge: the Fox Group subsidiary of News Corporation, which was owned by the Australian billionaire Rupert Murdoch. News Corporation was a media empire owning, among others, the *New York Post, TV Guide, New York Times,* Twentieth Century Fox, and the Fox television network. In May, Murdoch confirmed that the Fox Group had made a bid for the Dodgers. And on September 5 it was announced that O'Malley had agreed to sell the team and all its assets, including Dodger Stadium and the spring training facility at Vero Beach, to the Fox Group for $311 million—a then record amount for *any* sports team. The sale was approved by MLB and the other owners on March 20, 1998.

The Fox Group made all the right noises, but a niggling thought remained. Murdoch was not a baseball fan and had never even been to Dodger Stadium despite living in Los Angeles. Murdoch was a businessman first and foremost, and as long as the team made him money—not necessarily through the team itself, but through the Dodgers games being broadcast on the cable channel Fox Sports West—he would be happy.

## THE DODGERS

The Walt Disney Company had just purchased the California Angels, and there was a fear that Fox would lose the rights to broadcast Angels' games. At the time, it was rumored that Disney was considering launching regional television networks under its subsidiary, ESPN. By buying the Dodgers, the Fox Group secured the future television rights of the team. It did not take long for people to realize that the success of the Dodgers on the field was of little importance within the News Corporation empire.

* * *

It is fair to say that Mike Piazza was not exactly that happy with the Dodgers. He was understandably not pleased when Russell was asked by reporters who he believed was the 1996 NL MVP. Instead of saying Piazza, which was the logical thing for his manager to say, he replied "Ken Caminiti," the Padre third baseman. Caminiti went on to win the MVP Award, with Piazza finishing second. Piazza was also not exactly endeared with his two-year, $15 million contract signed in January 1997. Piazza was the fifth-highest paid player in baseball but felt as though he deserved a much larger payday. He was seeking a five-year deal worth around $60 million. However, O'Malley did not want to give out long-term, big-money contracts which could impact the team's selling price. The two-year contract with Piazza was a compromise, as neither side relished the prospect of going to arbitration and further straining the relationship.

Piazza was also not exactly pleased when, in March, his former teammate Brett Butler, who retired at the end of 1997, told Bill Plaschke, "Mike Piazza is the greatest hitter I have ever been around . . . but you can't build around Piazza because he is not a leader. . . . You know all that stuff that went down last year about Mike being the leader, calling out the team, all that stuff? It was all fabricated. Mike Piazza is a moody, self-centered, '90s player." Butler even claimed that Piazza did not care that much about winning. "We're in [crunch] time during pennant races the last two years, and all Piazza seems to care about is winning the MVP from Larry Walker or the batting title from Tony Gwynn. . . . We'd be winning games 8–0, but if he isn't getting his knocks [hits], he'd be all ticked off, walking up and down the dugout all mad."

Naturally, Piazza was not happy with such comments. He told Plaschke, "Maybe Brett, who's never won a World Series either, is very frustrated about something, and wants to make me a scapegoat. . . . I always looked up to him, tried to learn from him. That's why this is so disappointing. . . . We can't be concerned about what Brett Butler says about our club, because he's not on our club." Unfortunately, Piazza would not be in LA for much longer.

Piazza wanted to finalize a new contract with the Dodgers before the start of the 1998 season and set a deadline of February 15. Piazza was seeking a seven-year, $105 million deal. He was bewildered that the team seemed in no hurry to finalize such a deal and told the *Los Angeles Times* in April,

I'm not going to lie and say I'm not concerned about this, that I'm not confused and disappointed by the whole thing, because I am. . . . I'm mad that this has dragged into the season, and that it now has the potential to become a distraction. I'm not going to use this as an excuse if things aren't going well, because that wouldn't

be fair to the fans, my teammates or [team management].
But how can I not think about this?

The Dodgers eventually offered a deal worth $76 million over six years. Piazza later claimed in his book *Long Shot* that if the Dodgers increased that to $79 million he would have signed. However, rather than doing that, the press reported that Piazza turned down an $80 million deal. Piazza believed it was someone in the organization that planted that story to make him look bad, and it indeed did to a certain section of fans, so much so that Piazza was booed for weeks at Dodger Stadium after contract-extension talks had broken down. In his book, Piazza lays some of the blame on Scully: "The way the whole contract drama looked to them—many of whom were taking their view from Scully—was that, by setting a deadline and insisting on so much money, I was demonstrating a conspicuous lack of loyalty to the ballclub. . . Vin Scully was crushing me." However, all that Scully did was in one interview ask about Piazza's self-imposed deadline.

Despite all this, a deal between Piazza and the Dodgers could have still been worked out. Piazza wanted to stay with the Dodgers, but some within the organization had other ideas. On May 14, Piazza and third baseman Todd Zeile were traded to the Florida Marlins for Manuel Barrios, Bobby Bonilla, Jim Eisenreich, Charles Johnson, and Gary Sheffield. Of the five players received for Piazza and Zeile, only Sheffield live up to his billing, having several solid years in LA. However, Sheffield was a power-hitting outfielder, not exactly a rare commodity. Moreover, as part of the trade, the Dodgers ended up with $80 million more in payroll to cover the incoming player salaries.

In contrast, Zeile would have a good couple of years before declining; he retired after the 2004 season. In another positive for the Dodgers (although not known at the time), with Zeile traded, nineteen-year-old Adrián Beltré would become the Dodgers starting third baseman later in the year.

Nevertheless, it was clear why the Marlins made the trade with the Dodgers. After winning the 1997 World Series, the Marlins wanted to purge their squad of any high-priced contracts. Indeed, Piazza was traded by the Marlins on May 22 to the Mets. Piazza continued to be a decent-to-good defensive catcher and an outstanding power-hitting threat— the rarest of rare commodities. He was duly rewarded once his playing career was over by being voted into the Hall of Fame in 2016.

The trade, which was not even during the traditional trading period, was mind-boggling at the time—and with the benefit of hindsight even more insane. Thus, why did the Dodgers make the trade? Quite simply, the trade had nothing to do with the on-field success or otherwise of the team. Indeed, general manager Fred Claire did not orchestrate the trade—Fox executives made the deal without Claire's knowledge. Claire later claimed, "As bad as the deal itself was for the Dodgers, for a variety of reasons, the timing of it was absolutely bizarre. It had nothing to do with the team itself or any type of normal move that's ever been made. You can't go back in time and show me a player of his magnitude traded in May. That shows how out of balance it was. It was made for non-baseball reasons." It has long been rumored that the trade was made in an attempt by Fox to persuade Marlins owner H. Wayne Huizenga to sell them a regional cable network.

A lopsided trade always invites questions. However, a trade that was almost guaranteed to make a team worse and was done solely to try to secure a cable network makes this trade the worst in team history. The shake-up within the organization was, however, far from over. On June 4, the team traded Hideo Nomo and Brad Clontz to the Mets for Greg McMichael and Dave Mlicki. McMichael would eventually appear in 12 games for the Dodgers before being traded for Brian Bohanon later in the year. (Bohanon would go on and appear in 14 games for the Dodgers.) Mlicki played in twenty-two games for the Dodgers. Nomo would go on to have a number of decent-to-good years in the majors, including returning to the Dodgers in 2002.

Even with all the maneuvering, the Dodgers were not having a good year on the field; the team was ravaged by injuries and was 12½ games out of first by June 21. This is when the Fox group dropped another bombshell.

In one fell swoop they fired manager Bill Russell and general manager Fred Claire. Triple-A manager Glenn Hoffman was promoted, and Lasorda was named the new GM. Russell was understandably bitter about his firing and blamed it in part on Lasorda trying to undermine him. While Lasorda denied the accusation, he was not happy that Russell was his own man when it came to managing and rarely sought out Lasorda for advice. Likewise, at the Hall of Fame induction ceremony in August 1997, Lasorda claimed if he was given free reign Bobby Valentine would be the Dodger manager. Moreover, Lasorda was annoyed at his lack of decision-making powers as vice president. It should be noted that both Lasorda and Claire claim that the former skipper had no role in the GM's firing. However, Lasorda certainly wanted a greater role, and there were rumors he had been lobbying Fox executives for him to take over as GM.

One of Lasorda's first moves as GM, on July 4, was trading Paul Konerko and Dennys Reyes for closer Jeff Shaw. Reyes never truly distinguishing himself and was a baseball journeyman. Shaw was a good closer and would suit up for the Dodgers for three-and-a-half seasons before retiring following the 2001 season. However, why a team 12½ games out of first needed a closer is a mystery. Moreover, while yet to blossom, Konerko had all the attributes to be a future star. He went on to have a number of fine seasons with the White Sox, finishing his career with 439 home runs, 2,340 hits, and an OPS of .841. He was a six-time All-Star.

* * *

In terms of trade, 1998 was not the finest year for the Dodgers—nor was it their finest year on the field. The team finished the year with a record of 83–79—15 games out of first. With continued struggles on the field, there would be substantial changes before the season was out.

The Lasorda era in charge did not last long, as Baltimore assistant general manager Kevin Malone was named as the team's new GM on September 11. While Lasorda was happy to step aside (having a role in choosing his successor), Glenn Hoffman would have liked to have continued as the team's manager on a permanent basis. But this was not to be, as veteran manager Davey Johnson, who led the Mets to World Series triumph in 1986, became the team's new skipped in October 1998. Johnson was not Malone's first choice; Malone was hoping Expos manager

Felipe Alou would accept the position. Alou declined, deciding to stay with Montreal.

There would be, of course, even more changes before the 1999 season got underway. The biggest acquisition was veteran starting pitcher Kevin Brown. Brown was a very-good-to-excellent pitcher. It was a wise signing for the Dodgers, especially considering that the team was only middle-of-the road in regard to pitching the previous season. Brown signed a lucrative deal for seven years at $105 million. The figure shocked the industry, and there were a lot of complaints that Fox's vast resources were trying to buy a World Series ring. In response, Malone claimed, "Kevin Brown and the other moves we've made have brought the Dodger haters out of the closet. . . . To me, it's just sour grapes. Everyone is jealous of the Dodgers." Brown noted, "If they don't like it because you're trying to win, too bad. You're not here to try to be nice to the other team. You're trying to do everything you can to beat them."

The reality is that other teams, if they had the resources, also had no issues with spending megamoney on players. For example, the Mets gave Piazza a seven-year deal at $91 million. What was not so wise was giving the thirty-four-year-old Brown such a lengthy deal. Such a contract was guaranteed to be a problem in later years. However, as long as Brown was as dominant as he had been in recent years—and the Dodgers won—his guaranteed decline would be forgiven. Indeed, the Dodgers were favored in some quarters to win the World Series . . . then reality hit. For those hoping that all the changes inflicted upon the fan base would bear fruit, they were to be solely disappointed.

Gary Sheffield, Eric Karros, Mark Grudzielanek (who was acquired from the Expos in a multiplayer trade in June 1998), and

Adrián Beltré had good seasons. Indeed, the offense improved, albeit marginally, from fourteenth-best to eleventh-best in the NL. On the pitching side, Brown lived up to his contract; he went 18–9 with an ERA of 3.00, while being an All Star and leading baseball with 35 starts. Closer Jeff Shaw had a fine season, saving 34 games. Ismael Valdez was decent but suffered from a lack of run support. Yet despite the dominance of Brown, the pitching staff was actually worse than the previous year.

The Dodgers were still in contention, but went 8–17 in June and 11–18 in July, finishing with a losing record of 77–85—23 games out of first. It was a horrible season to say the least.

The season can be summarized by two statements. In August of that year, Raul Mondesi, who was having a down year, unloaded on the Dodger hierarchy. As recapped by the *Los Angeles Times*, Mondesi said,

> I told my agent to get me the [expletive] out of here as soon as possible. I can't take this anymore. I've had to deal with this all year. I told them to trade me because I don't want to [expletive] be here. [Expletive] Davey and [expletive] Malone, they try to put all of our problems on me. They're trying to say that all this [expletive] is my fault. That's the way they feel, fine. Just get me out of here. [Expletive] Davey. [Expletive] Malone. [Expletive] both of them.

Mondesi got his wish and was traded with Pedro Borbon to the Toronto Blue Jays for minor-leaguer Jorge Nunez and Shawn Green. As the team would find out, Green would be the prize piece in that deal.

As fine as Mondesi's statement was, the most misguided and foolish statement came from general manager Kevin Malone.

Before the season got underway, Malone told the press that he expected the World Series would be between the Dodgers and the Yankees and that there was a "new sheriff in town." Malone was correct insofar as the Yankees made and won the World Series, but his Dodgers were far from sheriffs—they were not even hall monitors.

The end of the decade would bring further change to ownership. In a sign that the Fox Group was losing interest in owning the Dodgers, on October 28 it was announced that Robert Daly, a former co-chairman at Warner Brothers, had purchased 10 percent of the club from Fox and would run the team. Daly claimed, "I knew everybody at Warner Bros. I knew the gardeners, I knew the guards at the gate. . . . I want us here, the guards, everyone who works for the Dodgers, to have a great feeling." A great feeling meant a successful ballclub. It was Daly, a Dodger fan since the age of six, when the team played in Brooklyn, who negotiated the Mondesi-Green trade. Daly's ownership stake and appointment was officially confirmed by the league's owners on January 24, 2000.

Thus, the 1990s ended with more ownership upheaval and the team not appearing in a World Series for the first time since the 1940s. Unfortunately, the 2000s would bring more of the same.

# 7

# 2000S: A DECADE OF UPHEAVAL
# AND DISAPPOINTMENT

**W**ITH A NEW man in charge, as well as a new year, decade, and century, the Dodgers were hoping to break their World Series drought. And several players were working toward that goal, having stellar seasons. Sheffield hit 43 home runs to tie the Dodger record set in 1956 by Duke Snider, while having an OPS of 1.081. Sheffield was an All-Star and finished ninth in MVP voting. Catcher Todd Hundley, who was acquired in 1999 (and was replaced on the Mets by Piazza), rebounded after a horrible offensive season the previous year by having an OPS of .954 (a career best) but was injured for most of the year and only appeared in 90 games. Fortunately, back-up veteran catcher Chad Kreuter also had a good year offensively; he had an OBP of .410 and an OPS of .827. Eric Karros broke the record for all-time Dodger home runs with his 229th, and Adrián Beltré continued his improvement, hitting 20 home runs with an OPS of .835—a very impressive achievement for a twenty year old.

Newcomer Shawn Green, however, was a slight disappointment. He hit .269 with an OPS .839 and 24 home runs—all well down on his previous year with the Blue Jays.

On the pitching side, Kevin Brown once again lived up to his contract, going 13–6 with a NL-best ERA of 2.58. South Korean Chan Ho Park, who began his career with the Dodgers in 1994, was developing into a very good pitcher. For the season he had a record of 18–10 with a career-best ERA of 3.27. However, the rest of the starting pitchers were mediocre at best, and the team committed the second-most errors in the NL with 135.

The team was number one, however, in fighting. On May 16, at a game at Wrigley Field, a Cubs fan reached over the bullpen wall, hit Chad Kreuter, and stole his cap. Hundley told *Newsday*,

> A fan came down and hit one of our guys in the back of the head. . . . Literally punched him in the back of the head when he wasn't looking. And he took his hat—that's how the whole thing started. If you wanted a hat that bad, be polite and ask for one. We'll give it to you. We've got a whole bunch of them. . . . When you come down and punch a guy in the head, then we're allowed to do whatever we want to do.

And "do whatever we want" meant that Kreuter and some other Dodgers chased the fan and got into tussles with some other spectators. In all, sixteen Dodgers were suspended for a total of 60 games and three coaches were suspended for a total of 24 games. Kreuter received the harshest among the players, being suspended for eight games. Johnson was not happy with the league's decision, telling the press, "It's very unfair as far as

I'm concerned. . . . My whole coaching staff was trying to keep our people from getting smoked. Some guys who got suspended didn't even go into the stands. They also didn't talk about security [at Wrigley] and that's disappointing."

Fighting aside, the Dodgers were an improved side and finished with a record of 86–76, good enough for second in the NL West, 11 games behind the Giants. However, for many this was not good enough considering that the team had the second-highest payroll in baseball at just over $90 million, second only to the Yankees. That the Dodgers were not blowing away the competition led to in-fighting well before the season ended. The fighting, however, was now coming from the front office.

The sniping started in early August with the Dodgers still, at that stage, in the pennant race. General manager Kevin Malone told the *Los Angeles Times*, "We did the things we needed to do with our moves in the off-season, and we added talent [through midseason trades]. We all have to perform at this time of year because that's what we're paid to do. We're paid to win."

Likewise, Daly and Malone wanted Johnson to manage the Dodgers more aggressively. In other words, if the team didn't win, it was the players' and Johnson's fault. And with them tumbling out of contention, Johnson knew his time in Los Angeles was coming to an end. With over a month still left in the season, Johnson told the *Los Angeles Times*, if he was to be fired "let's do it and not wait. . . . Let me put my house on the market instead of waiting eight weeks. Just do it. Hey, I know what's going on. These people have spent a lot of money and so you know there are going to be changes. A lot of money. There has to be."

Following the column Johnson and Daly had a meeting, with Daly asking the manager whether he wanted to quit. Johnson replied in the negative, and things were smoothed over. Johnson told the press, "I'm not a dead man yet." However, at that stage Johnson was indeed a dead man—he just didn't know it yet.

Johnson was fired as Dodger manager in October. On November 1, Jim Tracy, the bench coach for the previous two seasons under Johnson, became the team's new manager. After years of stability with Alston and then Lasorda, the Dodgers managerial position became a hot seat. It was Tracy's first major-league managing job. At the press conference to announce his hiring, Tracy said, "I'm very grateful I'm being given this opportunity. . . . I have no fear whatsoever taking on this situation. My focus will be on re-establishing the pride, re-establishing totally the tradition of this organization."

Malone was in favor of an internal candidate, noting, "We felt it was most important to promote within the organization. We've made a lot of progress in the last two years. We think Jim is the right man to lead us forward. Jim has the familiarity with the organization." A lot of progress is not how most people would summarize the Dodgers' last two years. And nor would it be how they described the 2001 season.

* * *

The 2001 Dodgers finished with an identical record of 86–76, this time only good enough for third in the NL West, six games behind the Arizona Diamondbacks (who joined the division in 1998). They were only one game out of first on September 7, but a bad run quickly eliminated them from contention. The team's core was essentially the same team as the previous year; the only reason why they were still in contention that late into the season is that the division was quite a bit weaker than in 2000.

Gary Sheffield and Shawn Green once again led the offense, with Green smashing 49 home runs to break the Dodger single-season record. Catcher Paul Lo Duca, who first saw action with the Dodgers in 1998, had a career year, hitting 25 home runs with an OPS of .917. On the pitching side, Chan Ho Park had another good year and led the team in wins, while Jeff Shaw, in his final season before retirement, posted 43 saves. Kevin Brown was excellent (when on the field), going 10–4 with an ERA of 2.65. However, he was injured for a good portion of the year and only appeared in 20 games.

Quite simply, for a team with the third-highest payroll in baseball, it was another disappointing year. And once again it was a year that will be remembered more for what happened off the field. Kevin Malone was on thin ice with part-owner Robert Daly, as he—as well as most of baseball—was getting tired of Malone's outlandish statements. In addition to the ones previously mentioned, the GM compared Brown's record-breaking deal to Jackie Robinson breaking the color barrier, as well as Gary Sheffield to Bill Clinton. Of course, if the Dodgers were winning and Malone was making good personnel decisions, his outlandishness would not have mattered. But Malone was failing on both of these counts. Things came to ahead in April after Malone got into an altercation with a Padres fan at Petco Park in San Diego. That was the final straw, as Daly forced Malone to resign. On a conference call announcing the decision, Daly said Malone

> sort of dug himself into a little bit of a hole. . . . It was an accumulation of things that took place. This has to do with distractions. We're here to play baseball, not

have people read about all these other things. . . . These distractions that kept coming up recently reached the point where I felt that they were taking away from what we were all trying to build. He became a distraction, a lightning rod.

In response, Malone claimed, "Throughout my career, I've played with passion, both on the field and in the front office. . . . That passion has, I'm sure, annoyed some, been misunderstood by others but respected by those who know me best."

As one could guess, there were a number of the "sheriff was run out of town" jokes made at the time. Dave Wallace became the interim GM, and Dan Evans was named as the full-time replacement in October.

It did not take Evans long to make his mark on the Dodgers. He re-signed Hideo Nomo to a three-year deal, signed Kazuhisa Ishii from Japan, and had to deal with a disgruntled Gary Sheffield.

Before the start of the 2002 season, as he did the previous year, Sheffield demanded that he be traded. The slugger was unhappy prior to the start of the 2001, as he was not given a so-called lifetime-contract extension to make him one of the highest paid players in the game. In January 2002, Sheffield claimed that Evans lied to him about trying to trade him to the A's; as such he either wanted to be traded or be given assurances that he would be with the club beyond 2004, when his contract expired. Sheffield told the *Los Angeles Times*,

The bottom line is that [the Dodgers] can't tell me anything now. You've got to show actions. It's not about them telling me I've got a title on this team, that I'm the franchise player. Until they say, "OK, Gary, this is what the case is, this is what we're going to do to prove what we're saying about you," I don't want to hear anything. Or, they can take the other course and trade me.

The Dodgers did take action. On January 15, Evans orchestrated a multiplayer trade with the Braves that sent Sheffield to Atlanta in return for Andrew Brown, Brian Jordan, and Odalis Perez. Brown never played for the Dodgers, Jordan had an average year for the Dodgers in 2002 and an injury-ravaged 2003, while Perez, who showed promise in three seasons with the Braves and was only twenty-four, would have two good seasons with Los Angeles and two-and-a-half not-so-good seasons before being traded to the Royals in July 2006. As for Sheffield, he would eventually retire at the end of the 2009 season. From 2002 to 2009, he was a three-time All-Star and won a Silver Slugger, finishing in the top three of MVP voting twice. In only one of those years, when he was thirty-nine years old, was his OPS below .800. In purely baseball terms, the Dodgers would have been a lot better signing Sheffield to a long-term contract than trading him, but whether he would have distrusted so-called team chemistry is another matter.

Considering that for the majority of those years the Dodgers were not that successful on the field, one must wonder whether the disruption Sheffield could have potentially caused would have been a minor talking point if the team regularly made the postseason. Of course, Sheffield alone could not drive the Dodgers toward the playoffs, and in that regard the Fox Group seemed to just be happy largely going with a pat hand.

The organization lost $55 million in 2001 and more than $88 million since Fox had taken over the team. Yet, despite the losses, Rupert Murdoch set out what he wanted to achieve. In December 2001, in an interview with Charlie Rose, Murdoch noted that the economic reason for purchasing the Dodgers "was that . . . we were trying to establish a second cable network in Southern California and Disney was trying to get one going too, around their teams. And, by getting in first . . . they didn't find any room to get in. So we really have that local sports business in Southern California as a result."

The Dodgers were not yet for sale, but it was only a matter of time. One got the sense that the Fox Group no longer wanted to chase any big-name free agents or, more to the point, the long-term big-money contracts that such free agents deserved.

As such, the Dodgers went into the 2002 season largely unchanged when it came to position players. Without Sheffield in the lineup the offense was bound to take a step back, and that is exactly how it went. The 2001 team had the eighth-best hitting side in the NL, while the 2002 side was twelfth. Only Shawn Green had an outstanding year, hitting 32 home runs, driving in 114, and having an OPS of .944. He led the team in almost all offensive categories. In a personal highlight, on May 23, he hit four home runs in a single game against the Brewers at Miller Park. Green hit it out of the park in the second, fourth, fifth, and ninth inning while going 6-for-7, scoring six runs and driving in seven. Following the game, Green said, "It definitely hasn't sunk in yet. . . . I wish I had a few days off so I could enjoy it. It's something I'll never forget." Green, who entered the Milwaukee series in a major slump, noted, "The ball had been looking like a Ping-Pong ball. . . . Today, it probably looked like a softball."

In contrast to the offense, the pitching staff was overhauled, with the big loss at the time being Chan Ho Park signing as a free agent with the Texas Rangers. Yet the Dodgers overcame his loss. Odalis Perez and Hideo Nomo had very good years, with all of the regular starters having an ERA below 4.30. Unfortunately, the wisdom of giving a long-term deal to Kevin Brown was looking even more foolhardy, as the thirty-seven year old was injured once again for a large portion of the season. He only appeared in 17 games with a then career-worst ERA of 4.81. While Brown was having a bad year, one pitcher found magic and turned into one of the most dominant closers baseball had ever seen: Eric Gagne.

The twenty-three-year-old Gagne broke in with LA as a starting pitcher in 1999, appearing in five games. In 2000 and 2001, he was an adequate back-of-the-rotation starter. He was good enough to make the team, but almost guaranteed to be a journeyman for his career. However, the decision to put him in the bullpen turned Gagne's career around. Going into the season, the team planned on going down the closer-by-committee route, but after a dominant outing against the Giants early in April he became the team's full-time closer. Gagne was more than happy with the situation, telling *USA Today,* "Mentally, it's been pretty easy because they say I've always had a closer's mentality. Physically, it was just a case of seeing how I could bounce back from back-to-back days or three straight days. I can pretty much pitch every day, so I feel good about it." There was one downside for Gagne about closing: the lack of plate opportunities. "I love to hit," said Gagne. "I was a huge Tim Wallach fan. Hitting—that's the reason I began playing baseball." Gagne would only make one plate appearance in the entire year (striking out). As for how he did as a closer, Gagne saved 52 and had an ERA of 1.97. He was an All-Star, finished twelfth in MVP voting, and came in fourth in the Cy Young vote. It was a remarkable season. And, moreover, Gagne brought life to Dodger Stadium. There is just something about closers and entrance music. For Yankee fans, Mariano Rivera coming into the game with Metallica's "Enter Sandman" playing was a highlight. But for Dodger fans, Gagne entering the game to the sound of Guns N' Roses "Welcome to the Jungle" with GAME OVER flashing on the scoreboard at Dodger Stadium was a sight to behold.

Unfortunately, as dominant as Gagne was, the same could not be said for the club as a whole. The improved pitching was the main impetus on the team winning six more games than the previous season, finishing with a record of 92–70. But, once again, they finished six games behind the Diamondbacks and had to settle for third place in the NL West. Gagne and Green aside, it was another average season. And there was more of the same in the following season, at least on the field; off of it was another matter entirely.

The offseason started on a sad note when the Dodgers traded Eric Karros and Mark Grudzielanek to the Cubs for Chad Hermansen and Todd Hundley. As was seemingly the norm, the trade was not that successful. Hermansen appeared in 11 games for the Dodgers and hit .160, while Hundley appeared in 21 games, hitting .182. Both were out of the organization by the following year. Grudzielanek was unhappy with his decreased playing time with the Dodgers and repeatedly voiced this to manager Jim Tracy. Grudzielanek, who was not necessarily living up to his high-priced contract, went on to have a number of good seasons in the majors before eventually retiring in 2010. All this taken into consideration, one could make an argument—although not necessarily a good one—that trading him was good for team chemistry and payroll flexibility.

The trade of Karros is another matter entirely. Karros wanted to finish his career with the Dodgers so much so that in November he agreed to a modification in his contract to eliminate a vesting option that would have guaranteed him a $9 million payday in 2004 if he had 500 plate appearances in 2003. Instead, the Dodgers could buy out Karros's contract for $1 million. Karros, who turned thirty-five in 2003, was in the waning stage of his career. Like Grudzielanek, he was not exactly happy with how Tracy had been managing the team, which was related to a number of heated discussions the two had engaged in the previous season. Thus, for team chemistry and for Tracy to have authority over the clubhouse, trading Karros was for the best. However, the slugger was a Dodger legend, and it would have been good if a way could have been found for him to finish his career with the club. He was understandably disappointed not to finish his career with the Dodgers. While Karros and Tracy had indeed gone through a few squabbles together, the former felt that they were now on good terms. Karros told the *Los Angeles Times*, "I had a very honest relationship with Jim [Tracy], we were both very candid. . . . He was very honest with me, and I was very honest with him. . . . But did I ever influence a decision or make out a lineup for him? Saying that is an insult to Tracy."

One could not help but get the impression that the trade was more about saving the team money than clubhouse relationships. While it was claimed at the time the trade would allow the team to pursue big-name free agents, this did not materialize. The Dodgers, in fact, went into the 2003 season with a weaker lineup.

Quite simply, the Fox Group did not want to sign an expensive free agent as they were looking to sell the team. In early January 2003, News Corporation denied that it wanted to get out of the baseball business, but it was reported a few days later that the company retained an investment banker to openly find a buyer for the team. The following day it was reported that Dave Checketts, a former Madison Square Garden chairman, was willing to buy the Dodgers for $650 million on the proviso that the cable channel Fox Sports Net West 2 was included in the sale. Fox was not willing to part with the channel, so the search for a buyer continued. In May, it was reported that Fox was negotiating exclusively with Malcolm Glazer, the owner of the NFL's Tampa Bay Buccaneers. The talks fell through, as both MLB and the NFL were concerned about Glazer complying with the respective league's cross-ownership policies.

Finally, in October, Fox found a buyer for the Dodgers: Frank McCourt. McCourt was seemingly desperate to own a baseball team, as he tried to buy the Red Sox in 2001 and the Angels in 2003. McCourt was officially listed as a real estate developer, but in divorce proceedings his wife, Jamie, stated that he basically made his living by suing people. McCourt bought the Dodgers for $430 million, and he claimed more than $200 million of that was his own money, with News Corporation loaning him $145 million. At the time, it was reported as a highly leveraged deal, and there were doubts as to whether McCourt actually used any of his own money to purchase the team. Nevertheless, MLB commissioner Bud Selig said, "This transaction meets all of baseball's debt service rules and financial requirements in every way. . . . We at Major League Baseball are confident that

Mr. McCourt, as a rabid and knowledgeable fan and successful businessman, will devote the time and energy necessary to make the franchise a great success."

It was later revealed that McCourt did not even use a single cent of his own money in the deal, which shows how desperate Fox was to sell the Dodgers. As Molly Knight noted in *The Best Team Money Can Buy*, McCourt "put up his parking lot [he owned] as collateral against the $145 million loan he got from Fox to complete the sale of the Dodgers. And when McCourt defaulted on that loan, Fox foreclosed on the lot and sold it to be done with him. In the end, McCourt traded a parking lot for one of Major League Baseball's flagship franchises."

Can you imagine it? The storied Los Angeles Dodgers were bought by a person who used none of his own money to purchase the team. This would not have necessarily mattered if the Dodgers were successful under McCourt's ownership, but the new order instead made the Dodgers a laughingstock. However, their futility was still to come.

As for the 2003 season, the highlight was Eric Gagne truly being "lights out," as he was perfect in 55 save opportunities. He was an All-Star, finished sixth in the MVP voting, and was the NL Cy Young Award winner. It was another remarkable season from Gagne. The same was not true for the rest of the Dodgers. While the pitching staff, led by Gagne, Nomo, and, in a bounce-back year, Brown, was the best in the NL, the offense was the worst in the NL. Shawn Green was the only regular to have an OPS of above .800, and even then he had a down year with only 19 home runs. The Dodgers were not in contention after late June and finished with a record of 85–77, good enough for second in the NL West, 15½ games behind the Giants. The best way to note the 2003 season was of a team treading water.

And considering that the sale of the Dodgers was not approved by the other owners until January 29, 2004, it looked as though the upcoming season would be a carbon copy of the previous year. As the approval did not come well into the new year, the Dodgers were not in a real position to negotiate with free agents.

For example, both Nomar Garciaparra and Vladimir Guerrero expressed an interest in joining the Dodgers, but in the end the team did not try to work out a deal with either player. Not helping matters, GM Dan Evans was unsure whether he would continue in the position once McCourt formally took over. Indeed, a little over a week after the owners approved the sale, Evans was out, with thirty-one-year-old Paul DePodesta taking over the position. It was a bold signing, as DePodesta was a proponent of sabermetrics. While common place in baseball today, at the time such thinkers were viewed as outsiders by a number of those involved in the sport.

The only off-season move of significance was orchestrated by Evans and led to Kevin Brown being traded to the Yankees in return for Brandon Weeden, Yhency Brazobán, Jeff Weaver, and cash considerations. In other words, the Dodgers were happy to be rid of Brown and his high-priced contract. Weeden never played a game in the majors and instead took his talents to the NFL. Brazobán would have a decent year for the Dodgers in 2004, while Weaver would have two average seasons for the Dodgers. Considering Brown would be often-injured in his two subpar seasons with the Yankees, the trade worked out well for LA.

There was one more trade of significance for the Dodgers, this one occurring midyear. On July 30, the Dodgers traded Paul Lo Duca, Juan Encarnacion, and Guillermo Mota to the Florida Marlins for Hee-Seop Choi, Bill Murphy, and Brad Penny. Murphy was traded in a multiplayer deal a few days later, with the Dodgers getting outfielder Steve Finley among others. Whether the trade strengthened the Dodgers is debatable, but trading your starting catcher—and team captain—who had many years left in the game and was having a good season was interesting to say the least. Choi never lived up to expectations, Finley played well for the rest of the season, and Penny was a potential ace. Thus, the trade was not as bad as it seemed on the surface.

Considering Lo Duca was beloved by the fans and was a club-house leader, while Mota was the set-up man to Gagne, it was not surprising that many fans and the media ripped DePodesta. If he was an old-style GM, it is doubtful he would have received as much criticism. But he was ahead of his time when it came to analytics, so-called moneyball. Thus, he was seemingly fair game from shock jocks and journalists looking for controversy.

Not helping DePodesta was that Lo Duca cried during his farewell interview. He said, "It was a little surprising, just because we were playing so well. . . . I could understand it if we were tailing off a little bit, but we hadn't been. . . . This team has a chance to go a long way. We have fallen short in the past, and the fans of LA were really excited this year to maybe make it to the playoffs, so it makes it difficult. I felt like I was a decent part of what's been going on. So it makes it a little tougher."

Despite DePodesta supposedly ripping the heart and soul out of the team and destroying team chemistry, the Dodgers led the division for a large portion of the season. They were in first place starting on July 7, and, despite stumbling at times, went into the final three games of the season with a three-game lead over the second-place Giants. As fate would have it, the two teams would meet at Dodger Stadium.

The Dodgers lost the first game, 4–2, and it looked like the second game would go the same way, as the Giants led 3–0 heading into the bottom of the ninth. However, they weren't done yet. Shawn Green led off the inning with a single, which was followed by a walk to Robin Ventura. With two on and nobody out, Alex Cora stuck out looking. Knowing the game—and the season—were on the line, Tracy pinch-hit for the soft-hitting catcher David Ross and brought in José Hernández. Hernández walked to load the bases, and Tracy made another move to bring Hee-Seop Choi in to hit for the pitcher Yhency Brazobán. But just like Hernández, Choi didn't need to swing as he was walked to bring in a run. This was followed by César Izturis reaching on an error to cut the lead to one. Jayson Werth then singled home the tying run. The bases were still loaded, and Dodger Stadium was rocking. Up to the plate stepped Steve Finley, and he spent longer than usual looking around the stadium. Following the game, Finley said, "I was just enjoying the atmosphere. . . . I thought about this a couple weeks ago. I wanted this situation. I wanted to get the hit." And a he got that hit. On an 0-1 fastball, Finley deposited the ball over the right-field fence for a walk-off grand slam. The Dodgers were NL West champions and were heading to the postseason for the first time since 1996.

The Dodgers were led by a breakout season by Adrián Beltré, who batted .334 with 200 hits, 32 doubles, 121 RBIs, a 1.017 OPS, and a league-leading 48 home runs. Beltré finished second in MVP voting and won the Silver Slugger Award. It was a mesmerizing season for the twenty-five year old.

On the pitching mound, Gagne was dominant once again. He saved 45 games and finished seventh in the Cy Young voting. However, on July 5 the unthinkable happened: Gagne blew a save opportunity, his first since August 26, 2002. During this period Gagne successfully saved 84 games, blowing away the previous record of 54, which was held by Tom Gordon. Even though he failed to convert the save opportunity, the crowd at Dodger Stadium rightfully gave Gagne a standing ovation. He later called the ovation one of the most fun times he has had in baseball, while players hugged him in the dugout at the end of the inning. Records are indeed made to be broken, but Gagne's record may well stand the test of time.

With the best third baseman and closer in the majors, the Dodgers were hoping their first season under new ownership would result in playoff success. However, the Cardinals and a reality check awaited. The Cardinals, led by Albert Pujols, Jim Edmonds, and Scott Rolen, were by far the best team in the NL. In Games One and Two of the NLDS, the Dodgers were blown out by identical scores of 8–3 in St. Louis. They came back in Game Three, winning 4–0 in Los Angeles, but the Cardinals once again had a cakewalk in Game Four, winning 6–2 to advance to the NLCS and end the Dodgers season. Nevertheless, 2004 should have been the building block for upcoming seasons, but 2005 proved to be a nightmare.

* * *

The nightmare began in the offseason, when slugger Adrián Beltré signed with the Seattle Mariners. The Mariners gave Beltré a five-year deal worth $64 million. In contrast, the Dodgers offered Beltré a six-year deal at $60 million. It was alleged that the Dodgers had a promise from Beltré's agent, Scott Boras, that they would be given an opportunity to match any contract offer, but this did not materialize. By not signing Beltré, the Dodgers had payroll flexibility to sign J. D. Drew, another Boras client.

Drew was coming off a number of great years and seemed like a very good signing by DePodesta. Unfortunately, the failure to sign or find a suitable replacement for Beltré meant that third base would be an issue for the team throughout the season. Less than a month after signing Drew, the Dodgers traded Shawn Green to the Diamondbacks for highly regarded catcher Dioner Navarro, as well as Beltran Perez and minor leaguers William Juarez and Danny Muegge.

Nowadays, one often reads that the trade was bad for the Dodgers. It is true that Navarro never panned out for Los Angeles and only appeared in 50 games in 2005. In contrast, Green had a good 2005 for the divisional rival Diamondbacks. Yet Green was highly paid and clearly in decline. Thus, while the trade did not work out, these things do happen—although the failure of Navarro meant that Jason Phillips would have to be the everyday catcher. (And he had an average year behind the plate and a horrible one at the plate.)

The Dodgers, however, were not done revamping their roster. Thirty-seven-year-old Jeff Kent signed on to be the Dodgers everyday second baseman and rewarded the team with a great year on the way to making the All-Star team and winning the Silver Slugger Award. And on the pitching side, fresh off helping the Red Sox to World Series glory, Derek Lowe signed with the team.

Quite simply, the Dodgers seemed to be an improved side and started the season going 15–8 for the month of April. But then the baseball gods looked down, and, before one knew it, the team was struggling mightily and had a plethora of injuries, including to J. D. Drew, Jayson Werth, and Eric Gagne. Gagne underwent season-ending shoulder surgery in June, which he never truly recovered from.

The Dodgers ended the season with a 71–91 record, 11 games behind the first-place Padres. Tracy was one of the first casualties, as he and the organization decided it was best for him to step down. And before the month was out, general manager Paul DePodesta, who was conducting interviews for the manager's job, was fired by owner Frank McCourt. This brought joy to certain sections of the media that hounded DePodesta all year, calling him numerous less-than-flattering nicknames, including "Google Boy." These scribes constantly ridiculed DePodesta because he believed in sabermetrics and supposedly did not understand that chemistry is most important to a baseball team. Also not helping DePodesta was that McCourt's wife, Jamie, disliked him (and eventually disliked Frank too). And then there was the role of Tommy Lasorda, who publicly praised DePodesta. Yet respected journalist Ken Rosenthal reported at the time that Lasorda, who often sat next to McCourt during home games, was less than flattering about the job DePodesta was doing. In response, Lasorda claimed Rosenthal was "a big fat liar." Considering that Rosenthal was and still is highly respected in baseball and never issued a correction or retraction is telling. In addition, McCourt made it very clear that he valued the advice of the former Dodger manager:

> I appreciate his advice and counsel. . . . I encourage it. I named him special advisor to the chairman last year, and it wasn't just a title. I want to know what he's thinking. This is a man with almost 60 years of baseball experience, someone who truly, truly loves the organization. Shame on me if I don't reach out to Tommy and say, "What do you think?"

McCourt decided to hire Ned Colletti to run the team. In contrast to DePodesta, Colletti was an experienced baseball person. He first joined the Cubs front office in 1982 before moving to the Giants, where he was eventually promoted to assistant GM in 1996. There was a major difference between DePodesta and Colletti; Colletti was seemingly disdainful of advanced analytics. Indeed, the analytics department was for all intents and purposes disbanded after Colletti's arrival, as everyone hired by DePodesta left early in Colletti's reign. In fact, it was not until 2011 that the Dodgers once again had an analytics department—one of the last teams in baseball to adopt such a department.

## 2006–09: THE RISE OF THE YOUNG GUNS AND MANNYWOOD

One of Ned Colletti's first moves was hiring Grady Little as the new Dodger manager. Grady had previously managed the Red Sox in 2002 and 2003. Colletti also traded talented but troubled outfielder Milton Bradley and infielder Antonio Pérez to the Athletics for minor-league prospect Andre Ethier. Six days later he signed shortstop Rafael Furcal, already a veteran at age twenty-eight, and Nomar Garciaparra. And in the new year, the Dodgers signed Takashi Saito from Japan. Saito would go on to become the closer during the season. By midyear, Colletti traded infielder César Izturis for the veteran All-Star and future member of the Hall of Fame Greg Maddux. Maddux proved invaluable down the stretch.

The 2006 season would be notable for the blooding of a number of rookies. Among the players making their major-league debuts included Andre Ethier, Takashi Saito, Russell Martin, Matt Kemp, James Loney, and Chad Billingsley. All would go on to have successful careers in the big leagues. Thus, while the Dodgers were struggling for a number of years, the scouting department, led by Logan White, was unearthing a nucleus of future Dodger teams. It was White who played the leading role in preventing the organization from sinking further into the abyss during the lean years. And in 2006, that scouting department was beyond ecstatic to choose a Texas high school pitcher as the seventh pick in the draft. The pitcher was future All-Star, multiple Cy Young winner, and one of the best pitchers *ever*: Clayton Kershaw. That, though, was still to come.

As for the 2006 side, they were inconsistent in the first few months of the season. They went 12–13 in April, 18–10 in May, 11–15 in June, and a deplorable 9–17 in July. No team, however, dominated the NL West, and the Dodgers were only 5 games out by the end of July. After such struggles, the team turned it on in August, going 21–7, but the inconsistency returned in September as the Dodgers went 16–12. What did this all mean? Well, the Dodgers trailed the Padres by two with five games remaining. They proceeded to win all five games (and the final nine out of eleven), including sweeping the Giants in San Francisco in the final three games to tie the Padres atop the NL West. In 2006, there was no one-game tiebreaker. The Padres had a better record against the Dodgers, and as such won the NL West with Los Angeles settling for the wild-card spot. The offense, led by J. D. Drew, Nomar Garciaparra, Jeff Kent, and Andre Ethier, had a great year with the third-best OPS in the NL. Meanwhile, Derek Lowe, Brad Penny, and Takashi Saito all had fine individual seasons for the fourth-best pitching staff in the NL.

The Dodgers faced the Mets in the NLDS, and the less said about that series, the better. The Mets swept the Dodgers to end the season. While they were competitive in every game (losing 6–5, 4–1, and 9-5), the series was seemingly doomed in the top of the second in Game One. Kent and then Drew singled to start the inning. With runners on first and second, Martin hit a ball to deep right field that hit the base of the wall. Kent, not the fastest runner, was tagged out at the plate. That would have been bad enough, but Drew kept running and was also tagged out at the plate. That is not a typo; both Kent and Drew were out at home. It was just mind-numbingly awful.

What was not awful was the famous "4+1" game against the Padres on September 18 at Dodger Stadium. Entering the bottom of the ninth, the Dodgers trailed 9–5. The game was seemingly over. Indeed, as the Padre lead was more than three runs the Padres did not even bother to bring in one of the greatest closers of all time in Trevor Hoffman to start the inning. Instead, Jon Adkins was brought in to get the final three outs. Unfortunately for Adkins, it did not quite work out that way. On a 1-0 count to start the inning, Kent hit a home run to cut the deficit to three. This was followed by Drew, who *also* hit a home run. Padres' manager Bruce Bochy had seen enough and brought in Hoffman. Martin, the next batter up, greeted Hoffman with *another* home run, this time on the very first pitch he saw. The crowd, which had thinned out, was going wild, and people who had left were trying to rush back into the stadium. Next up to the plate stepped Marlon Anderson. He swung at the first pitch he saw, sending it clear over the fence. The Dodgers had hit four home runs in a row to tie the game, and there were still none out in the inning. That was the fourth time in major-league history that a team had hit four consecutive home runs. Hoffman then retired the next three batters to send the game into extra innings.

The Padres scored in the top of the 10th to take a 10–9 lead. The four home runs in a row seemed all for naught. However, Kenny Lofton walked to start the bottom of the 10th. Then the magical night in Los Angeles had its fairytale ending, as on a 3-1 count Nomar Garciaparra hit a walk-off home run. The Dodgers had staged a miraculous comeback and won the game, 11–10. The Dodgers hit seven home runs in the game, tying the Dodger Stadium record. Garciaparra told the *Los Angeles Times*, "When I was rounding the bases, I couldn't wait to get home and hug everybody. It was like a group hug, because it was a group effort." He said, "It was so loud at the end. They [the remaining fans] were still there, waiting, when—believe me—it would have been easy for them to say it was over. We didn't give up, and neither did they." The 4+1 game is one of the greatest in Dodger history. That game and the 2006 season as a whole should have been an impetus for an even better 2007 season. It was, however, not to be.

* * *

The Dodgers' 2007 woes began in the offseason, when Ned Colletti signed former Giants pitcher Jason Schmidt to a three-year, $47 million contract. There was one slight problem: Schmidt had a torn rotator cuff. That would be bad enough, but the Dodgers *knew* that Schmidt was injured before he signed. To say that it was a foolish decision to sign someone to a long-term contract who had a major injury is a massive understatement. Schmidt only appeared in 10 games over the life of the contract. Likewise, while Garciaparra had a good first half of the 2006 season, his second half left a lot to be desired (yet he still signed a two-year contract extension). And Drew, who had an opt-out clause, decided to exercise that right and signed with the Red Sox.

The odd off-season decision-making continued at the start of the season. Despite Kemp, Loney, and Billingsley being more than ready, Colletti decided to place his faith in veterans. Billingsley's first start was on June 21, Loney did not make the team out of Spring Training and was finally called up in late May, and Kemp was sent back to the minors in early April and did not reappear for the big-league team until June.

Yet, despite this, the Dodgers were in contention for most of the year and on July 21 had the best record in the NL. Then things gradually fell apart. They were six games out on August 11 but clawed their way back and were 3½ games back by mid-September. Alas, they then proceeded to lose seven in a row and 10 out of 11 to see their playoff chances dissipate. The team finished the season with a record of 82–80, eight games out of first.

During the waning days of the season, the locker room was revealed to be less than united. Kent decided to vent his frustrations about the young players on the team to the *Los Angeles Times*, saying "I don't know why they don't get it. They don't understand a lot of things. Professionalism. How to manufacture a run. How to keep your emotions in it. There's just a lot of things that go on with playing 162 games. But I think experience can help more than inexperience. And it's hard to give a young kid experience."

Thirty-nine-year-old Luis Gonzalez, coincidently the same age as Kent, was also critical of the young players. As is common in almost all sports, the older players were becoming bitter when their playing time was reduced and it was clear that their days were numbered. Kemp eloquently responded to the criticism by noting, "If you take the younger guys away, do you have a team?"

While Gonzalez made it clear he would not re-sign with the Dodgers, it was not like the Dodgers wanted him back. But Kent decided to exercise his option. In a total random occurrence, he decided to go public with his frustrations once he could invoke the option. Also not returning was manager Grady Little. He technically resigned but, like Gonzalez, it was exceedingly unlikely he would be brought back. Taking over in the manager hot seat was long-time Yankee manager and future member of the Hall of Fame Joe Torre.

One new face in the Dodgers lineup was offseason-signing Andruw Jones. At one time, Jones was one of the best players in the game, but he was coming off the worst season of his career. Colletti decided to splurge and sign Jones for a $36.2 million, two-year contract. Jones was so pleased he showed up to Spring Training overweight. In his one year for Los Angeles, he hit .158 with an

OPS of .505 in 75 games. Jones may well be the worst signing in Dodger history. And considering that Schmidt fiasco, arguably the two worst signings in Dodger history were orchestrated in consecutive years by Colletti. The Dodgers released Jones in January 2009, preferring to release him and pay the money he was owed rather than have him take up a roster spot for the 2009 season.

There was also another controversial signing during the midyear trade period: Casey Blake. Blake was a decent third baseman and helped the Dodgers down the stretch. What was controversial about the deal is that the Dodgers sent Carlos Santana to the Indians. Santana was the team's best catching prospect, a star waiting to happen. During the trading period teams often give up highly rated prospects for rentals, like was the case with Blake. However, the Dodgers allegedly included Santana in the trade because McCourt was having trouble balancing the books and declared that no trades could increase payroll. Thus, by including Santana in the deal, the Indians agreed to cover the remainder of Blake's salary. While it was later claimed that the Indians insisted that Santana be included in the deal, the trade still could have been done without the young catcher. What lends credence to the claim is that another deal was in place to secure former Cy Young Award winner CC Sabathia but McCourt nixed it as it would increase payroll.

By late July, the Dodgers continued to struggle; they were coming off losing months in May and June. They played a lot better in July, but were clawing just to be .500 on the season. However, the putrid state of the NL West meant they were only two games out of the NL West lead. And that is when the Dodgers pulled off the greatest midseason signing in their history. As part of a three-team trade, the team acquired a perennial All-Star and one of the best hitters in the game: Manny Ramirez. In return, the Dodgers sent fringe major leaguer Andy LaRoche and minor leaguer Bryan Morris to the Pirates. And to cap it off, the Red Sox so badly wanted to get rid of Ramirez that they agreed to pay the remainder of his 2008 salary. If one considers short-term signings, while Jones may be the worst in Dodger history, Ramirez was clearly the best. As a Dodger in 2008, Ramirez hit .396 and had an OBP of .489, a slugging percentage of .743, an OPS of 1.232, 14 doubles, and 17 home runs—all in the span of 53 glorious games. Ramirez was a phenomenon in Los Angeles. Dubbed Mannywood, the Dodgers had seen nothing like it since the peak days of Fernandomania.

While it is often assumed that Ramirez turned the season around, on August 29 the Dodgers were still 4½ games back and had a record of 65–70. They then went on a tear, winning eight in a row and 12 out of 13 to take over the divisional lead. They finished the season with a record of 84–78, NL West champions and playoff bound.

As was the norm throughout Dodger history, it was the pitching staff that dominated—the best in the NL. Chad Billingsley led the starters in wins (16) and ERA (3.14); Lowe had another fine season, going 14–11 with an ERA of 3.24; thirty-three-year-old "rookie" Hiroki Kuroda suffered due to a lack of run support, but his ERA was only 3.73; and Jonathan Broxton was becoming a dominant closer. On the downside, Brad Penny had a below-average year, as he tried to pitch through injury. The 2008 season also saw the major-league debut of Clayton Kershaw, as he was called up in late May at the ripe old age of twenty. He went 5–5 on the season with an ERA of 4.26. While the numbers do not leap off the page, Kershaw showed enough signs for anyone looking that he had the potential to turn into one of the greats.

Awaiting the Dodgers in the NLDS were the Cubs, who held the best record in the NL. However, just having the best record doesn't mean the game is already decided, as the Dodgers dominated the series. The Dodgers were trailing by two after four innings in Game One, but first baseman James Loney hit a grand slam in the fifth to give the Dodgers a 4–2 lead. They went on to win, 7–2, with Russell Martin and Manny also hitting home runs. The Dodgers did even better in Game Two, with Billingsley pitching a strong 6⅔ innings and the offense firing on all cylinders, as they won 10–3. The series then came to Los Angeles. In Game Three, the home team scored two runs in the first, which would prove to be more than enough, as they eventually ran out winners 3–1 to sweep the Cubs. Kuroda was excellent, Martin hit two doubles, Ramirez went 1-for-2 with two intentional walks, while Broxton secured a four-out save. And then reality hit hard in the NLCS against the Phillies.

In Game One at Citizens Bank Park in Philadelphia, the Dodgers were leading 2–0 heading into the bottom of the sixth. Things then fell apart, as Chase Utley hit a two-run shot, following by a solo blast from Pat Burrell. The Dodgers never threatened after that and lost, 3–2. The Phillies jumped out to a quick 8–2 lead after three innings in Game Two, and held on to win 8–5. Game Three was a different matter entirely. The Dodgers scored five runs in the first, and the game was as good as over. They recorded a 7–2 victory.

In Game Four, Los Angeles led after seven innings in front of 56,800 hometown fans. In the top of the eighth, with one out and a man on first, Shane Victorino homered off of Cory

Wade to tie the game. Wade then retired the next batter before allowing a single to Carlos Ruiz. Skipper Joe Torre had seen enough and brought on Broxton to face pinch hitter Matt Stairs. On a 3-1 count, Stairs homered to give the Phillies the lead and break the home fans' hearts. The Phillies scored four runs in the inning and went on to win, 7–5. The Dodgers were mentally destroyed. Two days later, the Phillies clinched the NLCS with an easy 5–1 victory at Dodger Stadium.

While blame was cast all over for the Dodgers capitulation, one player was beyond reproach. Manny Ramirez had hit .520 with four home runs, an OBP of .667, and an OPS of an astounding 1.747 for the playoffs. It was a herculean performance to say the least. And after protracted contract negotiations in the offseason, the Dodgers were hoping for more of the same the following season after signing Ramirez to a two-year, $45 million contract.

* * *

The Dodgers started the season with guns blazing and a healthy lead in the division by early May. Manny Ramirez's contract was looking like a bargain. He was hitting .348 with six home runs and an OPS of 1.133. On May 6, things came crashing down. It was announced that Ramirez had failed a drug test during Spring Training. His drug of choice was the female fertility drug human chorionic gonadotropin. The drug is on the banned list because hCG helps to restore a person's natural testosterone levels after a steroid cycle (as steroids shut down a person's ability to create testosterone).

While Ramirez blamed the failed test on prescribed medication, he later failed a test for testosterone and eventually admitted to using PEDs. Not surprisingly, Ramirez was not the same hitter after his suspension. In his final 68 games he only hit .255 with an OPS of .838. In other words, he was a good player rather than an out-of-this-world superstar. One would assume that losing their greatest offensive threat would have heavily impacted the team.

After a hot start, the Dodgers led the NL West by 6½ games when Ramirez was suspended; when he returned they led the division by seven games. However, a five-game losing streak late in the season almost cost them the pennant; with two games remaining their lead was cut to one. Their final games were against the team battling them for the pennant: the Colorado Rockies.

On October 3, Clayton Kershaw took the mound and proceeded to throw six innings of shutout ball while striking out 10. The game was a tight and tense affair. Both teams were scoreless until the bottom of the seventh, when the Dodgers piled on five runs to effectively end the Rockies hopes. Another NL West crown was secured by the Los Angeles Dodgers. And for good measure, they defeated the Rockies on the final day of the season by a score of 5–3. They would finish the season with a record of 95–67, the best record in the NL.

Andre Ethier and Matt Kemp carried the offense. Ethier led the team with 31 home runs, finished sixth in MVP voting, and won the Silver Slugger Award. In a breakout year, Kemp hit .297 with 26 home runs, 101 RBIs, and 34 stolen bases; he was rewarded by finishing tenth in MVP voting while winning a Gold Glove and the Silver Slugger Award.

As for their NL-best pitching staff, veteran Randy Wolf went 11–7 with an ERA of 3.23. Chad Billingsley led the team in wins with 12, but, showing how wins are more a team statistic, his ERA ballooned to 4.03. Jonathan Broxton made the All-Star team while picking up 36 saves. Kershaw once again suffered through a lack of run support, as his ERA was 2.79 (best by a starter by far), yet his record was only 8–8. The Dodgers were confident heading into the playoffs, but history once again repeated itself.

The Dodgers faced the St. Louis Cardinal in the NLDS. The Cardinals struck first in Game One, but following a Rafael Furcal walk to start the bottom half of the inning, Kemp homered on the first pitch he saw to give the Dodgers the lead. Despite some tense moments and a less-than-stellar 2-for-15 with runners in scoring position, the Dodgers held on to win 5–3.

The Cardinals looked to level the series in Game Two and were leading 2–1 with two outs in the bottom of the ninth. The Dodgers last hope was first baseman James Loney, and on a 2-2 count he hit a soft liner to Matt Holiday in left field. Holiday came charging in and proceeded to drop the ball, allowing Loney to reach second. Following a walk to Blake, Ronnie Belliard singled to tie the game, and a walk to Martin loaded the bases. Up to the plate stepped pinch-hitter Mark Loretta. In his fifteenth and final year in the majors, Loretta had struggled mostly coming off the bench. But on this night he would forever be remembered in Dodger folklore, as he singled to bring home the winning run. Loretta said it was the biggest hit in his career: "It's crazy. . . . You never know in this game. It's a crazy game." Andre Ethier, who homered in the game, told the *New York Times*, "Absolutely, we stole one. . . I thought it was over. Show me one person out there who didn't think it was over. We needed a little magic." As for Holliday, he said, "I had it. . . . I was coming in to get it, then all of a sudden it hits the lights. You can't see. Obviously, I can catch a ball hit right at me. It wasn't a lack of effort. I just couldn't see it."

The dropped catch basically doomed the Cardinals, and the Dodgers scored an easy 5–1 victory in Game Three with Ethier hitting a double, triple, and a two-run home run. As in 2008, the Dodgers roared into the NLCS through sweeping an opponent in the divisional series. And, once again, awaiting the Dodgers were the Philadelphia Phillies. Once again, history would repeat itself.

In Game One at Dodger Stadium, the Dodgers took an early 1–0 lead before the Phillies scored five runs in the top of the fifth. The Dodgers came back with three runs in the bottom of the inning to make things interesting, but the Phillies held on to win 8–6. In contrast to that high-scoring affair, the Dodgers defeated the Phillies 2–1 in Game Two due in part to a bases-loaded walk by Ethier in the bottom of the eighth. Game Three was over as a contest after the Phillies scored four runs in the first and two in the second, going on to win 11–0. This brings us, as in 2008, to the pivotal Game Four.

The Phillies scored early once again—this time two runs in the bottom of the first. However, RBI singles by Loney and Martin in the top of the fourth tied the game. A solo home run by Kemp in the fifth and an RBI single by Casey Blake in the sixth gave the Dodgers a two-run advantage, but the Phillies got one back in the bottom of the inning. That would end the scoring for a while.

The Phillies threatened in the bottom of the eighth, but Joe Torre, who became Dodgers the manager in 2008, brought on Jonathan Broxton to get the final out of the inning and end the threat. In the bottom of the ninth, Broxton quickly recorded the first out, but followed that with a walk and a hit batter. He got

Greg Dobbs to line out, and the runners did not advance. But just like 2008, Game Four of the NLCS would once again cause heartache for LA. On a 1-1 pitch, Jimmy Rollins doubled to right field to score both runners; the Phillies walked it off. And as in 2008, the loss destroyed the Dodgers, and they were never in Game Five, getting blown out 10–4. If 2008 was a tragedy, then 2009 was a farce.

Thus, the decade ended on a depressing note, as the Dodgers had once again failed to appear in, let alone win, a World Series. But with the rise of the young guns, the Dodgers and their fans had to be optimistic heading into 2010. Unfortunately, the year did not turn out quite as expected.

# 8

## 2010–17: BANKRUPTCY, NEW OWNERSHIP, AND THE "BEST TEAM MONEY CAN BUY"

**THE DODGERS DID** not have the best start to 2010, with the team going 9–14 in the month of April. Not helping matters was that GM Ned Colletti called out the players and outfielder Matt Kemp in particular, stating, "Some guys, I guess, think that they're better than they are. They think the opposition's just going to roll over and get beat by them. That obviously doesn't happen. The baserunning's below average. The defense is below average. Why is it? Because he got a new deal? I can't tell you."

Kemp, who had signed a two-year, $10.95 million contract in the offseason, was not happy in the slightest, telling reporters, "Of course, it's good to make money. But that's not why I started playing this game. I started playing this game because I love the game, and I'm going to continue to love this game."

At the time of the criticism Kemp was leading the team in homers and was hitting .294 with an OPS of .942. It is true that Kemp had made mental gaffes in the field and on the basepaths, but it was odd for Colletti to single him out. The GM, however, may have been more concerned with what was happening to Kemp off the field. Kemp was enjoying the Hollywood life a bit too much, and it had affected his play. He slumped for the majority of the year, and the team's old-school skipper Joe Torre and bench coach Larry Bowa got into a very public feud with Kemp during the year.

For the hometown fans, all they saw was Kemp not living up to his potential and not playing the game the "right way." To them, he seemed like just another lazy multimillionaire who went Hollywood. However, how wealthy a person is, who someone is dating, how good-looking someone is has no bearing on what a person feels inside. Unbeknownst to many, Kemp was battling unseen demons and was often downright despondent. As he told Molly Knight, "So many nights I just went home and cried." Baseball and indeed life can be the cruelest of the cruel. It can bring a strong person to his knees and then grind him further into the ground.

It was not just Kemp struggling on the field of play during the 2010 season. The Dodgers finished with a record of 80–82, 12 games out of first place. James Loney had another below-average year, as did Russell Martin before a torn labrum in his right hip curtailed his season. As Martin was seemingly already in decline and it was unknown whether he could successfully come back from the injury, the Dodgers decided to not offer him salary arbitration at the end of the season, making him a free agent. He went on the sign with the Yankees and had a number of decent to good seasons with several clubs before rejoining the Dodgers prior to the start of the 2019 season.

As for the pitching staff, outside of Clayton Kershaw, Chad Billingsley, Hiroki Kuroda, and relief pitcher Hung-Chih Kuo, they left a lot to be desired. Kershaw began his ascent into one of the all-time greats, as he led all starters in games pitched (32), wins (13), and ERA (2.91).

Likewise, Andre Ethier had another very good year, as did Manny Ramirez, albeit in only 66 games. But with the Dodgers out of contention for a playoff berth and owner Frank McCourt looking to save money, Ramirez was traded midseason to the Chicago White Sox. Thus, the curtain came down for the final time on Mannywood. Likewise, Torre's managerial reign came to an end. He retired at the end of the season and was replaced by hitting coach and Yankee great Don Mattingly.

* * *

In the lead-up to the 2011 season, the Los Angeles media had an overwhelming desire for the Dodgers to cut ties with Matt Kemp, but the outfielder wanted to stay a Dodger. Don Mattingly always had a good relationship with Kemp and wanted him to remain in Los Angeles as well. And when the dust settled after the nonstop rumors of the offseason, Kemp was still a Dodger. The outfielder responded by having one of the best seasons for a player in team history. He hit .325 with 39 home runs, 115 runs scored, 126 RBIs (leading the league in these three categories), and a .986 OPS. That the Dodgers only played 161 games due to a postponed match-up against Washington not being replayed potentially deprived Kemp of joining the elite 40-40 club. Kemp was an All-Star while winning a

Gold Glove and the Silver Slugger Award. He finished second in MVP voting behind Ryan Braun, who was later revealed to be using PEDs. Kemp dominated the Dodgers offense so much so that the player with the next highest OPS among his teammates was Andre Ethier; his OPS was .789. Kemp's 2011 was historic, as was Kershaw's.

Kershaw, who was still only twenty-three years old, was outstanding. He went 21–5 while leading the NL in strikeouts (248) and ERA (2.28). He was an All-Star for the first time in his career, won a Gold Glove, and was a clear winner for the Cy Young Award. The scary thing, if you want to call it that, is that Kershaw was only getting better. His 2011 season was just the beginning of an unparalleled run of unsurpassed domination. Yet Kershaw and Kemp were lone bright flames on an easily forgettable season. The Dodgers finished 2011 with a record of 82–79, 11½ games out of first. What was not forgettable, though, was the drama surrounding the Dodgers off the field due to the issues with ownership.

On October 14, 2009, the day before the Dodgers played Game One of the NLCS against the Phillies, Frank and Jamie McCourt announced they were getting a divorce. The timing of the announcement certainly left a lot to be desired. Two days later, signaling that things were going to get messy, Frank McCourt declared he had 100 percent ownership of the Dodgers; Jamie declared that she owned 50 percent of the team, while later that month she was fired from her chief executive position. On December 7, 2010, a judge ruled that the couple's prenuptial agreement was invalid. As such, there was confusion about who actually owned the Dodgers. And all of this was just the precursor to the downright debacle that 2011 would bring.

In April 2011, there were fears that the Dodgers were running out of money. Major League Baseball finally had enough, and on April 20 took control of the team. League Commissioner Bud Selig said in a statement,

> I have taken this action because of my deep concerns regarding the finances and operations of the Dodgers and to protect the best interests of the club, its great fans and all of Major League Baseball. . . . My office will continue its thorough investigation into the operations and finances of the Dodgers and related entities during the period of Mr. McCourt's ownership.

On the surface, it looked like the Dodgers would get out of this nightmare when the McCourts announced they had agreed to a settlement as long as the league approved the sale of the Dodgers' TV rights to Fox.

There were just a couple of issues: the deal was below market-value and there would be an up-front payment of $385 million, of which $173.5 million would go to the McCourts and their legal representation. As such, MLB rejected the sale three days later. Then, on June 27, the organization hit the lowest of lows. The team filed for bankruptcy protection, as it was unlikely they would be able to cover their $30 million payroll. In filing the protection, McCourt blamed Bud Selig: "He's turned his back on the Dodgers, treated us differently, and forced us to the point we find ourselves in today. . . . I simply cannot allow the commissioner to knowingly and intentionally be in a position to expose the Dodgers to financial risk any longer."

In response, Selig said the Dodgers' woes were "caused by Mr. McCourt's excessive debt and his diversion of club assets for his own personal needs. . . . The action taken today by Mr.

McCourt does nothing but inflict further harm to this historic franchise." It was a sad state of affairs caused not by MLB or Bud Selig, but by Frank McCourt. The Dodgers were now a laughingstock, and fans of the once storied franchise had to deal with McCourt and MLB battling it out in bankruptcy court. Finally on November 1, McCourt conceded defeat and agreed to sell the team. McCourt said, "I know the last couple years were very, very difficult. . . . I'm very, very sorry about that. We're going to move forward and handle the situation now in as professional a way as possible and make sure the baton is passed here in a classy way." Classy is not how most people would characterize McCourt's ownership of the Los Angeles Dodgers.

The 2011 fiasco came to an end with the Dodgers once again for sale; the team was a league-wide laughingstock. Fans had seemingly had enough, as attendance had declined by 22 percent since 2009. And in 2011, only 2,935,139 fans attended games at Dodger Stadium; only "good" enough for sixth in the NL. While the first two years of the decade were a never-ending nightmare, 2012 would be a turning point in the team's fortunes both on and off the field.

## 2012: THE GUGGENHEIM ERA

The New Year started without a buyer for the team in place. On March 25, there were only three bidders remaining, including St. Louis (now LA) Rams owner Stan Kroenke. Two days later, and a mere few hours after MLB approved the final three bidders, the Dodgers had a new owner. A consortium headed by Mark Walter, the chief executive officer of Guggenheim Partners; Stan Kasten, former President of the Braves and Nationals; Peter Guber, Chairman and CEO of Mandalay Entertainment;

and Los Angeles Lakers legend Magic Johnson agreed to pay $2 billion to buy the Dodgers. The amount was the highest ever for a sports franchise. Kasten would take the mantle of president and CEO.

On May 1, the sale was officially completed, and the McCourt era was thankfully brought to a close. Proving that sometimes the "bad" guys win, despite almost bankrupting the Dodgers and making them a laughingstock, through the sale of the team McCourt earned net profits of approximately $1 billion. McCourt, who did not use even one singly penny of his own money to buy the Dodgers and basically bought the team with a Boston parking lot, was now a billionaire. And in a bitter irony, McCourt retained a 50 percent ownership in the Dodger Stadium parking lots.

With the specter of the sale looming over the team, they were largely quiet in the offseason with no big-name signings. Yet that did not seem to matter; the Dodgers won nine out of their first ten games, led the division by 3½ games at the end of April, and still had a five-game lead in the division on June 17. The team then went into a horrible slump, losing 11 out of 12 to see their lead in the division washed away. And in July the team lost seven out of eight before going on a five-game win streak. Inconsistency summed up the year in a nutshell.

The new ownership seemingly had enough and on July 25 traded young pitcher Nathan Eovaldi and minor leaguer Scott McGough to the Miami Marlins. In return they received pitcher Randy Choate and Hanley Ramirez. McCough was a fringe prospect and as of 2017 had only appeared in six games with the Marlins. Despite having a world of promise, Eovaldi has not quite lived up to his potential, although he has had a decent major-league career thus far. Choate was a good left-handed relief pitcher, but the real prize in the trade was Ramirez. A former Rookie of the Year and three-time All-Star, Ramirez had grown disgruntled in Miami, and they had grown disgruntled with him. It was on the surface a great coup for the team. But in 2012, Ramirez never quite gelled at the plate, hitting .271 with an OPS of .774. Nevertheless, Ramirez was a clear upgrade at shortstop.

Of course, not all trades work out. At the trade deadline of July 31, the Dodgers acquired Shane Victorino for Josh Lindblom, Ethan Martin, and a player to be named later (Stefan Jarrin). The trade was a failure for the Dodgers, not because of any of the players given up, but because Victorino did not play well for his new team, hitting only .245 with an OPS of .667—well below his norm.

Nevertheless, the Dodgers were a long way from being done in the trade market. And on August 25, well after the "official" trade deadline, they pulled off a monster deal with the Red Sox. The team traded Ivan De Jesus Jr., James Loney, Allen Webster, and two players to be named later (which would end up being Ruby De La Rosa and Jerry Sands) to the Red Sox in return for Josh Beckett, Carl Crawford, Adrian Gonzalez, Nick Punto, and cash considerations. Beckett was a former All-Star and helped the Red Sox break its World Series curse, Crawford (who was recovering from Tommy John surgery) was at one time a hitting- and base-stealing machine, while Gonzalez was a premier first baseman long coveted by Dodger fans. While Punto wasn't on the same level as the other three, he was still a solid utility infielder. His inclusion in the trade was humorous to many Dodger fans, so much so that the trade is now known and forever will be as the Nick Punto trade. The Red Sox acquired some good prospects and a decent first baseman in Loney. Moreover, they shed millions of dollars in payroll in an instant, and the trade allowed them to rebuild (which resulted in a World Series victory the following year, and in 2018 when they defeated the Dodgers). For the Dodgers, Beckett pitched reasonably well the reminder of the year, Gonzalez performed slightly below expectations, while Punto did better than expected.

On the day of the trade, the Dodgers were two games out of first. Their season arguably came to an abrupt end three days later. Matt Kemp, who had two stints on the disabled list due to hamstring problems, was still having a great season. In 77 games he was hitting .337 with 17 home runs and an OPS of .987. Kemp, and to a less extent Andre Ethier and catcher A. J. Ellis, were the leading lights offensively for the Dodgers. But on August 28 at Coors Field, Kemp tried to make a running catch and at top speed crashed into the center-field wall. While he only missed a few games, he was not the same player; in the remaining 28 games he hit .214 with an OPS of .686. Kemp should not have been playing, and it was later revealed that he had a torn labrum which would need surgery to repair.

With Kemp struggling and no one covering the void, the Dodgers quickly slipped out of contention. They finished the season with a record of 86–76, eight games behind the Giants. That the Dodgers did not make the playoffs arguably cost Kershaw another Cy Young victory. The team's ace finished the season with a record of 14–9 despite leading the NL in ERA (2.53). The lack of run support cost Kershaw in the win column, as six of his losses occurred with the team scoring one run or less. Thus, the 2012 season came to the end with the Dodgers missing the playoffs once again. Unlike in the McCourt era, the

Guggenheim consortium was willing to spend in an attempt to secure World Series success.

* * *

In a two-day span in December 2012, the Dodgers made two astute signings. On December 9, Hyun-Jin Ryu was signed from the Hanwha Eagles of the Korea Baseball Organization. And the next day, in a big coup, free agent Zach Greinke agreed to join the Dodgers. Hyun-Jin Ryu responded by going 14–8 with an ERA of 3.00, while Greinke was even better with a record of 15–4 and an ERA of 2.63. Greinke was also the catalyst for a huge brawl between the Dodgers and the Padres on April 11. In just his second start for the team, Greinke hit Carlos Quentin with a pitch. There was a history of bad blood between the two—well at least there was in Quentin's mind. This led Quentin to charge Greinke and in the process break the pitcher's collarbone, causing him to miss a little over a month.

Just like Greinke's collarbone, the 2013 season was looking like a total bust; on June 21, the team was a pathetic 30–42, 9½ games out of first. There were numerous reports that manager Don Mattingly was on the verge of being fired.

But then something miraculous happened: the Dodgers went on a 42–8 run. That run equaled those of the 1941 Yankees and 1942 Cardinals. At the end of the record-tying 50-game run, the Dodgers had an 8½ game lead in the division and would cruise to the NL West crown, winning the division by 11 games.

The record run can be attributed to many factors. Both Greinke and Kershaw were magnificent during the run, with Greinke going 8–1 with an ERA of 2.25 while Kershaw was even better at

7–2 with an ERA of 1.40. For the season, Kershaw finished with a record of 16–9 and a NL-leading ERA of 1.83. He was duly rewarded at the end of the year with his second Cy Young Award.

Apart from Greinke and Kershaw, the offense catching fire was a big factor in the team's resurgence. And no two players had a bigger impact than Yasiel Puig and Hanley Ramirez.

Yasiel Puig, who defected from Cuba, was signed by the Dodgers to a seven-year contract worth $42 million on June 29, 2012. It was Logan White who implored the front office to capture the signature of the future "Wild Horse." Puig started 2013 in the minors despite an awe-inspiring Spring Training where he hit .517, but with the Dodgers struggling he was brought up on June 3. He collected two hits in his first game and sealed the victory by making a great catch in right field and throwing out the retreating baserunner at first base. Not to be known as a one-game wonder, he hit two home runs in his second career game.

And with that, Puigmania (or whatever you wanted to call it) was born. While raking with the bat, the young Cuban also had maturity issues (which was largely why he did not make the club out of Spring Training). Puig was not exactly humble, and this greatly annoyed a certain section of players, media, and fans who believed the game should be played the "right way." What the "right way" is can be open to debate, but bat flipping and showing up opposing pitchers—which Puig was prone to do—should never be tolerated under such a system.

As a result of his behavior, on June 11 the Dodgers were involved in another brawl. Diamondbacks pitcher Ian Kennedy hit Yasiel Puig on the tip of his nose with a fastball. Puig was very lucky that the ball did not hit him flush in the face. Kennedy seemingly threw at Puig because, as Kennedy later remarked,

Puig "plays with a lot of arrogance." In retaliation, Greinke hit Miguel Montero with a fastball in the middle of the back. Teams usually accept the payback in these types of situations, but not the Diamondbacks. In the bottom of the inning, Kennedy threw at Greinke's head. Luckily Greinke shrugged his shoulder and the ball bounced off of it. This led to a full-on brawl. Under baseball's unwritten rules, bat flips and showing excessive emotion are frowned upon; it is not playing the game the "right way." But throwing at players' heads that do not play the game the "right way" is seemingly suitable punishment. To say this is strange is quite the understatement.

Foolishness aside, Puig dominated once he was called up, and during the 42–8 run hit .332 with an OPS of .913. For the season as a whole he hit .319 with 19 home runs and an OPS of .925. Yet for all the platitudes that went to Puig for igniting the team, Ramirez was even better. Due to injury, Ramirez only played four games in April and May (two each month). He returned to the lineup in early June, mostly as a pinch hitter, and was inserted back into the everyday lineup on June 19 against the Mets in a doubleheader. He immediately made up for lost time, going 6-for-8 with a double and a home run. From that point on, he did not just catch fire; he went nuclear. During the 42–8 run, Ramirez hit .358 with 10 home runs and an OPS of 1.064. He ended up playing in 86 games and hit .345 with an OPS of 1.040 to go along with 20 home runs. With Puig and Ramirez dominating at the plate, the Dodgers ended up with a record of 92–70 and won the division by 11 games.

Considering the bad blood between the teams, it was fitting that the Dodgers clinched the division with a win against the Diamondbacks in Arizona. The Diamondbacks home field,

Chase Stadium, has a small swimming pool in right field pavilion. A number of Dodger players decided that the best way to celebrate clinching the division would be to have a pool party. As such, they frolicked in the water. During the celebrations, Kemp jokingly said someone urinated in the pool. Someone overheard Kemp and the next thing you knew it was all over the Internet how the Dodger players had pissed in the pool. Diamondbacks President Derrick Hall raged, "I could call it disrespectful and classless, but they don't have a beautiful pool at their old park and must have really wanted to see what one was like." To call the Chase field pool beautiful and implicitly criticize Dodger Stadium for not having a pool is certainly laughable. Even politicians got into the act; Senator John McCain, a Diamondbacks fan, tweeted, "No-class act by a bunch of overpaid, immature, arrogant, spoiled brats!" Because of the Dodgers' celebration we now know that celebrating in an opponents' pool is now considered as not playing the game the "right way." Of course, not all Diamondback players were outraged by the Dodgers' celebration. Then Arizona pitcher and future Dodger Brandon McCarthy tweeted, "I don't care how and where you do it. Only thing to care about is what we need to do to celebrate in our pool next year."

The Dodgers had more celebrating to do after the NLDS. Opposing the team in the divisional series would be the Atlanta Braves. In Game One at Turner Field in Atlanta, on the back of seven strong innings from Kershaw in which he only gave up one run while striking out 12, the Dodgers easily won 6–1. Atlanta evened the series following Game Two with a 4–3 victory. Apart from Ramirez, who hit two doubles and a home run, the offense was subdued.

But the bats woke up in Game Three. After trailing by two going into the bottom of the second, they went on an onslaught, thanks to a three-run home run from Carl Crawford and a two-run home run from Juan Uribe, taking back the series lead with a 13–6 victory. Ramirez was slightly subdued in this game; he went 3-for-4 with a walk, a double, and a triple.

Kershaw pitched on short rest in Game Four. Thanks to two solo home runs by Crawford (in the first and third), the Dodgers were cruising. But Atlanta tied it up in the bottom of the fourth, thanks to two unearned runs and scored the go-ahead run in the top of the seventh. Not to be undone, in the bottom of the eighth, Puig hit a lead-off double. Rather than bringing in their dominant closer Craig Kimbrel in the most important part of the game, Atlanta manager Fredi Gonzalez chose to stick with David Carpenter. It was a costly mistake, as on a 2-2 pitch Uribe hit a two-run home run to give the Dodgers a 4–3 lead. Kenley Jansen then struck out the Braves in the ninth, and the Dodgers were heading back to the NLCS.

For Uribe, it was the icing on a glorious season. He was signed by GM Ned Colletti following helping the Giants win the 2010 World Series. The Dodgers certainly paid more than Uribe was worth, but no one could imagine how horrendous his 2011 and 2012 seasons would be. In 2011, he had an OPS of .557, and was even worse in 2012 when it dropped to .543. He was so bad that Mattingly refused to play him. Rather than sulk and be a clubhouse cancer, Uribe was his usual upbeat self and an asset to the locker room. And in 2013, Uribe once again began to hit; his OPS rose to .769, and while once he was scorned by fans, he was now beloved. As happy as Uribe was with his game-winning home run, his teammates were even more ecstatic. After the game, catcher A. J. Ellis said, "You ask everyone in that clubhouse who's their favorite teammate and 95 percent of them are going to say Juan Uribe. . . . He deserved this night. He deserved this moment."

Mattingly, who wanted Uribe to bunt Puig over to third, noted that "The smile on his face when he hit that home run was priceless. . . . He's had a rough couple of years, but he's been great." Uribe's smile could light up the blackest of black nights, and it was a moment no Dodger fan will ever forget.

Unfortunately, no Dodger fan will ever forget the first inning of Game One of the NLCS against the Cardinals either. With a man on first, on a 1-2 pitch Cardinals starter Joe Kelly drilled Hanley Ramirez with a 95 mph fastball. Ramirez stayed in the game and hobbled to first, eventually going 0-for-2 with three walks, two being intentional. The Cardinals eventually won the game in 13 innings, 3–2.

Losing in extra innings was not great, but most concerning was the considerable pain Ramirez was in after the game. The X-ray on his ribs came back negative, and he was scheduled to start Game Two. However, he was scratched moments before the game, as he could not swing the bat due to pain. In Molly Knight's book, *The Best Team Money Can Buy*, it was revealed that Ramirez, who was terrified of needles, refused to be injected with the painkiller Toradol. Toradol is so powerful that a person withering in pain ends up feeling nothing. Indeed, Crawford was injected with the painkiller following Game Two of the NLDS because of his shoulder pain. And, as noted above, he homered twice in Game Three. That Ramirez refused the injection did not exactly make the rest of the locker room happy. Nevertheless, what was merely thought to be bruising was actually a hairline fracture. Also not making the locker room happy was Andre Ethier, who refused to play in Game Two because of a hurt shin.

And with no Ramirez and no Ethier, the Dodgers' offense was virtually nonexistent in Game Two. Kershaw was saddled with the loss after giving up one run in six innings, but the one run was all the Cardinals needed, as they won the game 1–0. From that point forward the Dodgers were behind the proverbial eight-ball. While they won Game Three at Dodger Stadium 3–0, thanks to seven shutout inning from Ryu and a 2-for-4 performance from Ramirez, Hanley was held hitless in the remainder in the series. Playing with a hairline fracture of the ribs is not conducive for hitting. And with the red-hot Ramirez not being able to swing a bat properly, it was all the advantage a very good Cardinals team needed. In Game Four the Cardinals scored three runs in the top of the third, and with a moribund Dodger offense the game was as good as over. The Cardinals eventually won, 4–2. The offense came back from the dead in Game Five. Two home runs from Gonzalez and solo shots from Crawford and Ellis, as well as seven strong innings of work from Greinke, saw the Dodgers win 6–4. The series then returned to St. Louis. With Kershaw taking the mound and the offense bouncing back, Dodger fans were optimistic that their team could force a deciding Game Seven . . . but it was not to be. In a performance most Dodger fans wish to forget, Kershaw gave up seven runs in only four innings while the offense could only muster up two hits, as the Cardinals easily won 9–0 to advance to the World Series. Following the game, Kershaw, with his winner-take-all mentality, noted, "What does it really matter, making the playoffs or coming in in last place, if you don't win the World Series? It doesn't really matter."

While the Dodgers did not make or win the World Series, the 2013 season will always be fondly remembered for Greinke. The Dodgers were close to clinching the division when they started losing games. Mattingly held a team meeting and said the usual things (do not worry about winning the division, play day-to-day, etc.). Once he was done speaking, Greinke asked to address his teammates. It was a surprise, as Greinke is often quiet both with the media and his teammates, plus he was pitching that day (and most starters are usually quiet on the day they pitch). Greinke did not want to address the team on any on-field issues but rather on bathroom hygiene. As recounted by Knight, Greinke began by saying "I've been noticing something. . . . Some of you guys have been doing the number two and not washing your hands. . . . It's not good. I noticed it even happened earlier today. . . . So if you guys could just be better about it that would be great."

\* \* \*

The offseason began on an interesting note when the Dodgers had an end-of-season press conference with Ned Colletti and Don Mattingly. The two looked like a feuding couple. Colletti spoke first and gave out the usual clichés. In contrast, Mattingly threw hand grenades. He said "My option [to manage in 2014] vested once we beat Atlanta. . . . That doesn't mean I'll be back. . . . I love it here. But I don't want to be anywhere where you're not wanted."

Mattingly was eventually confirmed as the Dodgers manager for the upcoming season, as he was given a three-year contract extension. Apart from the press conference, it was a relatively quiet offseason for the team. The owners had already outlaid vast amounts of money to turn the team's fortunes around and expected the current squad, with only minimal changes, to once again make the playoffs and hopefully do better than the previous season.

Like the previous season, however, the team got off to an average start. On June 8, they had a record of 33–31 and were a whopping 10 games behind the first-place Giants. However, the Giants lost 9 out of 10, and the Dodgers played good baseball and were tied for the division lead at month's end. The teams would battle for the division lead the rest of the season. There would be no collapse by the Dodgers this year; despite some stumbles, they held their nerve. Their biggest lead of the season was six games, which occurred on the final day of the season. The Dodgers finished with a record of 94–68 and were once again headed to the postseason.

The offense had a fine season—ranked second-best in the NL. Gonzalez was once again very good, leading the team in doubles (41), home runs (27) and RBIs (116). While not as hot as the previous season, Hanley Ramirez still posted an OPS of .817, but it became clear during the season that his career as a Dodger was coming to an end, as the front office was not interested in discussing a possible contract extension. Ramirez responded by sulking for the majority of the season. He also wanted to play as often as possible to make himself attractive to potential suitors. Unfortunately, at times this cost the Dodgers, as Ramirez refused to go on the disabled list even though he was clearly injured. There was also talk that he did not exactly go all out in the field.

One person who gave his all was Justin Turner. As a nonroster invitee during Spring Training, Turner defied all expectations. In 106 games, he hit .340 with an OPS of .897. Turner would go on to have many outstanding seasons with Los Angeles and is arguably the best nonroster invitee ever.

While Turner was an unexpected bonus, the Dodgers were hoping that Matt Kemp would rediscover his old form. In an injury-ravaged 2013, Kemp was restricted to only 73 games and was still suffering the effects of shoulder surgery. Additionally, he severely damaged his ankle in a game against Washington that effectively ended his season. Likewise, the 2014 season was looking to be a bust. On June 4, Kemp was hitting .238 with an OPS of .689. He slowly improved, but by July 23 his OPS was still only .755. During the season, Mattingly informed Kemp that he would no longer be the starting center fielder. Kemp did not take the news well and was benched for a few days, as he refused to play in left field. After the failed stint in left he was moved to right. There was continued talk that Kemp was going to be traded, and the slugger responded by getting nuclear. For the remainder of the season (58 games) he hit .315 with an OPS of .998 to go along with 17 home runs. Kemp was a large reason why the Dodgers reached the postseason.

Likewise, in his first full season in the majors, Puig had a fine season; he hit .296 with an OPS of .863. The Dodger players and coaches, however, were getting tired of the youngster's antics. In the offseason Puig was caught speeding, going 110 mph. And if that didn't help bring ire, the coaching staff was far from pleased when Puig showed up to Spring Training twenty-five pounds overweight.

To his credit, when the season started, he had dropped most of the excess weight, but his commitment to baseball began to be called into question. At the first workout of the year at Dodger Stadium, Puig showed up at 10:27 a.m. The workout was scheduled for 10:30 a.m. Puig then went to talk to Mattingly and emerged asking his teammates what he could do better. Uribe and Ramirez, among others, told him to show up on time, and Ramirez, who was not exactly loved by the end of his tenure in Miami, told Puig not to make the same mistakes as he had. What should have been a turning point was anything but. One week later, in a game he was scheduled to start, Puig showed up late to the Dodgers' home opener and was benched. There were other incidents throughout the season. As Knight recounts, on the bus from O'Hare International Airport in Chicago to their hotel

> some players asked to stop for pizza, the rest told the driver to continue to the hotel and circle back for the guys getting food. But Puig had opened the door to the luggage bay on the bus so he could retrieve his bag, and the driver couldn't move until the door was shut. Greinke got out and threw Puig's bag into the street. Puig responded by pushing Greinke, but J. P. Howell intervened to stop Puig.

Quite simply, many of Puig's teammates were sick of his antics and believed that the twenty-three year old cared more about fame than putting in the hard work to succeed at the major-league level.

In addition to throwing Puig's bag into the street, Greinke had another very good season on the mound. He finished with a record of 17–8 and an ERA of 2.71, making the All-Star team and winning a Gold Glove. While Greinke flourished as a Dodger, one pitcher who did not was Josh Beckett. After making only eight appearances in 2013, going 0–5 with an ERA of 5.19, he bounced back in 2014 to finish with a record of 6–6 and an ERA of 2.88. Injury, though, curtailed his season, limiting him to 20 starts, and he retired at season's end. There was one moment of brilliance, however, for Beckett. On May 25 at Citizens Bank Park in Philadelphia, Beckett pitched nine scoreless innings, walking three, striking out six, and not giving up a hit. Beckett had no-hit the Phillies. Following the game Beckett noted, "I don't think I had no-hit stuff." The no-hitter was the first and only of his career. "It was awesome. . . . You think about it pretty much from the fourth on. I'm not one of those guys that carried a lot of no-hitters deep into games." It was the first Dodger no-hitter since Nomo's one in Colorado in 1996. The Dodgers did not have to wait anywhere near that long for their next no-hitter, as it came 24 days later.

It seemed impossible, but Kershaw was becoming an even better pitcher. In 2014 he went 21–3, led the NL with six complete games, and lowered his ERA to 1.77. Kershaw was once again an All-Star and Cy Young winner. Moreover, he was named the NL MVP for the first time. And in another first, on June 18 against Colorado at Dodger Stadium, Kershaw pitched a no-hitter. The Dodgers ace gave up no walks and struck out a career-high 15, and was only denied a perfect game due to a Ramirez throwing error in the seventh. It was one of the greatest pitching performances in team—if not baseball—history.

Following the game, Kershaw told the *Los Angeles Times,*

> I guess I really haven't thought of the ramifications, of throwing one of these things. . . . It's definitely special company. I don't take for granted the history of this or what it means. I definitely understand all that. But as far

as individually, though, it's right up there with winning playoff games and World Series games and all that stuff. It's pretty cool.

Kershaw also made a note to mention Beckett: "Beckett told me he was going to teach me how to do that [pitch a no-hitter], so I have Josh to thank." With the best pitcher on the planet, the Dodgers were confident heading into the NLDS where they were set to meet their old nemesis: the St. Louis Cardinals. However, for the players, front office, and long-suffering fans, history would repeat itself once again.

In Game One in Los Angeles, the Dodgers were cruising with a 6–2 lead after six innings with Kershaw on the mound. And then the most infamous seventh inning in Dodgers history happened. Kershaw gave up four straight singles. He struck out the next batter before allowing another single, and then struck out another Cardinal. A two-out double from Matt Carpenter then cleared the bases. Mercifully, Mattingly then replaced Kershaw. Matt Holliday then hit a three-run homer off Pedro Baez. That was the end of the scoring for the inning, with the Cardinal notching eight runs. While the Dodgers scored two runs in the eighth and one in the ninth, they could not plate the tying run, and the Cardinals won Game One, 10–9. Following the game Kershaw said, "I couldn't hold it [the lead], it's a terrible feeling. . . . It doesn't feel good right now. I don't think it will feel good for the rest of the night." Unfortunately for Kershaw and the Dodgers, things would only get worse.

The Dodgers came back to win Game Two, thanks in a large part to Matt Kemp. The Dodgers were leading 2–0 after seven, but in the top of the eighth Carpenter hit a two-run homer off of Howell to tie the game. In the bottom of the inning, Kemp led off the inning with a home run to left field.

The series reverted to St. Louis for Game Three where once again the seventh inning would haunt the Dodgers. The score was tied 1–1 with the Cardinals coming up in the bottom of the seventh. After a lead-off double by Yadier Molina, Kolten Wong hit a two-run home run off of reliever Scott Elbert. The Dodgers threatened in the ninth, but it amounted to nothing, as the Cardinals won 3–1.

In Game Four, the Dodgers had a 2–0 lead after six innings and with Kershaw pitching on three days' rest. There was room for optimism that a Game Five would be needed. Once again, though, the seventh inning would be cruel to the Dodgers. After singles by Matt Holliday and Jhonny Peralta, Mattingly allowed Kershaw to remain in the game. Considering that Baez was prone to giving up crucial hits (as seen in Game One), the skipper was in a conundrum.

On an 0-1 count, Kershaw threw a curveball to left-hander Matt Adams. At that point in his career, Kershaw had never allowed a home run to a left-handed batter on a curveball. Adams changed all that with one swing, as he took Kershaw deep for a three-run shot. And once again the Dodgers threatened in the ninth, which amounted to nothing, as the Cardinals held on to win 3–2 and advance to the NLCS. Following the game, Kershaw told the assembled media, "The season ended and I was a big part of the reason why. . . . It doesn't feel good, regardless of how you pitched. I can't really put it into words right now. Just bad déjà vu, all over again."

For Kershaw, history repeated itself: Game One was the tragedy; Game Four was the farce. In addition, Kershaw was beginning to be labeled as someone who could not handle the pressure of the postseason. As the narrative went, he was a choker. Likewise, with another failed postseason in the books and the Giants once again winning the World Series (their third in five years), it was often claimed that the Dodgers lacked the grit and heart needed to win in October. The upcoming 2015 season would do nothing to convince people who held on to these narratives that they were wrong.

* * *

The offseason got off to a newsworthy note when the Dodgers hired Andrew Friedman as the president of baseball operations, who had previously been the GM of the Tamp Bay Rays. Freidman is a firm believer in analytics—such an approach was almost the opposite on how Colletti operated. As such, there was no surprise when Colletti was replaced by Farhan Zaidi. Zaidi was former director of baseball operations and assistant GM of the Oakland Athletics. And to complete the front office signings, former Padres GM Josh Byrnes was hired to be the vice president of baseball operations. The Guggenheim consortium believed that money alone could not buy a World Series victory; what was also needed was advance analytics in the front office.

Among the major offseason moves, rather than offer Ramirez a long-term contract that he was seeking, the front office only offered him a one-year qualifying offer. As expected, Ramirez rejected it and eventually signed a four-year deal with the Red Sox. In return, Los Angeles received a draft pick. Before the year was over they traded away another of their power hitters, sending Matt Kemp to the San Diego Padres in a multiplayer deal. The prize for the Dodgers was catcher Yasmani Grandal.

On the pitching side, the big acquisitions were Brett Anderson on a one-year contract and Brandon McCarthy. Neither player was a superstar, while both were prone to injuries, but they were solid pitchers who would hopefully fit nicely in the middle of the rotation. With Kershaw and Greinke being undisputed aces, the Dodgers rotation was arguably the best in baseball—at least on paper.

A shoulder injury put Hyun-Jin Ryu on the shelf for the entire 2015 season, and he only appeared in one game in 2016. Brandon McCarthy required Tommy John surgery after only four starts. Brett Anderson, however, appeared in a career-high 31 games, going 10–9 with an ERA of 3.69. Considering Anderson was only on a one-year contract and accepted the qualifying offer following the 2015 season, it was a good signing by the front office. Of course, the baseball gods can be cruel, and injury limited Anderson to only four games in 2016.

As for the Dodgers 2015 season, following a win against the Rockies on April 17, they were tied for first. Apart from May 29, they held on to the division lead for the rest of the season. Despite the usual hiccups along the way that even the best teams go through, the Dodgers eventually won the NL West by eight games. Offensively, Justin Turner, Adrian Gonzalez, and Andre Ethier had great seasons. Gonzalez led the team in hits, doubles, home runs, and RBIs.

There were, however, issues for the Dodgers heading into the postseason. Rookie center fielder Joc Pederson had an outstanding first half of the season. His OPS was .851, and he made the All-Star team. Unfortunately, Pederson went into a horrendous slump in the second half; he hit an awful .178 with an OPS of .617. Likewise, the trade that sent Kemp to the Padres for Yasmani Grandal seemed to be magnificent for the Dodgers. In the first half of the season, in addition to being a fine defensive catcher, Grandal hit .282 with an OPS of .927. He then played through a shoulder injury—never a smart approach (especially for a catcher). In the second half, he hit an awful .162 with an OPS of .498. As for Puig, injuries curtailed the majority of his season, but when he played he seemed a shell of his former self. He hit .255 with an OPS of .758, well down from the previous season and a long way from his stellar rookie year.

On the pitching side, apart from Brett Anderson, Mike Bolsinger (acquired from the Diamondbacks in the offseason) proved to be a valuable back-of-the-rotation guy. He appeared in 21 games with an ERA of 3.62. As for the big two of Kershaw and Greinke, Kershaw "struggled" early on, so much so that there were articles along the lines of "What's Wrong with Kershaw?" Apparently, he was not allowed to be human and have a few bad games. Eventually, he reverted back to the pitching machine he seemingly is, finishing the season with a record of 16–7 and an ERA of 2.13 while leading the league in complete games, innings pitched, and strikeouts. He was once again an All-Star, finished tenth in MVP voting, and came in third in Cy Young voting. Kershaw was great, but Greinke was even better. During the season, he pitched 45⅔ innings straight of scoreless ball, had a record of 19–3, and turned in a minute 1.66 ERA, which led the league. Greinke made the All-Star team, finished seventh in MVP voting, won a Gold Glove, and finished second for the Cy Young Award. No team had a more potent one-two punch than the Dodgers. And no team arguably had a better closer than the Dodgers.

Kenley Jansen, who was born in Willemstad, Curaçao, was a failed catching prospect. Quite simply, he could not hit. But he did have a proverbial cannon for an arm. This led to the Dodgers attempting to convert him to a pitcher starting in 2009. And to say it was a success would be an understatement. In 2010, Jansen made his major-league debut. In May 2012, Jansen became the Dodgers' closer and excelled in the role. However, the front office did not have faith in him, and former closers were brought in to fill the role. Once they failed, Jansen once again became the "ninth inning guy." In 2014, he saved 44 games—the first Dodger to save more than 40 games since Eric Gagne. In 2015, injuries delayed the start of Jansen's season, but he had another fine year by saving 36 games.

With Kershaw and Greinke leading the way, and with a dominant closer in Jansen, the Dodgers were feeling confident about their chances of capturing their first World Series title since 1988. Yet once again the baseball gods cast down fire and brimstone on the team's postseason chances.

Facing the Dodgers in the NLDS would be the New York Mets. In Game One, the Mets took the lead in the fourth inning when Daniel Murphy hit a solo home run off Kershaw. The seventh inning would once again prove to be unkind to the Dodgers, as following Kershaw walking the bases, Mattingly replaced him with Pedro Baez. And as sure as night follows day, David Wright singled off of Baez to plate two. While Gonzalez got one back in the eighth, the Mets held on and won 3–1. Once again, Kershaw suffered a loss in the postseason in a large part to being left in too long and the relievers being unable to rescue him.

In Game Two, the Mets once again jumped to an early lead after two solo shots off of Greinke in the second by Yoenis Cespedes and Michael Conforto. The Dodgers got one back in the fourth, thanks to an Ethier double. This time, however, the seventh would prove kind to the Dodgers. They scored four runs, thanks to a large part to doubles from Gonzalez and Turner, and went on to win 5–2. The series then headed to New York, and Game Three was one to forget for LA. Despite taking a 3–0 lead in the first, the Dodgers fell apart. The Mets scored four runs in the bottom of the inning, two in the third, and four in the fourth. They eventually won, 13–7. Game Four saw Kershaw pitch once again on short rest. He was magnificent, only giving up one run on three hits in seven innings, as the Dodgers won 3–1.

The teams then flew to Los Angeles for the deciding Game Five. Once again, the Mets scored early, this time a double by Murphy. The Dodgers came back in the bottom of the frame and took a 2–1 lead, thanks to singles from Corey Seager, Adrian Gonzalez, Justin Turner, and Andre Ethier off Mets starter Jacob deGrom. The game turned in the top of the fourth, as Murphy led off the inning with a single and advanced to second on a walk. However, not a single Dodger was covering third, which allowed Murphy to take the base. It was great baserunning from Murphy and Little League defense from the Dodgers. Murphy then scored on a sacrifice fly to tie the game. In the top of the sixth, Murphy put the Mets ahead with a solo home run. The Dodgers offense, which for the first five innings had at least one runner in scoring position, could only muster a single walk in the remaining four innings. The Mets won, 3–2. After the game the players were still uncertain who should have been covering third. Seager said, "I should have at least gone halfway to the bag. I was talking about the next play, and unfortunately I wasn't paying attention and he got to sneak by. That's something we have to discuss beforehand and work out." In contrast, Greinke claimed, "Just someone is supposed to be there—either me or

Seager or Yas [catcher Yasmani Grandal]. . . . Someone should be there. A bunch of people made mistakes. It wasn't any one person." Who was at fault in the end is immaterial; it was another postseason disappointment for the Los Angeles Dodgers.

＊ ＊ ＊

Unfortunately for Dodgers players and fans, postseason disappointment would once again reign its ugly head in 2016. However, this time it would not occur with Don Mattingly in charge. During the offseason, the Dodgers and Mattingly agreed to a mutual parting of the ways. Mattingly would then go on to become manager of the Miami Marlins. Taking charge of the LA club was former Padres bench coach and ex-Dodger Dave Roberts. Roberts, whose mother is Japanese and father is African American, is the first minority to lead the Dodgers. Roberts proved during the season he was prepared to make the tough choices. On April 8 against the Giants in San Francisco, Roberts pulled rookie Ross Stripling in the rookie's major-league debut after 7⅓ innings due to a high pitch count. What made the move controversial is that Stripling was pitching a no-hitter. Moreover, on September 10, Roberts pulled Rich Hill (acquired in a trade midseason) from a perfect game after seven innings. Hill, who was suffering from blisters on his pitching hand (which had previously caused him to miss games), was understandably upset. However, Roberts was putting the good of the team above any individual accomplishment. Such an approach was respected in the clubhouse and throughout baseball. And by year's end, Roberts was rewarded by winning NL Manager of the Year honors.

In addition to the managerial change, the other major move of the offseason was Zack Greinke opting out of his contract and signing a megadeal with the Diamondbacks. However, like the Padres in the previous season, the Diamondbacks' strategy of heavy spending on free agents and trading for talent to unseat the Dodgers from the top of the NL West was an unmitigated disaster, and they were never in contention.

There was also a major move during the season when A. J. Ellis was traded to the Phillies for catcher Carlos Ruiz. Even though Ellis was a back-up catcher, he was beloved in the clubhouse and, moreover, was best friends with Clayton Kershaw. Ellis noted that after saying goodbye to his teammates, "I'm almost out of tears now." The trade arguably made the Dodgers somewhat stronger, but at what cost? In an email correspondence with author Molly Knight, she noted:

> Players were devastated when it came down, but they understand it's a business, so they moved on. More of the impact has to do with the fact that [Yasmani] Grandal struggles with managing games, which frustrates the team's pitching staff to no end. . . . That's why this trade was different than a trade of an emotional leader who played any other position. Fair or not, many around the team saw it as a power move over Kershaw—taking away his ability to ask for Ellis to catch him in the playoffs. In that context it's quite bizarre. He can opt out of his contract in 2018, so it's probably not smart to upset him. . . . The problem is all of the other pitchers wanted to throw to Ellis as well. I guess they wanted to make the change to avoid a mutiny.

Yet for all the hand-wringing that went down at the time of the trade, just like with the trade of Lo Duca years earlier, the players are professionals and had a job to do. Their job was made easier, thanks to the Giants' disastrous second half of the season.

In the first half, the Giants had the best record in baseball, going 57–33 (the Dodgers, beset by injuries, went 51–40). In the second half, the Giants were one of the worst teams in baseball with a record of 30–42. The epic collapse allowed the Dodgers to clinch another NL West crown. That the Dodgers were even able to capitalize on the Giants' collapse is remarkable considering that Kershaw, who was having a season for the ages, missed over two months due to a back injury and only made his return in early September. When he succumbed to injury, the Dodgers were eight games out of first but a little over a month later were only one game out of the lead and when he returned led the division by five games.

It was not just Kershaw who went on the disabled list in 2016. The Dodgers set an all-time MLB record with twenty-eight different players going on the DL that season. The starting pitchers were particularly ravaged: Scott Kazmir (signed as a free agent) was restricted to 26 games, Alex Wood pitched in 14 games, Brandon McCarthy (who recovered from Tommy John surgery the previous year but then had a case of the yips) appeared in 10 games, Rich Hill only appeared in six games, Brett Anderson appeared in four games, and Hyun-Jin Ryu only made one appearance for the Dodgers.

Yet with all those injuries, there were still positives. Signed in the offseason from Nippon Professional Baseball (Japan), Kenta Maeda led all starters in innings pitched and appeared in 32 games. He was rewarded at the end of the season by finishing third for the Rookie of the Year Award. There was also the emergence of nineteen-year-old Julio Urias, who showed more than enough glimpses of his vast potential. Even though he was shuffled from the starting rotation to the bullpen and back again (and back again and back again), Urias emerged as a potential star. Unfortunately, serious injury has curtailed Urias's rise, and it is uncertain whether he can come back and pitch to anywhere near his former potential. While people can be envious of the high salaries many players command, injury can very easily and cruelly curtail a player's career at any moment.

One player who looks to be an All-Star for a long time to come is Corey Seager. Seager hit .308 with 40 doubles and 26 home runs to go along with an OPS of .877 and solid defense at short. In addition to being the unanimous choice for Rookie of the Year, Seager made the All-Star team and finished third in MVP voting. It would have been a remarkable season for a veteran, let alone a twenty-two year old.

While Seager will hopefully have a long career with the Dodgers, Vin Scully will not be calling them in action. Scully first started calling the Brooklyn Dodgers in 1950. When the team moved to Los Angeles, he followed suit.

The 2016 season began on a sad note when, on January 31, Scully announced that it would be his final year in the booth. His last game was the Dodgers' final game of the season on October 2, an apathetic 7–1 loss to the Giants in San Francisco. However, most fans would prefer to remember his final home game on September 25, with the Dodgers needing a win to clinch the division. Things were not exactly going to plan with the team trailing 3–2 with two outs in the bottom of the ninth. Then up to the plate stepped Seager, and on a 2-0 count he hit one out of the park to tie the game. And in the bottom of the 10th, journeyman Charlie Culberson, in the biggest hit of his career, deposited the ball over the left-field fence to walk it off. It was his only home run for the year, but a hit that clinched the division. As Scully said in his final home call, "Would you believe a home run?" It was a fitting end to an incredible career and, quite simply, the Los Angeles Dodgers will never be the same without the soothing tones of Scully calling the action.

Unfortunately, the last few years of Scully calling the action were marred, as the majority of Angelenos were unable to view the games due to the Dodgers' television deal. In January 2013, the Dodgers and Time Warner Cable announced a twenty-five-year deal valued at $8.35 billion for Dodger games to be exclusively on a new cable channel, SportsNet LA. The huge sum paid by Time Warner Cable, now known as Charter, in turn led them to seek an exorbitant amount from other cable providers and satellite providers to allow SportsNet LA on their platforms. Not surprisingly, they were not willing to play ball. Thus, fans who had a cable or satellite provider other than the Charter-owned Spectrum could not view Dodger games unless they changed companies. Charter was counting on this, as well as the other cable and satellite providers agreeing to air SportsNet LA. The reality has been something different. While the money has been a boon to the Dodgers, viewership for their games has been halved. For the Dodgers, the money is magnificent, and the club is still tops in attendance but only ranks fifteenth out of all MLB clubs when it comes to television viewership. Not every fan can afford to attend games, let alone be a season-ticket holder. The television deal, while being a benefit to the club's finances and helping toward on-field success, has the potential to cost the club in the long run if future generations of fans gravitate toward sports they can actually see on television.

Nevertheless, a World Series triumph would have been a fitting end to Scully's Dodger days, but it was not to be.

The story of the playoffs was the performances of Kershaw and Jansen. In Game One of the NLDS against the Washington Nationals, Kershaw was not at the top of his game, going only five innings and giving up three runs. It was enough, though, as the Dodgers won 4—3 with Jansen dominant in 1⅔ innings to record the save. The Dodgers then proceeded to drop Games Two and Three with a dormant offense. In Game Four, with Kershaw pitching on short rest (again), the Dodgers dominated early and took a 5–2 lead to the top of the seventh. But the seventh-inning blues once again struck for Kershaw and the Dodgers. Following a lead-off single by Danny Espinosa, Kershaw retired the next two batters, but the next two Nationals reached on a single (Trea Turner) and a walk (Bryce Harper). With the bases loaded Roberts replaced Kershaw with Pedro Baez. Baez then hit Jayson Werth to allow a run to score, and then Daniel Murphy drove in two runs with a single to tie the game. Luckily for Baez, the Dodgers scored in the bottom of the eighth to retake the lead, and Kenley Jansen retired the Nationals in order in the ninth. If Baez retired Werth everyone would have been talking about the great job Kershaw did. Instead, the narrative was that Kershaw could not perform under pressure; he was again a choker. It did not matter to such people that Kershaw was often pitching on short rest and cursed by a subpar bullpen. With the deciding Game Five in Washington, the Dodgers needed to work out a game plan for their bullpen.

Going into the top of the seventh inning, the Dodgers trailed 1–0. The seventh inning was once again to be one of the main talking points. The Dodgers scored four runs in the top of the inning, and the Nationals replied with two. With the bullpen once again faltering, Roberts turned to Jansen. . . and he did not let Roberts down. Jansen pitched 2⅓ innings, 51 pitches in total, and took Los Angeles to two outs from advancing. However, he was noticeably tiring and allowed back-to-back walks. In a shocker, Kershaw entered the game two days after throwing 100 pitches in Game Four and recorded the final two outs to pick up the save and send the Dodgers to the NLCS. Following the game, Jansen told the media it was "the best feeling in the world . . . to know the best pitcher in the game has your back."

"It's a satisfying feeling tonight, no doubt," Kershaw said, "and we're going to enjoy it and we're going to celebrate tonight and we're going to have a lot of fun doing it. . . . But tomorrow we're going to Chicago." And that is where the Dodgers season finished.

The Dodgers dropped Game One of the NLCS to the Cubs, 8–4, but won Game Two, 1–0, thanks in a large part to Kershaw being masterful in seven innings and Jansen recording a two-inning save. The series then went to Los Angeles, and in Game Three the Cubs were never in the contest, eventually losing 6–0. Dodger supporters everywhere were optimistic that the long World Series drought would finally be over. However, it was not to be. The Cubs defeated the Dodgers 10–2 in Game Four and 8–4 in Game Five. Back in Chicago for Game Six, Kershaw pitched off short rest. He gave up five runs (four earned) in only five innings of work. That was the fifth time that Kershaw had conceded at least five runs when starting elimination games, giving further ammunition to critics who claim he is not clutch. Recapping the game in the *Los Angeles* Times, Andy McCullough wrote, "Down five, Kershaw left the game on his own accord. He struck out [Ben] Zobrist for the third out and shuffled toward his dugout. He kept his head down as the ballpark vibrated with noise. He slipped out of sight, his season finished, his legacy still undetermined."

Fair or not, unless Kershaw leads the Dodgers to World Series glory there will always be a question mark on Kershaw's career.

The Cubs eventually won the game, 5–0, to advance to the World Series where they defeated the Cleveland Indians in seven games. The Cubs had wiped away their monumental World Series drought. As for Dodger fans, players, staff, and the front office, they were hoping that 2017 would be *the* year.

\* \* \*

The new season began on a positive note, with Los Angeles re-signing Rich Hill, Justin Turner, and Kenley Jansen. Jansen got married in the offseason in Curaçao. Turner was at the wedding. During their time on the island before the big day, the two had a talk about unfinished business in Los Angeles, and this eventually led to both staying with the Dodgers. On Jansen's wedding day, Turner noted later, "I told him [Jansen] on the dance floor, I said, 'Hey, I'm coming back.' And I don't think I talked to him again the rest of the night."

It was a very fortuitous wedding for Los Angeles. Turner is truly a worthy All-Star, and Jansen is now acknowledged as one of the preeminent closers in the game in large part due to his performance in the 2016 postseason. On July 25, 2010, Jansen recorded his first save for the Dodgers. On June 20, 2016, Jansen recorded his 162nd, surpassing Eric Gagne for the Dodgers franchise record. Jansen told reporters, "Being in Dodger history, that's awesome. . . . I'm honored to just be a part of the history now. It's a great day." And in a nice touch Gagne called Jansen following the game to congratulate him for breaking the record.

The 2017 regular season was more of the same. After a slow start, the Dodgers turned it on and headed into the All-Star break with a comfortable 7½-game lead in the division. They continued strong and won 18 of their last 19 games for the best record in the majors. The first half of the season also witnessed a sequel to the famous 4+1 game; while not as exciting as the original (very few sequels are), it was still exhilarating. On April 29, the Dodgers trailed the Phillies 5–2 in the bottom of the ninth. Puig promptly deposited a ball over the wall to cut the deficit. While some misguided commentators used to foolishly call home runs when a team was trailing rally killers, this was anything but. Rookie Cody Bellinger then hit one out, as did Turner. His first home run of the season tied the game. The Phillies then retired the next two Dodgers, but they rallied again and got runners at first and second with Adrian Gonzalez coming to the plate. He hit a slow roller to short, but what was generously called a hit allowed Austin Barnes to score. The Dodgers pulled off a miraculous victory in what I call the "3 + D'oh" game.

As for the second half of the season, it seemed it was going to be more of the same. The Dodgers were dominating like few teams in history and at one point went on a 52–9 run. *Sports Illustrated* proclaimed that the "Dodgers Might be the Greatest Team of All-Time." Whether such pronouncements upset the baseball gods is uncertain, but somehow the Dodgers just . . . forgot how to win. The team lost 16 out of 17 games, which included an

11-game losing streak. The losing streak was the longest in LA Dodger history, with only the 1944 Brooklyn Dodgers having a worse run (16 straight losses). The streak included nine straight loses at home, tying the 1987 team in futility. The Dodgers also lost 20 out of 25 games. Nothing could go right.

However, the team eventually steadied to win eight out of their last ten and finished with a record of 104–58, winning the NL West by 11 games. The 104 wins was a Los Angeles Dodgers' record. Even with the horrendous run, the team had best record in baseball, ensuring that they'd secured home-field advantage throughout the postseason. The team was led on offense by Justin Turner, who had an OBP of .415 and a slugging percentage of .530. The other standout was rookie Cody Bellinger. Bellinger set a NL rookie home run record of 39 while slugging .581.

As for the pitching staff, Kershaw had another injury-plagued season. Yet he still appeared in 27 games (tied for second-best with Alex Wood behind Maeda) with a record of 18–4 and had an ERA of 2.31. This was the ninth-straight season in which Kershaw had lowered his career ERA (now standing at 2.36). Wood also had a fine year, going 6–3 with a career-best ERA of 2.72. As for Jansen, he continued to be one of the best closers in baseball. He led the NL with 41 saves while having an ERA of 1.32.

One game stands out during the team's awful stretch—not for a thrilling victory, but an agonizing defeat. Rich Hill struggled for quite a bit of the season before turning things around. On August 23, one day after *Sports Illustrated*'s bold statement, at the majestic PNC Park at Pittsburgh, Hill had perfect stuff. Indeed, he pitched a perfect game through eight innings. Unfortunately, the dominant Dodger offense could not muster a run through nine innings. Some things are just not meant to be; on the first pitch in the bottom of the ninth, third baseman Logan Forsythe booted a grounder for an error. That was the first time in major league history that an error in the ninth derailed a perfect game. Not to be deterred, Hill retired the next three batters to keep the no-hitter alive. Once again, the Dodgers could not score in the top of the 10th. In the bottom of the inning with Hill still on the mound, Josh Harrison deposited one in the stands just out of reach of Curtis Granderson and ended the no-hitter and the game. In another one for the record books, Hill was the first pitcher in one hundred seasons to record a loss despite throwing nine or more innings while walking none and giving up a single hit. Following the game, Hill told Andy McCullough of the *Los Angeles Times*, "I try to keep everything as simple as possible, and don't think of it as anything bigger than what actually is going on. . . . We lost a ball game. That's it." He further added, "It falls on me, on this one. . . . One bad pitch."

Hill was stoic and was following cliché 101, but such actions only underline how heartbreaking it truly was. It is a team game, and wins and losses are the only things that matter, but one would suggest that World Series triumph would vanquish any despair Hill had over the flirtation with perfection.

And the postseason began on a perfect note, with the Dodgers sweeping the Diamondbacks in the NLDS. In Game One, the Dodgers scored four runs in the first and eventually won the game, 9–5. The only negative note was that after cruising through six innings, Kershaw gave up back-to-back home runs in the seventh. Even so, he only allowed four runs, but the narrative was reinforced that Kershaw struggles in the latter innings of postseason games. In the postseason, including this start, Kershaw's ERA was 3.31 in the first six innings. From the seventh onward it ballooned to 18.25. Before the seventh, it was clear that Kershaw was laboring and should have been pulled. Thus, it is better for Kershaw and the team that he does not go past six innings in the postseason unless he clearly has his best stuff.

In Game Two, the pitchers struggled, once again giving up five runs. Luckily, the offense picked them up by scoring eight as the Dodgers eased themselves to victory.

The series then moved to Arizona, and unlike the first two games, Game Three was a pitching duel. Solo home runs from Cody Bellinger and Austin Barnes proved to be the difference. Midseason acquisition Yu Darvish only gave up a solidarity run in five innings of work, and the bullpen did not allow a run, with Jansen picking up his second save of the series as the Dodgers won 3–1 and swept the Diamondbacks. In a comical note, following the game mounted police protected the pool in the center-field pavilion to ensure that the Dodgers did not celebrate in the pool as the team did in 2013. To make the situation even more laughable, one of the police horses pooed on the field. So, for the Diamondbacks it is better that a horse poos on their field than opposition players swim in their pool.

Awaiting in the NLCS were the Cubs and a rematch from the previous year. Would history once again repeat itself for the Dodgers? It seemed that was a distinct possibility when Seager was ruled out of the series with a back injury. However, for a rare time in team history, the cycle was broken.

In Game One, the Cubs took an early two-run lead, thanks to a home run from Albert Almora off Kershaw in the top of the fourth. While Kershaw only lasted five innings, the bullpen did not allow a hit for the rest of the game. The Dodgers tied it up in the bottom of the fifth through an RBI double from Yasiel Puig and a sacrifice fly from Seager's replacement, Charlie Culberson. A home run from Chris Taylor in the sixth gave Los Angeles the lead for good, eventually running out winners, 5–2.

Game Two was a pitcher's duel with the scores tied at one after the top of the ninth. In the bottom of the inning, with two on and two outs, Justin Turner came to the plate. On a 1-0 pitch, Turner hit a walk-off home run to center field. That was only the second walk-off in Los Angeles Dodger postseason history, as the first was Gibson's walk-off blast in Game One of the 1988 World Series. With a case of history repeating itself, Turner's home run was on the 29th anniversary of Gibson's blast.

Turner later shared that he had watched Gibson's home run on the floor of his grandmother's house. The walk-off home run was the first of Turner's baseball life. Following the game, he said, "I can't even put into words right now. . . . It's incredible. The most important thing, obviously, was helping us get another win. But hopefully, many, many years from now, I'll get to tell stories about it."

As in the first two games of the series, in Game Three the Cubs jumped out to an early lead. Yet the lead was short lived, as LA tied it in the second. Darvish pitched well, only giving up one run in 6⅓ innings of work. And the bullpen was once again stunning, surrendering only a single walk. Home runs by Andre Ethier (who missed almost all the season through injury) and Chris Taylor were more than enough, as Los Angeles took the game, 6–1. The Dodgers were unable to sweep the Cubs, losing

Game Four 3–2 as they were unable to get the big hit when it mattered. However, this was not the case in Game Five.

Kershaw pitched well, going six innings and only giving up one run. His performance was more than enough. The offense was magnificent, led by outfielder Enrique "Kiké" Hernandez. It is fair to say that Kiké is not a star. He is a solid player who in four years in the big leagues had only hit 28 home runs. Kiké struggled personally in recent times, as his dad battled cancer and as his native Puerto Rico was affected by Hurricane Maria, which devastated the island. His mother watched Game Five on a TV powered by a generator, as 80 percent of the island was still without power weeks after the hurricane. Prior to the game, Kiké texted his mother and told her he was going to hit a home run. In good parental advice she told him, "Don't think about hitting a homer, just think about putting the ball in play." And as sons often do, he ignored his mother's advice, telling her, "I was thinking about doing that the first two games and it didn't work, so I'm just going to try to hit a homer. Who cares about making contact? Everybody just wants homers."

To say Kiké's approach worked is an understatement. He hit three home runs (a Dodgers' postseason record and tying the MLB record), including a grand slam, with an NLCS-best seven RBI. The Dodgers won 11–1 and the series in five games, and were headed to the World Series for the first time since 1988. Following the game, Kiké told *Sporting News*,

> It's crazy. I don't have a lot of words for it. It's truly special to get to the World Series, and it's pretty cool that I just had that game. But more importantly, that just tells you what this team is all about. This team has

had a different guy come up big every single night, for 162 games and the eight games that we've played this postseason. Every single night there's a different guy coming up big and tonight it was my night.

Awaiting the Dodgers were the Houston Astros, who finished the season with a record of 101–61 before defeating Boston in four games in the ALDS and the Yankees in five in the ALCS. The Dodgers were ready for a fight. On the whiteboard in the Dodgers' clubhouse were the following words: "Everybody's got plans . . . till they get hit in the mouth. Hit these boys in their fuckin' mouths and don't look back!"

The Dodgers received a boost before the Series began, with Seager medically cleared to play. On a scorching-hot 103-degree day in Los Angeles, the Dodgers were electrified in Game One, as Chris Taylor hit the first pitch in the bottom of the first for a home run. Taylor, who was acquired in 2016, was an average player prior to the 2017 season. However, a swing change revitalized his game. In his previous major-league seasons he had hit only one home run. In 2017, he hit 21 in 140 games, with an OPS of .850. His previous best OPS was .692 in his rookie year when he played in 47 games. Taylor was also the co-MVP, with Turner, in the NLCS.

With Kershaw dominating, the solo shot looked like all the Dodgers would need, but the Astros tied it in the top of the fourth after a solo home run from Alex Bregman. The Dodgers, however, were not to be denied. Turner hit a two-run shot in the bottom of the sixth, as the Dodgers won the game, 3–1. With the two RBIs, Turner collected his 27th RBI of the playoffs, which tied Duke Snider for the Dodger postseason RBI record.

Following the game, Turner noted, "My first two at-bats, I was swinging a little bit bigger bat. . . . And I got beat in a couple of times. So I'm going to switch back to [my bat] that I normally use, a little smaller bat. Good thing I did, because I didn't get beat in the third time." Kershaw was magnificent on the mound, going seven innings and striking out 11 while only allowing three hits.

There was an unwelcome distraction for the clubhouse prior to Game Two with Adrian Gonzalez, who had missed the post-season because of injury. Rather than stay with the team, he watched the NLDS from his home and was in Italy for the NLCS to help his wife and daughters settle in, as his wife was taking a five-month course in the country. He returned before the start of Game One of the World Series, but was not at Dodger Stadium. Gonzalez later told the *Los Angeles Times*, "They swept the division series, so I'm like, OK, we're all superstitious guys, it's a superstitious sport. I don't want to show up and all of a sudden they lose and be like, 'Oh, man, I'm bad luck.'"

Following Game One, Gonzalez claimed he talked to Turner and Puig who told him they wanted him to be with the team. While Turner and Puig may well have been happy with Gonzalez being back, his decision not to be with the team up to that point did not sit well with the majority of the clubhouse. Gonzalez, not exactly a popular figure within the clubhouse to begin with, was traded to the Braves in December in a multiplayer trade. He was promptly released before signing a one-year contract with the Mets in the offseason.

Unfortunately for the Dodgers, while Game Two may well go down as one of the greatest World Series games in history, the outcome was not what the hometown players or fans wanted.

The Astros took an early 1–0 lead in the top of the third after an RBI single by Alex Bregman. Astros pitcher Justin Verlander was dealing and took a no-hitter into the bottom of the fifth, but Joc Pederson broke up the no-hitter and tied the game with a solo home run.

Following a walk to Chris Taylor, Corey Seager hit one out of the park to give the Dodgers a 3–1 lead. The home run shots were the only Dodger hits in the first nine innings.

With a runner on second in the top of the eighth, Jansen was summoned to the mound in an attempt to get the final six outs. Jansen allowed the inherited runner to score after a Carlos Correa single, which broke a streak of 28 innings of the bullpen not allowing a run. Worse was to come, as, shockingly, a solo home run in the top of the ninth by Marwin Gonzalez tied the game. It was unlucky 13, as Jansen had successfully converted his previous 12 save opportunities in the postseason. As Jansen stated, "I'm human. . . . You can't do nothing about it."

In the top of the 10th, back-to-back home runs by José Altuve and Carlos Correa seemingly won the Astros the game. However, thanks to a solo shot from Puig and a two-out RBI single from Kiké, the game was tied at 5–5 after 10 innings. The single was the first non-home-run hit for the Dodgers that night.

In the top of the 11th, a two-run home run by George Springer off Brandon McCarthy gave the Astros a 7–5 lead. Charlie Culberson hit a solo shot of his own in the bottom of the inning, but Puig struck out to end the game. The eight home runs are a World Series record, and the Astros hitting home runs in the ninth, 10th, and 11th inning is the first time such a thing occurred in the postseason. It was a thrilling game but one that left the Dodger players and their fans reeling.

The onslaught by the Astros early in Game Three compounded the misery. Darvish could only retire five batters and gave up four runs in the shortest start of his career. While the Dodgers fought back, they could not get the big hit when it mattered most and eventually lost 5–3. The game, however, will always be remembered for the disgraceful actions of Astros first baseman Yuli Gurriel. Once he was in the dugout after homering off of Darvish, Gurriel made a slanty-eyed hand gesture and said, "*Chinito*," which is a derogatory Spanish word for Asians. Following the game, Gurriel apologized, saying, "I didn't try to offend anybody. . . . I was commenting to my family that I hadn't had any good luck against Japanese pitchers here in the United States. . . . I didn't think anybody would think about what I meant with all those kinds of things like that. I offer my apologies to baseball and anyone offended." Darvish claimed, "Houston has Asian fans and Japanese fans, and there are Asians all over the place. . . . Acting like that is disrespectful to people all over the world. To the Houston organization, it's just not a nice thing." To say it is not a nice thing is quite the understatement; Darvish took the high road. Rather than suspend Gurriel during the World Series, MLB took the easy way out and imposed a five-game ban at the start of the 2018 season.

And things were not much better for the Dodgers at the start of Game Four. The team could only muster one hit against Houston starter Charlie Morton through the first five innings. Nevertheless, Alex Wood kept the Dodgers in the game by not allowing a hit through five. Alas, his no-hit bid was broken up by a George Springer home run in the bottom of the sixth. Almost miraculously, in the top of the seventh, Cody Bellinger, who was horrid throughout the World Series up to that point, doubled and was driven home, thanks to a two-out single from Logan Forsythe. The score remained tied until the top of the ninth. Seager singled, Turner walked, and Bellinger drove in Seager with another double. Puig struck out, and the Astros intentionally walked Forsythe to bring catcher Austin Barnes to the plate. Barnes hit a sacrifice fly and the Dodgers wrapped up the game thanks to a three-run home run by Pederson. While Jansen gave up a solo shot in the bottom of the ninth, the Dodgers held on to a 6–2 victory.

The hot offense continued in Game Five in a second all-time great World Series game. However, it was another one to forget for the Dodgers and their fans. The Dodgers scored three runs in the first and another in the fourth. The four runs should have been enough for the Dodgers, especially with Kershaw on the mound. However, he did not have it and allowed four runs to score in the inning, including a three-run home run to Gurriel.

The Dodgers jumped back ahead, thanks to a three-run blast from Bellinger in the top of the fifth. Kershaw then proceeded to walk two batters with two outs in the bottom of the inning before he was pulled. Kershaw was replaced by Kenta Maeda, who had been lights-out coming out of the bullpen in the postseason. However, he was overworked, and this was the first time he pitched with men on base. His fatigue showed, as José Altuve tied the game with a three-run blast of his own. While one can make the case that a reliever once again allowed Kershaw's inherited runners to score, the sad reality is that once again in a crucial game, Kershaw was not at his best. Even though he pitched a couple of very good, even great, games in the 2017 postseason, he gave up eight home runs. That is a postseason record and one that Kershaw undoubtedly wishes he did not own.

As much as the previous pages have argued that Kershaw is still a very good pitcher in the postseason despite the narrative, in the biggest game of his career he pitched a stinker. Kershaw now possessed a postseason ERA of 4.50. In contrast, Kershaw's regular-season ERA is 2.36—a very substantial difference. He has been unlucky in that nine out of eleven runners he has left on base eventually scored. Even taking this into consideration, the sad reality is that Kershaw has been nowhere near as dominant in the postseason as he is during the regular season.

The offense bailed out Kershaw in the top of the seventh, as Bellinger hit a single that was played into a triple, thanks to Springer in center field, which allowed Kiké to score from first. Once again, the Dodgers had come back.

The Dodgers then brought Brandon Morrow in to start the seventh. Morrow had been great out of the bullpen in both the regular and postseason. Yet Morrow had also pitched four times in five days. He also did not have his best stuff. While not giving up a single home run in the regular season, Morrow allowed two home runs and four earned runs and did not record an out that night. Quite simply, he should not have pitched in the game. Moreover, that no one was warming up as Morrow was melting down was a managerial mistake from Roberts. Before the game, Roberts told the media and Morrow himself that he would not be pitching in Game Five. However, Morrow convinced Roberts that he was good to go. After the game, Morrow admitted he was "selfish" and did not put the best interests of the club first.

The Dodgers clawed one back in the top of the eighth and arguably should have had another run. With one out and runners at second and third, Turner hit a ball that was caught in left. Third-base coach Chris Woodward shouted, "Go! Go!" but the stadium was so loud that Taylor, who was at third, thought Woodward was shouting, "No!" The Dodgers would not score again in the inning, and the Astros piled on more misery in the bottom of the eighth, thanks to another home run, this one by Brian McCann.

Yet the Dodgers came back in the top of the ninth through a two-run home run from Puig. That was the 22nd home run of the World Series—a new record. Barnes doubled to put the tying run in scoring position, and Taylor tied the game at 12 with a two-out RBI single. The scores remained tied until the bottom of the 10th.

With Jansen in his second inning of work, he quickly retired the first two batters. But after hitting McCann and walking Springer, it brought Alex Bregman up to the plate. Bregman hit a single into the outfield, and the Dodgers allowed the winning run to cross home plate. It was a wild game. Nevertheless, in the end the Dodgers were simply not good enough and on the losing end of another heartbreaking loss. For those that care about pitcher wins and losses, Jansen recorded his first postseason loss and first for the year. In a monumental understatement, after the loss Kershaw said, "Everybody's pretty exhausted after that one, emotionally and physically."

Reeling, the Dodgers at least had the advantage of playing the remainder of the series at home. In Game Six, the Astros took the lead in the third, thanks to a home run by Springer. The Dodgers responded in the sixth by scoring two, and a solo shot by Pederson in the seventh, who was arguably the Dodgers MVP in the World Series, finished the scoring, with Jansen recording the final six outs as Los Angeles ran out winners 3–1.

The first World Series Game Seven in Dodger Stadium history would decide which club would end their long World

Series drought. And as Lasorda told Roberts after Game Six, "You haven't done shit until you win tomorrow."

Unfortunately, on the biggest stage with everything to play for, the Dodgers didn't show up. With Darvish looking for redemption after his horrid start in Game Three, he somehow was actually worse. Darvish gave up five runs while only recording five outs. It was later revealed that Darvish was tipping his pitches. That ended the Astros scoring for the game, as the Dodgers bullpen, including Kershaw pitching four innings, kept Los Angeles in the game. But despite having numerous chances to make the game a contest, the Dodgers were an awful 1-for-13 with runners in scoring position, with the lone hit belonging to Andre Ethier in his final plate appearance for the team.

The Astros won the game, 5–1, and captured their first World Series. The Dodgers were once again mired in tragedy. Kershaw had a depressing, sad, and realistic take on the Dodger season that promised so much: "Maybe one of these days I won't fail, we won't fail and we'll win one of these things. . . . There's only one team that can succeed. There's only one team that wins the last game, so that's tough." He went on to note, "I think once the dust settles and we go home, we can realize that we had a pretty amazing season and we finished in second place, which nobody cares about or remembers."

In a postscript, there have been serious allegations that the Astros used sophisticated means to steal signs throughout the 2017 season. MLB is currently investigating (as of 2019), and if the allegations are proven, it will forever cast a shadow over their World Series triumph.

Unfortunately, despite some glorious moments and achievements, the Los Angeles Dodgers were mired in tragedy and farce once again in the postseason. As for the long World Series drought, in many ways that depends on luck. If we were to play the what-if game—if Hanley Ramirez did not receive a fastball to the ribs—the Dodgers may well have been 2013 World Series champions.

A regular season of 162 games truly determines the best team in each league. The postseason, on the other hand, is such a small sample size that, as the cliché goes, anything can happen. ESPN senior writer Keith Law notes that "the playoffs are largely random so it's really about getting into the postseason—now about winning the division. They're [the Dodgers] doing that pretty regularly and I think they've got the system to keep that up. But they've been unlucky in October."

The Dodgers have experienced more than their fair share of tragedy and farce, but the club and their fans have also experienced so much joy throughout their time in Los Angeles. With an ownership that wants to win and is willing to outlay the necessary resources, cutting-edge management, and a very good farm system, the Dodgers are well placed going forward. There is no reason why the club cannot continue to dominate the NL West in the foreseeable future, and if the baseball gods smile on them in the postseason, World Series triumph is almost assured. The Dodgers have had a wonderful 60 seasons in Los Angeles, and their future promises to be even better.

# POSTSCRIPT: 2018–2019:
# MORE HEARTBREAK

## 2018: ANOTHER WORLD SERIES LOSS

**C**OMING OFF WORLD Series heartbreak, and a Fall Classic that the team had numerous chances to win, was hard for the Dodgers and their fans. Nevertheless, the front office was happy with the players and like days gone past, did very little to improve the team. Yu Darvish left to join the Cubs, while the big signing was the return of Matt Kemp. After leaving the Dodgers, Kemp had up-and-down seasons with the Padres and Braves. His 2017 season was one to forget, as hamstring troubles led to his weight ballooning. Kemp was signed by Los Angeles as a salary dump; he was not expected to make it to Spring Training. Yet Kemp devoted himself, lost the excess pounds, and showed up to Spring Training in peak physical fitness. Even then, he was not expected to make the team. Yet, Kemp had a mighty fine pre-season, but there was constant chatter he would be traded. However, come Opening Day, Kemp was on the twenty-five-man roster. After a slow start in his first few games, there was even more talk that he would be on the way out. However, he then began started to rake, looking like the Kemp of old. And it was great to see.

Unfortunately, the rest of the Dodgers were largely putrid. On May 16, the club had a record of 16–26—a mammoth 8.5 games from the NL West summit. Yet, slowly but surely, they turned it around and were only four games out of first by the end of the month. Rather than run away with the division, the Dodgers were in a dogfight with Arizona and Colorado for the remainder of the season. The first to fall was Arizona. On September 1, in a game at Dodger Stadium, the Diamondbacks led 2–0 heading to the bottom of the eighth. With runners on first and second with one out, a slumping Kemp stepped up to the plate. On a 1-2 count, Kemp belted a three-run jack. The Dodgers had the lead and would go on to win the game, securing a memorable victory. The following day, Arizona led 2–1 heading into the bottom of the ninth. Los Angeles rallied again, and with one out and runners on second and third, Kemp came on to pinch-hit. Once again it was Archie Bradley on the mound. Kemp came up hacking and, on the first pitch, hit a double off the fence for a dramatic walk-off victory. The two losses were demoralizing for the Diamondbacks, and their season imploded.

That left a two-team race, and neither the Rockies nor the Dodgers wilted under the pressure. Finishing the season in a tie, a one-off game at Chavez Ravine would decide who would win the NL West; the loser would have to be satisfied with a Wild Card place in the postseason. Rather than a tight-tense affair, Los Angeles were never behind, easily winning 5–2. Another NL West crown was theirs.

Individually, during the regular season, Kemp hit .290/.338/.481. Justin Turner had another great season, going .312/.406/.518, while Max Muncy, in his first season with the club after two below-average years in Oakland and spending 2017 in the minors, had a breakout year with a slash line of .266/.369/.538. If one just looked at batting average, the team as a whole was decidedly…well…average (eighth in the NL). However, they were second in OBP and first in slugging and OPS. The boys in blue also led to NL in home runs with seven players smashing over twenty long balls: [Muncy (35), Bellinger (25), Pederson (25), Grandal (24), Puig (23), Hernandez (21), and Kemp (21)]. On the pitching side, Kershaw had another good, but injury-filled season, finishing with a record of 9–5 and an ERA of 2.73. Rookie Walker Buehler had an ERA of 2.62 while picking up eight wins, while Rich Hill led the team in wins (11).

First up in the playoffs were Atlanta. While the Dodgers were coming off a tight divisional race, the Braves won the NL East by eight games. Atlanta were rested; Los Angeles were tired. As such, of course in Game One at Dodger Stadium, the boys in blue stomped all over Atlanta. Pederson led off the bottom of the first with a solo shot. The home team added three more in the second and Los Angeles ended up winning 6–0 with Ryu pitching seven strong innings where he struck out eight and only gave up four hits. There was a similar story in Game two. The Dodgers scored in the first through a two-run home run from mid-season signing Manny Machado. Grandal also went deep, while Kershaw went eight while only giving up two hits. Los Angeles won, 3–0, and the series was as good as over. The Braves performed a dead cat bounce in Game Three. They scored five in the second before narrowly hanging on winning, 6–5. Game Four saw Atlanta leading 2–1 heading to the sixth. In the top of the inning, with runners at second and third and two out, pinch hitter David Freese (a mid-season signing from the Pirates) singled bringing both runners home. Los Angeles had the lead and the game was as good as over next inning. Turner singled to open the frame, Muncy walked, and then on a 1-2 count Machado homered to deep left. That ended the scoring for the day as the Dodgers won 6–2 and were headed to the NLCS. Awaiting them were the Milwaukee Brewers. The Brewers had the best record in the NL and swept the Rockies in the NLDS.

Game One in Milwaukee witnessed another poor postseason start from Kershaw. He gave up five runs (four earned) in only three innings of work. While Los Angeles made it close in the end, ultimately, they fell short losing 6–5. Not helping was the team committed four errors. Things were also not looking good after six innings of Game Two; the Dodgers were down 3–0. However, they clawed two back in the seventh and a two-run blast from Turner in the eighth ended the scoring for the day. The Dodgers won 4–3 and were feeling confident being back in Los Angeles for Game Three. However, the Dodgers were never in the game, losing 4–0 while only collecting a measly five hits. In Game Four, the Dodgers opened the scoring in the first through a Brian Dozier RBI single. The Brewers tied up the game in the fifth. And that ended scoring until the bottom of the thirteenth. Machado singled with one out and eventually moved to second on a wild pitch. That was to be crucial. With two out Bellinger singled Machado home. There was pandemonium at Dodger Stadium. That momentum continued in Game

Five. Kershaw rebounded strongly from his performance in the opener by pitching seven great innings of one-run ball, while only allowing three hits. The Dodger bats, while not exactly hot, got going in the fifth. A run in that inning and two in the sixth and seventh saw the home team take the game, 5–2. Game Six back in Milwaukee witnessed David Freese open proceedings with a solo shot. After that it all fell apart from the Dodgers. The Brewers scored four in the bottom of the inning and wound up winning 7–2. In the deciding Game Seven, the Dodgers were a woeful one for ten with runners in scoring position. But it was enough. Milwaukee led 1–0 after one. In the top of the second Machado reached on a bunt and Bellinger hit one out to deep right and just like that the Dodgers were in the lead. In the top of the sixth with runners on second and third, Puig hit a long ball of his own. It was party time in Milwaukee. The Dodgers took the game, 5–1, and were headed back to the Fall classic.

The only problem is that their opponents were the Red Sox. Boston had a record of 108–54 during the regular season. In the ALDS they defeated fellow hundred game winner the New York Yankees three games to one. And in the ALCS they defeated another hundred-game winner (103, to be exact), the Houston Astros, four games to one. It is safe to say that the Red Sox were rightfully hot favorites heading into the World Series. And in a further boost to their chances, they had home field advantage with Game One being at Fenway Park.

Taking the ball for Boston was Chris Sale. Kershaw for Los Angeles. Sale was decidedly average. He gave up three runs in only four innings of work. One of the runs was a solo shot from Kemp. That was almost certainly the last hit Kemp ever recorded in a Dodger uniform. As blah as Sale was, Kershaw, and stop me if you have heard this before, was even worse. Kershaw also went four innings (it was only the fourth time that both starters failed to go longer than four innings in a World Series game), but gave up five runs. Somedays pitchers are unlucky. Kershaw did have the misfortune once again of a relief pitcher (this time Ryan Madson) allowing both inherited runners to score. Yet to say Kershaw was unlucky would be engaging in revisionist history. He gave up five hits and three walks. The sad reality is that history repeated itself; Kershaw cannot be counted on in a post-season game. Sometimes he is an ace and sometimes he is at best a fourth in the rotation starter. Boston took Game One, 8–4. Following the game, Roberts said about Kershaw: "I don't think he had the fastball command that he typically does, missing up in the zone....I don't think his slider had the depth that we're used to seeing. And those guys, to their credit, they put some good at-bats on him." Things did not get better from the boys in blue in Game Two.

Ryu started for the Dodgers and taking the ball for Boston was David Price. Going into the World Series, Price had a similar reputation as Kershaw. Great regular season pitcher who goes missing in the postseason. Both pitchers were efficient enough in the early going. Boston took the lead in the second through an Ian Kinsler RBI single. Price then got in trouble in the fourth with the first three Dodgers reaching base. Kemp brought a run home with a sacrifice fly and with two out, Puig brought another runner home. Los Angeles were in the lead, but things soon fell apart. In the bottom of the fifth with two outs, Boston rallied loading the bases. Roberts had enough; Ryu was out and into the game came Madson. It was not pretty. He walked Steve Pearce on five pitches. Game tied. Up next on a 1-0 count, J.D.

Martinez singled brining home two. Madson once again allowed all inherited runners to score. Boston led, 4–2. That ended the scoring for the day. Price picked up the win, the Dodger batters could only manage three hits, and if one just looked at the box score, Madson after two games had an ERA of 0.00 after two World Series games despite allowing five runs to score. It is safe to say that ERA for relievers is not necessarily the best statistic to measure their performance.

Once again, simply looking at the box score for Game Three may have led one to believe that it was an exciting game. Los Angeles took the lead in the bottom of the third due to a Joc Pederson solo shot. That ended the scoring until the eighth. Jansen was brought in trying to earn a six-out save. He got the first two batters, but the third, Jackie Bradley Jr. homered to tie the game. Another blown World Series save for Jansen. Scores remained tied until the top of the thirteenth when the Red Sox plated an unearned run (throwing error by pitcher Scott Alexander). The Dodgers then came back to tie it in the bottom of the inning through an unearned run of their own. Finally, Muncy hit a walk-off homer in the bottom of the eighteenth to give Los Angeles a much-needed win. Apart from the Dodger victory, the game was a bore. Players swinging for the fences and almost always certainly striking out (the Red Sox struck out nineteen times; a World Series record. The Dodgers fifteen times. The combined strikeouts were a World Series record). The Dodgers could only record 11 hits, the Red Sox seven. The game went an astonishing seven hours and twenty minutes. It was the longest postseason game ever. The length of the game was greater than the entire 1939 World Series. Forty-six players saw action; another World Series record. I think everybody was glad when the game was over.

The players were right back in action the same day (at least it was a night game). And things were looking great for the home team. Hill was great for Los Angeles not giving up a run in six innings of work. His counterpart, Eduardo Rodriguez held the Dodger scoreless for five innings. The Dodger bats came alive in the bottom of the sixth. With one out and the bases loaded the Dodgers scored through a Bellinger groundout. Puig the proceeded to hit a three-run bomb. The Dodgers were up by four and sitting pretty. Except from that point on it all fell apart. With one on and one out in the bottom of the seventh, Roberts replaced Hill with Alexander. Alexander then gave up a walk. Alexander was out and into the game for some unknown reason was Madson. He retired the next batter, but pinch hitter Mitch Moreland swung at the first pitch he saw. The result was a three-run homer. The lead was down to one. Madson was left in and got Mookie Betts to lineout to end the inning. Roberts said that Madson was trusted in that crucial spot because "Ryan has a very good track record of getting righties and lefties out, and actually left-handers considerably more, and we just didn't execute." Madson may have had a good track record prior to the World Series, but in the Fall Classic he was horrendous. Jansen was then entrusted with the ball to get a six-out save. And history repeated itself. With one out, Steve Pearce, a mid-season signing from Toronto, swung at the first pitch he saw and tied the ballgame. After the game Jansen said, "They're a good team...and it was just one bad pitch." Bad pitch or not, once again, Jansen had blown another World Series save. He got out of the inning without any further damage. The same was not true for Los Angeles in the ninth. The combined prowess of Dylan Floro, Alex Wood, and Kenta Maeda pitched the ninth. Five hits and two walks later the inning was over. Boston had scored five runs. Los Angeles got two runs in the bottom of the inning, but it was a dead cat bounce. Boston won, 9–6.

It was up to Kershaw to keep Los Angeles in the Series in Game Five. As we have seen in the preceeding pages, when faced with such a situation Kershaw has usually not been an ace by any stretch of the imagination. His opposite number was Price, pitching off a short rest and hoping to put to bed the claim that he was a postseason choker. Both pitchers did not get off to a good start. After retiring the first batter he faced, Kershaw gave up a single to Andrew Benintendi on an 0-2 count. This brought up Pearce. And he went up hacking. Once again on the first pitch Pearce swung for the fences. The result being a two-run blast. In the bottom of the inning, the leadoff batter for the Dodgers, David Freese, also went up hacking. And on the first pitch he saw Freese swung for the fences. The result cut the margin to one. While both Kershaw and Price started less than ideally there was plenty of time for them both to recover. And Price did exactly that. He went seven innings while only giving up two walks and two more hits, while striking out five. Another World Series game where Dodger bats were ice cold. In contrast, Kershaw was average. Mookie Betts took Kershaw deep for a solo shot in the sixth and for good measure J. D. Martinez hit a solo shot of his own off of the Dodger ace in the seventh. Kershaw went seven innings giving up four runs. Not bad, but certainly not good at all. Into the game came Pedro Baez, and with two out in the eighth, Pearce hit another home run for the Red Sox. That was all folks. Boston won 5-1 and so very easily captured another World Series while condemning the Dodgers to back-to-back Fall Classic losses. Kershaw record in the postseason was now a bad 9-10 with an ERA of 4.32. His regular-season ERA is 2.39.

Following the game Price said "This is why I came to Boston…and I knew it was a tough place to play. I knew it was challenging with everything that goes on there. I've been through a lot in three years since I came here, but this is why I came." His fellow Game Five hero Pearce claimed "Baseball is a funny game. The longer you stay in the game, great things can happen. I'm very blessed to be here right now." While Boston was celebrating, Los Angeles were once again in the doldrums. Kershaw said "This was a tough one for us tonight, it really was….Myself personally, it was tough. David pitched a great game. I got outpitched, and we lost the game. I've got three days now to think about all that stuff before anything happens. It will be an eventful three days for me, and I'll try to figure it out." As Kershaw alluded to, he had to decide whether he would opt out of his contract and become a free agent.

The Dodger legend decided not to test the free agent waters, instead re-signing with Los Angeles. A new three-year, $93 million extension replaced the final two years and $65 million on his old contract. Upon signing the deal Kershaw said, "It gives me a chance to prove a lot of people wrong….I think this year especially - maybe rightfully so—there's been a lot of people saying that I'm in decline or I'm not going to be as good as I once was. I'm looking forward to proving a lot of people wrong with that." At least in 2019, Kershaw did not prove people wrong. Instead, he gave further credence that he is just not the same pitcher in the postseason.

## 2019: MORE PLAYOFF MISERY

The other big Dodger signing in the offseason was not free-agent superstars like Machado or Bryce Harper, but often-injured outfielder A. J. Pollock. Pollock is a good player when healthy, but the trouble is that he was often injured. In that regard, 2019 proved no different. The other big addition to the roster was the return of Seager, who missed most of the 2018 season after having Tommy John surgery. Seager took a while to get going, but had a fine year hitting .272 with an OPS of .817 while leading collecting forty-four doubles to lead the league.

As expected, Kemp was traded in the offseason. As good as he was there were always rumors swirling that Kemp would not play out his career in Dodger blue. What was not expected that in addition to Kemp, Puig was included in the trade that sent Kemp to the Reds. Also included in the trade were Alex Wood, Kyle Farmer, and $7 million. In return the Dodgers received two prospects and Homer Bailey, who was almost instantly released. Apart from Kemp and Puig, the other notable loss was Yasmani Grandal who eventually signed with the Brewers. The Dodgers needed another catcher and somewhat shockingly they signed Russell Martin. While Kemp excelled being back in Dodger blue, Martin was primarily the back-up catcher and had an acceptable season behind the plate.

The standout for the Dodgers' offensively was Cody Bellinger. Bellinger grew up supporting the Yankees, but that changed when Los Angeles signed him in the fourth round of the 2013 draft. While he was always considered a very good prospect, no one could quite imagine how great he would be. Bellinger quickly progressed through the minors, and as noted above, made his debut in the 2017 season. However, following his rookie of the year season, he suffered a sophomore slump; his OPS dropped from .933 to .814. What made the drop even worse is that his splits against right and left-handed pitching were pronounced and he was beginning to be platooned. In 422 plate appearances against right-handed pitching, his OPS was a very good .880. In 210 plate appearances against lefties, his OPS was a dismal .681. Bellinger did not start in almost a third of the Dodgers' postseason games and had another World Series to forgot. He went 1-for-16 with six strikeouts. Bellinger told *The New York Times*, "I didn't like where I was at that point….I didn't really say anything, I let it play out. But I wasn't going to let it happen again, that's for sure. It's weird coming into a game in the later innings, in a World Series game. There just wasn't much fluidity going around." Likewise, before the start of the 2019 season he said to ESPN, "It obviously sucked because I want to play every day….But you kind of understand where they're coming from. I don't believe that it's like that in the future. I think it was just, 'We've got to win now, any way we can.' That's how I took it."

Despite how the season ended, Bellinger proclaimed before the beginning of the new campaign that he no longer wanted to be platooned. Los Angeles had quiet confidence and Roberts stated that Bellinger would be out there every day no matter who took the mound and Bellinger repaid the faith the team had in him. In 2019 Bellinger had a slash line of .305/.406/.629 while hitting 47 home runs, driving in 115, and leading the league in total bases (351). He would go on to win the NL MVP Award.

In addition, with the departures of Kemp and Puig, Pederson got more playing time and had an OPS of .867 with thirty-six home runs. Muncy also had another very good year. He only batted .251, but he hit for power and walked. An OPS of .889 with 35 home runs meant there was no sophomore slump for Muncy in Dodger blue. While once again Turner was Mr. Consistent for Los Angeles. A slash line of 290/.372/.509 further solidified his place in the annuals of Dodger history

Pitching wise, Kershaw had another great season although he was not as dominate as he used to be. He finished with a record of 16–5, was an All-Star, and had an ERA of 3.03. That was his highest ERA since his rookie year, but in the year of the juiced ball an ERA increase was to be expected. For Kershaw, no matter how good he is now in the regular season, all eyes were on how he performed in the postseason. Despite some hiccups along the way, Buehler had a strong season going 14–4, an ERA of 3.26, and he was tied for the league lead in complete games; two. Baseball is in many ways a different game now than in the past. The standout was Ryu a record of 14–5, a league-leading ERA of 2.32, an All-Star and in the running for the Cy Young Award (which would go to the New York Mets' Jacob deGrom).

As for the season itself, an April 13 loss to the Brewers saw the Dodgers fall three games behind the summit in the NL West. Was the Dodgers reign atop the division finally coming to an end? Hardly. Los Angeles ended the month with a two-game lead. This increased to 8.5 at the end of May. The boys in blue increased their lead in the division at the end of every month. Los Angeles eventually won the division by 21 games. The Dodgers won 106 games eclipsing the 105 wins by the 1953 Brooklyn team for the most wins in franchise history. Following clinching the division, Roberts told the *USA Today*, "To clinch the division for the seventh year in a row—it's important, and it's a byproduct of playing good baseball....I would rather the early than the late one. We did the late one last year—163 was aggressive. Just to get it past you, get guys rest, get guys in roles they may face in the postseason." Los Angeles had the best record in the NL, were well rested, and once again in a great position to end their World Series drought. Would there be World Series glory or like the 1953 Brooklyn Dodgers, playoff heartbreak?

Awaiting them in the NLDS were the Nationals who won a dramatic Wild Card game over the Brewers to advance. Game One saw Buehler, perhaps a surprise starter over Kershaw or Ryu, dominate. It was later revealed that the Dodger front office and Roberts wanted to be able to pitch Kershaw in relief if a Game Five was necessary. Buehler was superb as he fanned eight over six innings while only giving up one hit. Los Angeles scored one in the first without getting a hit; four walks in the inning brought home a run. An error in the fifth allowed the Dodgers to double their lead. A bases-loaded single by Muncy plated two in the seventh. And home runs to Gavin Lux and Pederson in the eighth saw the boys in blue easily take the contest 6-0.

Unfortunately, Game Two was another matter entirely. Kershaw was again average in a postseason game. He gave up three runs in six innings of work. While technically a quality start, three runs in six innings equates to an ERA of 4.50; well above Kershaw's 2019 season ERA of 3.03. Still, Kershaw battled back as he gave up those runs in the first two innings. Los Angeles had plenty of time to chip away at the deficit. In the bottom of the sixth, the Dodgers got one back though a Turner sacrifice fly and cut the deficit to one in the following inning thanks to a solo shot from Muncy. Alas, the Nationals doubled their advantage in the top of the eighth. In the bottom of the ninth, the

Dodgers loaded the bases with two out. On the eighth pitch he saw Seager struck out to end the game. That was Los Angeles's 17th strike out for the game; not good at all. Washington took the contest, 4–2. Kershaw told the assembled media after the game that "I was able to get out of the first inning with limited damage. That inning could have gotten bigger. That's not what killed us….That second inning was not good….You get two strikes, two outs on a hitter, they shouldn't score any runs. And they score two more, and that was the difference in the game."

There was more doom and gloom to start Game Three in Washington. The Dodgers left the bases loaded in the first while in the bottom of the inning Ryu gave up a two-run blast. However, Ryu did not give up another un in five innings of work and the Dodger bats erupted. In the top of the fifth Muncy launched a solo shot. And there was carnage in the sixth. With runners at the corners, two outs, and the count 2-2, Martin doubled home both runners. Taylor walked, Enrique Hernandez followed that by doubling scoring both runs, Muncy was intentionally walked, and finally Turner homered. Seven runs in the innings. While the Nationals got two runs in the bottom of the inning, it was dead cat bounce. For good measure, Martin hit a two-run jack in the top of the ninth for a 10–4 victory. Roberts said of Martin that "What he's done for our entire group, namely the young catchers, just the entire group of ballplayers—his insight, his experience, and now you talk about when he does get an opportunity to play….He's got some big hits for us this year, none bigger than the one tonight [the double in the sixth]. But a lot of that is experience. Just for him to be an extension of me, the coaching staff and the other veterans is a big reason why we are here." Los Angeles were one win away from advancing.

Things started off great in Game Four with a Turner home run in the first. However, the Nationals leveled proceedings in the third and also knocked Hill out of the game. And it all fell apart in the fifth. With Urias on the mound the Nationals scored one to take the lead and put runners in the corners with two out. Roberts pulled Urias and into the game came Baez. Baez, who has always been prone to give up homers, especially in the playoffs, did not "disappoint." On the second pitch he saw, Ryan Zimmerman blasted a fastball that was up in the zone to center for a three-run home run. Once again, Baez allowed inherited runners to score. Four runs in the innings and the Dodger players and coaching staff were already thinking about Game Five back in Los Angeles. Washington eventually won Game Four, 6–1, and the teams were off to sunny California for the decider.

Once again, things started off great for the home team. In the bottom of the first Pederson led off with a ground rule double and this was followed by Muncy, who was having an amazing series, launching one deep for a two-run bomb. Then in the bottom of the second Hernandez homered to start the inning; Los Angeles was flying high and Dodger Stadium was electrified. Buehler was dealing. He only gave up one run in 6 2/3 innings of work. However, when Buehler left the game there were runners at first and second. Surely the Dodgers would not implode and would advance; right? Roberts called to the bullpen, but rather than bring in an established reliever or Maeda who was lights out as a relief option in the playoffs, he called upon Kershaw. It was a curious choice in many ways, but as I noted above Roberts and the front office planned this before the first pitch in the series was even thrown. It seemed that the Dodgers' hierarchy was trying to prove the Kershaw is clutch. Kershaw proceeded to strike out Adam Eaton on three pitches. Everything was right with the world, but it would soon turn tragic. Roberts brought out Kershaw to start the eighth. On a 1-0 count, Anthony Rendon homered to left. Roberts still had faith in Kershaw. It was misplaced. Juan Soto went up hacking and on the first pitch he saw homered. Game tied. Kershaw was out, Maeda was in. Maeda then struck out the side. Joe Kelly came on to pitch the ninth. He did not have the best of seasons, but considering Kelly was horrendous early on that he was merely replacement level was a decent turnaround. However, he only appeared in two games during the final fortnight of the season. In Game One of the NLDS, he pitched an inning giving up one hit. In Game Three he was awful. Kelly gave up two runs on three walks and a hit while failing to record an out. Yet here he was in the most crucial game of the season. To Kelly's credit he breezed through the ninth. Unfortunately for him, the Dodgers could not walk it off and for some reason Kelly was out to start the tenth to face the heart of the National order. The last time Kelly went more than one inning was August 24, yet Roberts obviously believed in Kelly rather than Jansen. Indeed, up to this point Jansen, who did not have his best season, only pitched in a decidedly low-leverage situation in Game Three.

The Dodgers' season was resting on Kelly's shoulders. Eaton walked. Kelly remained on the mound. Rendon hit a ground rule double moving Eaton to third. Kelly remained on the mound. For some reason that no one can work out, Soto was intentionally walked and the bases were loaded. Kelly still remained on the mound. Up to the plate stepped former Dodger Howie Kendrick. Kendrick was having an awful series with the glove and the bat. That was soon forgotten. On a 0-1 pitch he homered to deep center; a grand slam. Kelly remained on the mound. He finally recorded an out before giving up a single. It was at this point that Roberts had enough and into the game stepped Jansen. Jansen had no trouble getting the final two outs, but it really did not matter. Los Angeles went quietly in the tenth. The Nationals won, 7–3, and the Dodgers' season was over.

Roberts, Kershaw, and Kelly were all roundly criticized following the defeat. Yet at the same time, Bellinger had another postseason (his third) to forget hitting .211 with an OPS of .549. Pollock was a mind-numbing 0-for-13 with one walk and eleven strikeouts. There was plenty of blame to go around.

Kiké Hernandez told the assembled press following the game that "Winning 106 games in the regular season and going home after one round sucks. Our season, you can put it as a failure…. Down the road when all of us retire, we can look back and look at all the records we broke as a team this year for a great franchise like the Dodgers. For us to be one and done, it's tough. I don't think anybody in this clubhouse expected us to be going home this soon. It sucks. There's no other way to put it, but it sucks." The last word should go to Kershaw: "I had one job to do, to get three outs. I got one out, and didn't get the other two. I cost us the game right there: That's a terrible feeling. No excuses, I just didn't make pitches and it got hit over the fence." Most telling was that his own postseason failures are now in his head. He is lost in his own mind: "Everything people say is true right now about the postseason and I understand that. There's nothing I can do about it right now. It's a terrible feeling."

Winning a Dodger record of 106 games, capturing another divisional title would have been a triumph, even with the early playoff elimination if it had occurred in 2013 or even 2014. Yet seven straight divisional titles have not resulted in championship glory returning to Los Angeles. The 2010s have ended and it is another decade of "failure." Of course, things are so much better now for the boys in blue compared to bankrupt days of the McCourt era. Thus, while there is life there is hope. Another World Series victory is surely just around the corner. Indeed, just wait 'til next year!

# ACKNOWLEDGMENTS

**W**HILE I AM a fan of the Dodgers, I am not a fan of long acknowledgements. To all the people I have talked to, let me say you know who you are and I cannot thank you enough. A few people, however, deserve a shout-out in print. Everyone at Sports Publishing, and especially my editor Jason Katzman, have been a delight to work with. Molly Knight, in addition to writing one of the best books on baseball, has been more than gracious with her time. Thank you, Molly.

The majority of photos in the book have come from Janine Roach and Stacie Wheeler. A Dodger Stadium regular, Janine captures the highs and lows of the Dodgers on a par with highly paid professionals.

As always, my wife Su Lan was a source of inspiration throughout the time spent on this book. She can always make me smile, and I am so thankful that she is part of my life. Finally, I would like to thank our daughter and Dodger fan Valentina. I have always enjoyed watching the Dodgers, but watching them with Valentina while we have a tea party, build things, or play with her dolls has made the games extra special. I dedicate the book to her and my amazing wife.

# BIBLIOGRAPHICAL NOTES

**I** **AM HONORED THAT** I have continued the rich tradition of Dodger history books. Glenn Stout and Richard A. Johnson wrote a wonderful history of the Brooklyn Dodgers and Los Angeles Dodgers (*The Dodgers: 120 Years of Dodger Baseball*; Houghton Mifflin Harcourt, 2004). For those seeking an oral history of the Los Angeles Dodger up to 2001, Steve Delsohn has you covered (*True Blue: The Dramatic History of the Los Angeles Dodgers, Told by the Men Who Lived It*; Harper Perennial, 2002). Another very good oral history is from Carl Erskine (*Tales from the Dodgers Dugout: A Collection of the Greatest Dodgers Stories Ever Told*, Sports Publishing, 2017). *If These Walls Could Talk* (Triumph, 2014) by Houston Mitchell is a nice general overview of the key moments in LA Dodger History. J. P. Hoornstra has written an enjoyable book looking at the greatest games in Dodger history (*The 50 Greatest Dodgers Games of All Time*, Riverdale Avenue Books, 2015). And for people who want to argue who are the best players in Dodgers' history, a good place to start is Robert W. Cohen, *The 50 Greatest Players in Dodgers History* (Blue River Press, 2017).

Likewise, those looking for a comprehensive history of the Dodgers-Yankees rivalry look no further than Michael Schiavone's *Dodgers vs. Yankees: The Long-Standing Rivalry Between Two of Baseball's Greatest Teams* (Sports Publishing, 2020).

Of course, the Dodgers were not always the Dodgers. Peter Jensen Brown's "The Grim Reality of the 'Trolley Dodgers,'" (https://esnpc.blogspot.com/2014/04/the-grim-reality-of-trolley-dodgers.html) is an incredibly insightful article on how the Dodgers got their nickname.

For those looking for further insight into the often-tumultuous relationship between players and owners, see Michael Schiavone, *Sports and Labor in the United States* (SUNY Press, 2015).

The unexpected 1959 World Series triumph is chronicled beautifully in Brian M. Endlsey's aptly titled book *Bum's No More* (McFarland, 2009). Michael Leahy perfectly captured the rise and the fall of the Dodgers in the 1960s and how it related to the changing American society (*The Last Innocents: The Collision of the Turbulent Sixties and the Los Angeles Dodgers*; Harper 2016). Likewise, Michael Fallon's *Dodgerland: Decadent Los Angeles and the 1977–78 Dodgers* (University of Nebraska Press, 2016) combined baseball, politics, and life in the 1970s while looking at a Dodger team that was so close to glory.

Jason Turbow has written a very good book on the 1981 Dodgers, titled *They Bled Blue: Fernandomania, Strike-Season Mayhem, and the Weirdest Championship Baseball Had Ever Seen: The 1981 Los Angeles Dodgers* (Houghton Mifflin Harcourt, 2019).

Dodger history will forever be tied to Walter O'Malley. Michael D. Antonio's *Forever Blue* (Riverhead Books, 2009) is the definitive book on O'Malley. Another name that will always be linked with the Los Angeles Dodgers is Tommy Lasorda. Arguably the best book on his time at the Dodgers is *Tommy Lasorda: My Way* (Triumph, 2015) by Colin Gunderson. The Dodgers 1988 World Series triumph under Lasorda is vividly retold in Josh Sucon's *Miracle Men* (Triumph, 2013). Unfortunately, rather than turn into a dynasty, the Dodgers became a laughingstock. The dying days of the McCourt ownership and first few years under the Guggenheim Group are wonderfully recounted by Molly Knight in *The Best Team Money Can Buy* (Simon & Schuster, 2015). Ned Colletti had a front-row seat during this time. He relives this period in *The Big Chair: The Smooth Hops and Bad Bounces from the Inside World of the Acclaimed Los Angeles Dodgers General Manager* (G.P. Putnam's Sons, 2017).

Just like all of history, Dodger history is controversial. For two takes on the fight to build Dodger Stadium, see John H. M. Laslett, *Shameful Victory: The Los Angeles Dodgers, the Red Scare, and the Hidden History of Chavez Ravine* (University of Arizona Press, 2015) and Jerald Podair, *City of Dreams: Dodger Stadium and the Birth of Modern Los Angeles* (Princeton University Press, 2017).

Baseball-reference is an invaluable resource for any baseball historian as well as any fan. This book would not have been possible without it. Likewise, the *Sports Illustrated* and *Los Angeles Times* archives were a boon for this Dodger fan. Indeed, that so many newspapers have their archives online was a wonderful asset for me in researching this book.

# PHOTO INSERT CREDITS

## PAGE ONE

**Walter Alston (Top Left):** Public Domain

**Don Newcombe (Top Right):** Public Domain

**LA Coliseum, 1959 World Series (Bottom):** Ievenlostmycat, https://www.flickr.com/photos/61527130@N00/5989335364

## PAGE TWO

**Sandy Koufax (Top Left):** Public Domain

**Don Drysdale HOF Plaque (Top Right):** Penale52 (WikiCommons)

**Frank Howard (Bottom Left):** Public Domain

**Maury Wills (Bottom Right):** Cindy Murphy (WikiCommons, Flickr)

## PAGE THREE

**Tommy Lasorda (Top Left):** Public Domain

**Davey Lopes (Top Right):** Keith Allison, https://www.flickr.com/photos/27003603@N00/8666054473

**1988 World Series Trophy:** Peter Bond, https://www.flickr.com/photos/56141425@N00/4159690131

## PAGE FOUR

**Manny Ramirez (Top):** Barbara Moore, https://www.flickr.com/photos/40706303@N00/2739697556

**Dodger Stadium (Bottom):** Ron Reiring, https://www.flickr.com/photos/84263554@N00/642253142

## PAGE FIVE

**Clayton Kershaw (Top):** © Janine Roach

**Eric Gagne and Kenly Jansen (Bottom):** © Stacie Wheeler

## PAGE SIX

**Juan Uribe (Top Left):** © Janine Roach

**Yasiel Puig (Top Right):** © Janine Roach

**Matt Kemp (Bottom Left):** TonyTheTiger (WikiCommons)

**Cody Bellinger (Bottom Right):** Johnmaxmena2 (WikiCommons)

## PAGE SEVEN

**Zack Greinke (Top):** © Janine Roach

**Corey Seager (Middle):** © Stacie Wheeler

**Justin Turner (Bottom):** © Janine Roach

## PAGE EIGHT

**Orel Hershiser (Top):** © Janine Roach

**Fernando Valenzuela (Middle):** © Janine Roach

**Vin Scully (Bottom):** © Janine Roach